Viability of UNCLOS amid Emerging Global Maritime Challenges

Lan Anh T. Nguyen · Hai Dang Vu
Editors

Viability of UNCLOS amid Emerging Global Maritime Challenges

Springer

Editors
Lan Anh T. Nguyen
South China Sea Institute
Diplomatic Academy of Vietnam
Hanoi, Vietnam

Hai Dang Vu
South China Sea Institute
Diplomatic Academy of Vietnam
Hanoi, Vietnam

ISBN 978-981-97-5837-1 ISBN 978-981-97-5838-8 (eBook)
https://doi.org/10.1007/978-981-97-5838-8

This Springer imprint is published by the registered company Springer Nature Singapore Pte Ltd.
The registered company address is: 152 Beach Road, #21-01/04 Gateway East, Singapore 189721, Singapore

This project was funded with UK International Development from the UK government.
This material has been funded by UK International Development from the UK government; however, the views expressed do not necessarily reflect the UK government's official policies.

UK International Development

Partnership | Progress | Prosperity

The original version of the book has been revised: The funding statement and the logo of UK international development programme in cover page have been included. A correction to this book can be found at https://doi.org/10.1007/978-981-97-5838-8_13

Introduction

The United Nations Convention on the Law of the Sea (UNCLOS), signed on 10 December 1982 and entered into force on 16 November 1994, is not an international treaty like any other. With more than 300 articles, nine Annexes and an almost universal membership,[1] UNCLOS has been referred to as a "Constitution for the Oceans".[2] It is the most comprehensive international legal document to govern the most human activities at sea. The Convention is so important that it became the victim of its own success: it is very difficult if not impossible to amend its provisions.

This year marks the 30th anniversary of the entry into force of UNCLOS. This book would like to seize this opportunity to provide a critical review of the Convention from three different approaches. First and foremost, it confirms the primary importance of UNCLOS in establishing a comprehensive legal framework for governing all State activities at sea. However, it also points out that there are still some issues, both existing and emerging, which have not been regulated or not regulated clearly enough under UNCLOS. Finally, it ascertains how UNCLOS has been applied in the South China Sea, both by being a basis for gauging the claims of its coastal States and by guiding regional cooperation. The review is done through the lenses of well-known law of the sea scholars through their contributions in the book.

It is undeniable that UNCLOS has contributed to the creation of a strong legal regime destined to regulate all activities at sea. In the first chapter of the book, Kriangsak Kittichaisaree discusses the role and future developments of UNCLOS

---

[1] To date, 169 States have ratified UNCLOS, see Chronological lists of ratifications of, accessions and successions to the Convention and the related Agreements, online: Division for Ocean Affairs and the Law of the Sea https://www.un.org/depts/los/reference_files/chronological_lists_of_ratifications.htm#The%20United%20Nations%20Convention%20on%20the%20Law%20of%20the%20Sea

[2] The terminology was used for the first time by Ambassador Tommy T.B. Koh of Singapore, in his Openning Remarks as President of the Third United Nations Conference on the Law of the Sea, United Nations-Division for Ocean Affairs and the Law of the Sea, United Nations Convention on the Law of the Sea of 10 December 1982: overview and full text, online: United Nations – Division for Ocean Affairs and the Law of the Sea <http://www.un.org/Depts/los/convention_agreements/convention_overview_convention.htm>

through an analysis of decisions and advisory opinions rendered by the International Tribunal for the Law of the Sea (ITLOS). He chooses four areas of case study for his discussion: exploitation of non-living resources on continental shelf beyond 200 nautical miles and the realization of the Common Heritage of Mankind; climate change and sea-level rise, new movement of human rights at sea; and challenges caused by new technologies. Being an ITLOS judge himself, Kittichaisaree's analysis provides an insider's view on how ITLOS has been applying UNCLOS on these matters. For instance, for the exploitation of non-living resources on continental shelf beyond 200 nautical miles, to alleviate environmental concerns relating to deep seabed mining, the ITLOS' Seabed Disputes Chamber, in its *Responsibilities and obligations of States with respect to activities in the Area* Advisory Opinion has made it clear that a State sponsoring an application for activities in the Area must have the duty to respect relevant international environmental obligations and to make sure that its sponsored contractor to comply with UNCLOS and related instruments. In the second chapter, Kentaro Nishimoto is the opinion that despite its adoption more than 40 years ago, UNCLOS is still the legal framework within which all activities in the oceans and seas must be carried out". Furthermore, UNCLOS is a "living treaty" which can adapt to changing circumstances and address new challenges unforeseen at the time it was negotiated. According to Nishimoto, there are five mechanisms which allows UNCLOS to cope new challenges: adopting implementing agreements, rule-making by bodies created under UNCLOS, incorporating generally accepted international rules and standards, referring to subsequent state practices, and using the development of the law by international courts and tribunals. In the third Chapter, Rüdiger Wolfrum, President of ITLOS from 2005 to 2008, affirms that UNCLOS has many achievements, of which a major one is the establishment of a mandatory system for the settlement of maritime disputes. UNCLOS adopted in 1982 a modern dispute settlement system, which was tailored to the needs of an efficient ocean governance as it was seen 40 years ago and ensuring well a balance between a dispute settlement mechanism to ensure peace in the world and the respect of sovereignty of States. Wolfrum pointed out that today, one important challenge is that the dispute settlement mechanism under UNCLOS concern with disputes with regards to *erga omnes* obligations. Concretely, in such kind of disputes, who would have the standing to initiate the dispute settlement procedures and who would potentially be bound by the resulting decision. He also suggests, as a remedy to this challenge, the use of advisory opinions to resolve international disputes.

As a matter of fact, no law is perfect. Even though UNCLOS is the most complete and comprehensive legal instrument for ocean governance, it cannot help but have some important limits. These limits come from a number of issues: first, being a package deal instrument, there are still some areas where the provisions UNCLOS are not sufficiently clear. Second, there are areas where the application of UNCLOS provisions in specific cases have met with lots of challenges. Finally, there are issues which were simply not there when UNCLOS was adopted. All three limits are discussed in the second part of the book "UNCLOS and Emerging Global Challenges". In Chap. 4, James Kraska analyses the regime of marine scientific research under UNCLOS to explain that there are methods of marine data collection which fall outside of the regime of marine scientific research stipulated in Part XIII of UNCLOS. These are operational oceanography, data collection using remote sensing satellite, hydrographic surveys, exploring underwater cultural heritage exploration, environmental monitoring and assessment, military and intelligence activities, biologging, and citizen science. Each of these nine methods of ocean data collection either has a separate legal regime or lacks any controlling legal authority that would render them subject to foreign regulation. He concludes that UNCLOS rules relating to marine scientific research were designed for ship-based by non-military expeditions, which were the primary method for studying the ocean in the post-World War II era. Chapter 5, Clive Schofield provides an comprehensive approach in dealing with one of the most difficult issues for the law of the sea now: sea-level rising. First, Schofield pointed out a number of potential impacts of sea-level rise on baseline and maritime entitlements: shifting the location of the baseline and reclassification of insular features from a "full" island to rock, low-tide elevation, or worse, the sea floor. The changes in the location of baselines along the coast also impacts the delimitation of maritime boundaries as it may affect the construction of the equidistance line. There are a number of response options to this problem: from protecting the coast through the construction of coastal structures or land reclamation to more legal options such as declaring, fixing and thus stabilizing baseline limits as well as the delimitation of maritime boundaries. State practice seems to go in that direction. As the International Law Association and International Law Committee have been taking up this topic for studies, he concludes that it is reasonable to suggest that this is an area of international law of the sea that is in the process of evolution. Also touching upon the effect of sea-level rise on maritime entitlements, Vincent Cogliati-Bantz, in Chap. 6, considers sea-level rise more than just a challenge to existing coastal State maritime entitlement but an impetus for legal changes. Cogliati-Bantz argues that all efforts undertaken by coastal States to expand their jurisdiction at sea as reflected in the rules of UNCLOS relating to maritime entitlement are being challenged by sea-level rise. The suggestion of "freezing baselines" seems to receive lots of support by coastal States. However, this is just a contemporary solution that could undermine the integrity of UNCLOS as it may set precedents to validate the primacy of particular interests over self-restraint. For instance, some have argued that the special powers of coastal States remain even after the ice has reduced. According to Cogliati-Bantz, the solution to deal with sea-level rising should be best discussed thoroughly at the global level in order to reach an authoritative interpretation of UNCLOS, incorporation of compatible norms and principles, or the adoption of multilateral compatible complementary agreements. For Chap. 7, Minerva Batool and Yen-Chiang Chang explore the issue of marine scientific research for environmental protection. According to the authors, the regime of marine scientific research under UNCLOS does not cover suitably marine scientific research for marine environmental protection. Batool and Chiang Chang argues that an important basis for marine scientific research for marine environmental protection is the United Nations Sustainable Development Goal 14 "Life below water" (SDG 14) which calls for increasing scientific knowledge, research and technology for improving the ocean health. The cooperation for marine scientific research under SDG 14 lays the groundwork for developing international legal instruments to ensure the latest scientific knowledge to inform policies.

Finally, if there is a marine region in the world where UNCLOS has best proven its importance is the South China Sea. The South China Sea is generally defined as the body of water in the Pacific Ocean located between the Strait of Malacca in the Southeast and the Strait of Taiwan in the Northeast. Considered as one of largest semi-enclosed seas in the world, the marine region has an estimated area of about 3,500,000 km2 and is surrounded by China, including Taiwan, the Philippines, Brunei, Indonesia, Singapore, Malaysia, Thailand, Cambodia and Vietnam.[3] The South China Sea hosts very complicated territorial and maritime disputes between China, Philippines, Malaysia, Brunei, Indonesia and Vietnam.[4] UNCLOS has served as the most important legal basis if not the sole legal basis to evaluate limits of the maritime entitlements of claimant States. Indeed, the arbitral tribunal of Annex VII of UNCLOS was used by the Philippines against China in 2013. The resulting arbitral award in 2016 has provided much clarity to the status of maritime claims in the South China Sea, thus help narrowing down the scope of the South China Sea disputes.[5]

The Part Three of the book would however look at how UNCLOS can help promote the cooperation in the South China Sea. In Chap. 8, drawing from the experiences of cooperation in the Arctic, Suzette Suarez opines that ocean science research plays a critical role in motivating conflicting States to jointly address and overcome challenges relating to cross-border issues despite their conflicts. For the South China Sea, Suarez calls for its claimant States to cooperate in ocean science research in existing international institutions with mandates in ocean science, in particular the International Seabed Authority (ISA), an institution created under the framework of UNCLOS for the governance of the Area. While much seabed and subsoil of the South China Sea is part of continental shelves under the national jurisdiction, there is an area in the South China Sea which is part of the Area under the regulatory authority of the ISA. Hence, claimant States could harness the existing institutional structure and marine scientific research programme the ISA to collaborate in scientific research activities in the Area in the South China Sea. Nong Hong deals with the issue of cooperation to protect biodiversity in areas beyond national jurisdiction (ABNJ) in the South China Sea in Chap. 9, focusing on area-based management practice. The South China Sea is well-known for being one of the most biologically diverse marine ecosystems in the world. Hong examines regional and national practices in area-based management in the region from both sectoral and cross-sectoral

[3] International Hydrographic Organization, *Limits of the Oceans and Seas*, Special Publication No. 23, 3rd ed. (Monte-Carlo: International Hydrographic Organization, 1953) 30.

[4] Raul (Pete) Pedrozo, China versus Vietnam: An Analysis of the Competing Claims in the South China Sea (August 2014) CNA Occasional Paper and J. Ashley Roach, *Malaysia and Brunei: An Analysis of their Claims in the South China Sea* (August 2014) CAN Occasional Paper.

[5] Award on Jurisdiction and Admissibility, an Arbitral Tribunal Constituted under Annex VII to the 1982 United Nations Convention on the Law of the Sea between the Republic of the Philippines and the People's Republic of China, PCA Case N° 2013-19.

approaches. From these practices, she explores the potential challenges for the implementation of area-based management in ABNJ as there may exist an expanse of high seas in the South China Sea. These challenges include distinctive characteristics of the ABNJ environment, lack of funding mechanism for data collection, lack of overarching governance principles, fragmented institutional framework for resource management, and absence of a comprehensive mechanism to implement area-based management tools in areas beyond national jurisdiction. In addition to these general challenges, the adoption of area-based management in ABNJ in the South China Sea would face additional obstacles such as lack of mutual trust, marine environmental protection not top priority for South China Sea countries and lack of documentation relating to marine protected areas. For Chap. 10, Robert Beckman discusses challenges to navigation rights and high seas freedoms in the Indo-Pacific, in particular in the South China Sea, while suggesting cooperation to reach consensus on how relevant provisions of UNCLOS are interpreted to reduce tensions and conflicts in the region. Beckman first points out there are a number of disagreements between States in the region and China, which could be ranged in two categories. The first one is disagreements relating to China's excessive maritime claims such as the nine dash line or the claim of exclusive economic zone and continental shelf from insular features. The second one is disagreements concerning interpretation of certain provisions of UNCLOS such as naval exercises, restriction of survey activities in the exclusive economic zone and restriction of innocent passage. He suggests regional States should engage in discussions with China on how to interpret relevant provisions of UNCLOS to reduce tensions and preserve rules-based legal order set out in the Convention. In Chap. 12, Damos Dumoli Agusman, provides a very interesting perspective about the 2019's South China Sea "battle of *notes verbales*". It refers to the series of *notes verbales* from many States, both coastal States to the South China Sea and those outside the region,[6] triggered by Malaysia's submission of its extended continental shelf in December 2019. Curiously, most of the notes verbales are issued in response to China's reaction to Malaysia's submission. For Damos, this is a form of diplomatic lawfare based on UNCLOS. This battle of notes verbales has helped clarify the limits of coastal states' maritime entitlement in the South China Sea. For instance, Vietnam states that UNCLOS provides the sole legal basis for maritime entitlement in the South China Sea. Malaysia opposes claims that exceeds the geographic and substantive limits of maritime entitlement under UNCLOS. Indonesia argues that any historic rights existing prior to the entry into force of UNCLOS is superseded by the provisions of UNCLOS as per the South China Sea arbitration award. Such clarifications could be helpful to promote joint development in the South China Sea as a temporary arrangement until the resolution of the disputes. In the last Chapter, Hai Dang Vu evaluates how Southeast Asian coastal States implement provisions of UNCLOS relating to state jurisdiction over submarine pipelines. He does so by analysing relevant national legislations of the nine Southeast Asian coastal States, namely: Brunei, Cambodia, Indonesia, Malaysia,

[6] Notes verbales were sent by China, Malaysia, Philippines, Vietnam, Indonesia, United States, Germany, France, United Kingdom, Australia, New Zealand, and Japan.

Myanmar, Philippines, Singapore, Thailand, and Vietnam. Legislations analysed are those relating to national maritime entitlement, oil and gas activities, and shipping. He concludes that there is no harmonization in complying with the freedom of laying submarine pipelines under UNCLOS between Southeast Asian States and calling for the Association of Southeast Asian Nations to take action to improve this freedom and harmonisation of regulations relating to national jurisdiction relating to submarine pipelines in the region.

Contents

Part I
UNCLOS: An Established Legal Framework

Chapter 1
Roles and Future Developments of UNCLOS

Kriangsak Kittichaisaree

1 Introduction

The role and future developments of the 1982 UN Convention on the Law of the Sea (UNCLOS) may be better appreciated in light of Article 293 (Applicable law) of UNCLOS, stipulating that a court or tribunal having jurisdiction under the compulsory procedures entailing binding decisions under UNCLOS shall apply UNCLOS "and other rules of international law not incompatible with [UNCLOS]". In other words, the international law of the sea comprises the provisions of UNCLOS and treaty law as well as rules of customary international law insofar as the latter two bodies of law are not incompatible with UNCLOS. Such treaties may be related to UNCLOS in the sense that they provide detailed regulatory regimes to supplement UNCLOS, as in the case of the 1995 UN Agreement for the Implementation of the Provisions of the UN Convention on the Law of the Sea of 10 December 1982 relating to the Conservation and Management of Straddling Fish Stocks and Highly Migratory Species Fish Stocks.[1] Rules of customary international law may be regional or global ones arising from regional or global State practice, respectively, with *opinio juris* among the States concerned.

In this context, the roles and future developments of UNCLOS may be assessed from the following perspectives: (1) the exploitation of the non-living resources on continental shelves beyond 200 n.m. and the realisation of the Common Heritage of Mankind; (2) the phenomena of climate change and sea-level rise unforeseen at the time of drafting UNCLOS; (3) the new movement for human rights at sea and (4) challenges caused by new technologies and grey areas under UNCLOS.

---

[1] 2167 UN Treaties Series 88.

K. Kittichaisaree (✉)
Judge of the International Tribunal for the Law of the Sea, Hamburg, Germany
e-mail: kriangsakkitt@hotmail.com

L. A. T. Nguyen and H. D. Vu (eds.), *Viability of UNCLOS amid Emerging Global Maritime Challenges*, https://doi.org/10.1007/978-981-97-5838-8_1

2 Exploiting Non-living Resources of Continental Shelves Beyond 200 n.m. and the Realisation of the Common Heritage of Mankind

The outer limits of the continental shelf beyond 200 n.m. have to be determined so that the coastal States concerned can exploit the non-living resources thereof and the parameters of the Area subject to Part XI of UNCLOS determined. It would take decades before most of such limits can be recommended by the Commission on the Limits of the Continental Shelf (CLCS) pursuant to Article 76(8) of UNCLOS. The long wait can be drastically shortened by adjudication under UNCLOS, though.

In *Delimitation of the Maritime Boundary in the Bay of Bengal (Bangladesh/Myanmar)*, the International Tribunal for the Law of the Sea (ITLOS) became the first international judicial body to render judgment on the delimitation of the continental shelf beyond 200 n.m. ITLOS and its special chamber have since held they can delimit the continental shelf beyond 200 n.m. if there is no doubt, or no significant uncertainty, that such a continental shelf exists. ITLOS is careful when it posits that the fact that the outer limits of the continental shelf beyond 200 n.m. have not been recommended by the CLCS does not imply that ITLOS must refrain from determining the existence of the entitlement to the continental shelf and from delimiting the continental shelf between the parties concerned.[2] This reasoning is followed by the International Court of Justice (ICJ) in *Maritime Delimitation in the Indian Ocean (Somalia v Kenya).*[3]

Article 82 of UNCLOS obligates the coastal State to make payments or contributions in kind in respect of the exploitation of the non-living resources of the continental shelf beyond 200 n.m. The payments or contributions shall be made through the International Seabed Authority (ISA), which shall distribute them to States Parties to UNCLOS, on the basis of equitable sharing criteria, taking into account the interests and needs of developing States, particularly the least developed and the land-locked among them. However, a developing State which is a net importer of a mineral resource produced from its continental shelf is exempt from making such payments or contributions in respect of that mineral resource. Possible disputes may arise between the coastal States making payments or contributions and other States Parties to UNCLOS; between the former States and the ISA and/or between other States Parties to UNCLOS, in particular potential beneficiaries, and the ISA.

Deep seabed mining is likely to become a feasible reality in a foreseeable future. Yet, there is opposition to it for fear that it would destroy the marine environment. For example, in the report of 1 March 2022 by the UK House of Lords' International Relations and Defence Committee, entitled "The Law of the Sea in the 21st Century",

---

[2] Delimitation of the maritime boundary in the Bay of Bengal (Bangladesh/Myanmar), Judgment, ITLOS Reports 2012, p. 4 at p. 98. See also Delimitation of the Maritime Boundary in the Atlantic Ocean (Ghana/Côte d'Ivoire), Judgment, ITLOS Reports 2017, p. 4; Dispute concerning the Delimitation of the Maritime Boundary between Mauritius and Maldives in the Indian Ocean, ITLOS Judgment of 28 April 2023, paras. 449–451.

[3] Maritime Delimitation in the Indian Ocean (Somalia v. Kenya), Preliminary Objections, I.C.J. Reports 2017, p. 3 at p. 38.

which was a result of extensive consultations with a number of interested parties, recommends, in paragraph 290, that deep seabed mining should only be authorised when the minerals in question cannot be recovered in sufficient quantity from existing products and when the deep seabed mining of those minerals is less environmentally damaging than extraction on land. This opposition may delay the realisation of the Common Heritage of Mankind principle that was the genesis of UNCLOS.[4]

To alleviate such environmental concerns as regards deep seabed mining, the Advisory Opinion of ITLOS' Seabed Disputes Chamber in *Responsibilities and obligations of States with respect to activities in the Area*[5] can be useful. The Chamber reaffirms the obligation to conduct an environmental impact assessment as a direct obligation under UNCLOS and a general obligation under customary international law. The Chamber rules that States sponsoring an application to undertake activities in the Area pursuant to Part XI of UNCLOS have two kinds of obligations under UNCLOS and related instruments. The first kind of obligations is one of "due diligence" to ensure compliance by sponsored contractors with the terms of the contract and the obligations set out in UNCLOS and related instruments. The standard of due diligence may vary over time and depends on the level of risk and on the activities involved. This "due diligence" obligation requires the sponsoring State to take measures within its legal system. These measures must consist of laws and regulations and administrative measures. The applicable standard is that the measures must be "reasonably appropriate". The second kind of obligations are direct obligations with which sponsoring States must comply independently of their obligation to ensure a certain conduct on the part of the sponsored contractors. The five most important direct obligations of the sponsoring State are (a) the obligation to assist the Authority set out in Article 153(4) of UNCLOS; (b) the obligation to apply a precautionary approach as reflected in Principle 15 of the 1992 Rio Declaration on Environment and Development and set out in the Nodules Regulations and the Sulphides Regulations; this obligation is also to be considered an integral part of the "due diligence" obligation of the sponsoring State and applicable beyond the scope of the two Regulations; (c) the obligation to apply the "best environmental practices" set out in the Sulphides Regulations but equally applicable in the context of the Nodules Regulations; (d) the obligation to adopt measures to ensure the provision of guarantees in the event of an emergency order by the Authority for protection of the marine environment and (e) the obligation to provide recourse for compensation. In addition, the sponsoring State is under a due diligence obligation to ensure compliance by the sponsored contractor with its obligation to conduct an environmental impact assessment. The obligation to conduct an environmental impact assessment is also a general obligation under customary law and is set out as a direct obligation

[4] In its response to the House of Lords' recommendations, the UK Government states, on 31 May 2022, that the UK will maintain its policy position of not sponsoring or supporting the issuing of any exploitation licences for deep seabed mining projects until there is sufficient scientific evidence about the potential impact on deep sea ecosystems, and strong enforceable environmental Regulations, Standards and Guidelines have been developed by the ISA and are in place.

[5] Responsibilities and obligations of States with respect to activities in the Area, Advisory Opinion, 1 February 2011, ITLOS Reports 2011, p. 10.

for all States in Article 206 of UNCLOS and as an aspect of the sponsoring State's obligation to assist the Authority under Article 153(4) of UNCLOS. Obligations of both kinds apply equally to developed and developing States, unless specifically provided otherwise in the applicable provisions, such as Principle 15 of the 1992 Rio Declaration, referred to in the Nodules Regulations and the Sulphides Regulations, according to which States shall apply the precautionary approach "according to their capabilities". The sponsoring State incurs liability if it fails to carry out such responsibilities and damage is caused by such failure.

Instead of banning deep seabed mining altogether due to environmental concerns, the ISA and the international community can find ways and means to make this environmentally sound and yet cost-effective. And this is possible.[6]

Apart from these marine environmental implications, deep seabed mining will also entail possible conflicts between a contractor's activities and planned or existing marine scientific research in the Area that might lead to disputes involving States Parties, contractors, researchers and the ISA. The request for an advisory opinion from ITLOS' Seabed Disputes Chamber on this issue has been on the agenda of the Council of the ISA since 2016, but deferred due to the ISA's current focus on drafting the Mining Code. Another issue is that of the accommodation, compatibility and coexistence between activities in the Area and laying, operation, etc. of submarine cables in the same maritime location. This is where the high seas freedom and "due regard" under Article 87(1)(c) and (2) of UNCLOS will have to be balanced with the requirement for "reasonable regard for other activities" under Article 147(1)(3) in Part XI of UNCLOS.

3 Climate Change and Sea-Level Rise

Sea-level rise affects baselines and consequently maritime boundaries. Article 7(2) is the only provision under UNCLOS on highly unstable coastlines, allowing the use of straight baseline for deltas "and other natural conditions". According to Article 11, offshore installations and artificial islands shall not be used to delimit the territorial sea. Article 121 stipulates that islands are entitled to maritime zones measured from their baselines but rocks which cannot sustain human habitation or economic life of their own shall have no exclusive economic zone (EEZ) or continental shelf, whereas Article 13 allows the use of low-tide elevations as baselines if they are situated wholly or partly at a distance not exceeding the breadth of the territorial sea from the mainland or an island. Yet, sea-level rise may fully submerge geographical features previously used as basepoints to draw maritime boundaries—be they unilaterally, bilaterally in an agreement with another State or as result of international

[6] See, e.g. the recommendations in Matthias Haeckel, Annemiek Vink, Felix Janssen and Sabine Kasten, "Environmental Impacts of Deep Seabed Mining" in *Knowledge and Changing Circumstances in the Law of the Sea*, ed. Tomas Heidar (Leiden/Boston: Brill, 2020) 327 at 339–340.

adjudication. What used to be islands may lose their capacity to sustain human habitation or economic life of their own due to sea-level rise. In the worst-case scenario, some small island States may be entirely submerged under the sea, thereby raising a fundamental question of the continuity of their statehood and the related question of protection of persons displaced by sea-level rise. The issue of acquired rights under international law is also pertinent. UNCLOS must be interpreted in accordance with the international law of treaties as codified in the 1969 Vienna Convention on the Law of the Treaties,[7] Article 31 (General rules of interpretation) of which stipulates in paragraph 3 that the following shall be taken into account, together with the context: (a) any subsequent agreement between the parties regarding the interpretation of the treaty or the application of its provisions; (b) any subsequent practice in the application of the treaty which establishes the agreement of the parties regarding its interpretation; (c) any relevant rules of international law applicable in the relations between the parties.

For its part, the UN International Law Commission has set up the Study Group on Sea-Level Rise in relation to International Law, which has been working on this issue since 2019.[8]

On 12 December 2022, the Commission of Small Island Developing States on Climate Change and International Law (COSIS), established by Antigua and Barbuda and Tuvalu on 31 October 2021 and currently comprising 9 States Parties to UNCLOS,[9] requested ITLOS' advisory opinion on the following questions:

> What are the specific obligations of State Parties to UNCLOS, including under Part XII: (a) to prevent, reduce and control pollution of the marine environment in relation to the deleterious effects that result or are likely to result from climate change, including through ocean warming and sea-level rise, and ocean acidification, which are caused by anthropogenic greenhouse gas emissions into the atmosphere?
>
> (b) to protect and preserve the marine environment in relation to climate change impacts, including ocean warming and sea level rise, and ocean acidification?

Article 21 of the ITLOS Statute provides that the jurisdiction of ITLOS comprises all disputes and all applications submitted to it in accordance with UNCLOS and "all matters specifically provided for in any other agreement which confers jurisdiction on [ITLOS]". ITLOS has held that this provision provides the legal basis of jurisdiction to a full bench of ITLOS to give advisory opinions unrelated to a legal question arising within the scope of the activities of the Assembly or the Council of the ISA, which is within the purview of the Seabed Disputes Chamber.[10] Article 138 of its Rules does *not* establish ITLOS' advisory jurisdiction—it only furnishes the prerequisites to be satisfied before ITLOS can exercise its advisory jurisdiction;

[7] 1155 UN Treaty Series 331.

[8] Report of the International Law Commission, Seventy-fourth session (24 April–2 June and 3 July–4 August 2023), A/78/10, Chapter VIII.

[9] Antigua and Barbuda, Tuvalu, Palau, Niue, Vanuatu, Saint Lucia, Saint Vincent and the Grenadines, Saint Kitts and Nevis, and the Bahamas.

[10] Request for Advisory Opinion submitted by the Sub-Regional Fisheries Commission, Advisory Opinion, 2 April 2015, ITLOS Reports 2015, p. 4 at pp. 20–24.

namely, an international agreement related to the purposes of UNCLOS specifically provides for the submission to ITLOS of a request for an advisory opinion; the request must be transmitted to ITLOS by a body authorised by or in accordance with the aforesaid agreement; and such an opinion may be given on "a legal question".[11] ITLOS held oral hearings on this request in September 2023 and, as of this writing, will deliver its advisory opinion in this case in May 2024.

Other States Parties to UNCLOS may wish to request ITLOS to give an advisory opinion on legal questions on sea-level rise or climate change not asked by COSIS since their legal interests do not necessarily overlap. There could also be ramifications for other States of any "new" legal regime applicable to submerged island States.

As for the issue of State responsibility for climate change, one learned author argues that disputes concerning climate-related impacts on the marine environment are within compulsory jurisdiction under Part XV of UNCLOS since Articles 286 and 288 of UNCLOS cover any dispute concerning interpretation and application of UNCLOS *unless* excluded by Article 297 or 298 thereof, and neither Article excludes a dispute concerning interpretation and application of Article 192 (on the general obligation to protect and preserve the marine environment), Article 194 (on measures to be taken to prevent, reduce and control pollution of the marine environment), Article 207 (on the obligation to reduce marine pollution from land-based sources), nor Article 212 (on the obligation to prevent, reduce and control pollution of the marine environment from or through the atmosphere). Any State Party to UNCLOS may, according to this view, institute contentious proceedings for non-compliance with Part XII by another State Party.[12]

Global warming as a result of climate change has brought to the international attention the use of polar regions, including the rights of navigation in iced-covered areas, especially the Northwest Passage and the Northern Sea Route. Article 234 is the only provision under UNCLOS that specifically addresses "ice-covered areas", stipulating that coastal States have the right to adopt and enforce non-discriminatory laws and regulations for the prevention, reduction and control of marine pollution from vessels in ice-covered areas within the limits of the EEZ, where particularly severe climatic conditions and the presence of ice covering such areas for most of the year create obstructions or exceptional hazards to navigation, and pollution of the marine environment could cause major harm to or irreversible disturbance of the ecological balance, and that such laws and regulations shall have due regard to navigation and the protection and preservation of the marine environment based on the best available scientific evidence. It has been rightly pointed out that some of UNCLOS's principles and concepts like the general obligation of cooperation, the precautionary approach, the science-based approach, and the ecosystem-based management as developed in other legal instruments implementing UNCLOS could provide useful tools of governance for the Arctic Ocean governance, particularly concerning the protection and

[11] *Ibid.*, pp. 22–23.

[12] Alan Boyle, "Litigating Climate Change under Part XII of the LOSC", *Int'l J Marine & Coastal L* 34 (2019): 458, at 475, 477–81.

preservation of marine environment, especially conservation and management of marine living resources.[13]

4 Human Rights at Sea

ITLOS has consistently held that "[c]onsiderations of humanity must apply in the law of the sea, as they do in other areas of international law" and applied this principle whenever occasions arise.[14]

In this connection, there is a new movement for "Human Rights at Sea" as "a special regime of international law".[15] A draft Geneva Declaration on Human Rights at Sea, open for public consultation until 1 September 2022, proclaims the following four principles. First, human rights are universal; they apply at sea, as they do on land. Second, all persons at sea, without any distinction, are entitled to their human rights. Third, there are no maritime specific reasons for denying human rights at sea. Fourth, all human rights established under both treaty and customary international law must be respected at sea.[16]

The tragedies of a large number of deaths by drowning in the Mediterranean of irregular migrants travelling by ships from Africa to Europe has raised a question about the duty to render assistance to any person found at sea in danger of being lost and persons in distress at sea under Article 98 of UNCLOS, which has been subject to varying interpretations without any universally agreed solution.[17] Beyond this context lies the issues of human rights of seafarers, including fishers, whose working conditions and treatment by their employers and the States concerned—be they the flag States, States of nationality, coastal States arresting them or port States where their vessels are being docked—have caused international concerns.[18]

The human rights of sea gypsies and traditional/artisanal fishers should fall within the ambit of this movement, too. Articles 47(6) and 51(1) of UNCLOS specifically refer to the traditional rights, including fishing rights, in what is now the archipelagic waters of an archipelagic State. In the *South China Sea Arbitral Award*, the Arbitral

[13] Vonintsoa Rafaly, "The Law of the Sea in the Age of Building an Appropriate Arctic Ocean Governance Addressing Climate Change Issues", *Yearbook Polar Law* 13 (2021): 233 at 242–251.

[14] M/V "SAIGA" (No 2) (Saint Vincent and the Grenadines v. Guinea), Judgment, ITLOS Reports 1999, p. 10 at pp. 61–62; "Juno Trader" (Saint Vincent and the Grenadines v. Guinea-Bissau), Prompt Release, Judgment, 18 December 2004, ITLOS Reports 2004, p. 17 at pp. 38–39.

[15] Steven Haines, "Developing Human Rights at Sea", *Ocean Yearbook* 35 (2021): 18. See also Sofia Galani, "Assessing Maritime Security and Human Rights: The Role of the EU and its Member States in the Protection of Human Rights in the Maritime Domain", *Int'l J Marine & Coastal Law* 35 (2020): 325.

[16] https://www.humanrightsatsea.org/GDHRAS.

[17] See further, Kriangsak Kittichaisaree, *International Human Rights Law and Diplomacy* (Cheltenham: Edward Elgar Publishing 2020) at pp. 313–321.

[18] See also UN Office on Drugs and Crime, *Maritime Crimes: A Manual for Criminal Justice Practitioners* (3rd edn, Vienna: UNODC, 2020) 71–83 (Human rights in the maritime domain).

Tribunal states that in the EEZ, traditional fishing rights are extinguished, except insofar as Article 62(3) specifies that "the need to minimise economic dislocation in States whose nationals have habitually fished in the zone" shall constitute one of the factors to be taken into account by the coastal State in giving access to any surplus in the allowable catch. The Arbitral Tribunal notes that UNCLOS does not preclude that States may continue to recognise traditional fishing rights in the EEZ in their legislation, in bilateral fisheries access agreements, or through regional fisheries management organisations, but such recognition is not required by UNCLOS, except to the extent specified in Article 62(3).[19] Some regional human rights mechanisms have reaffirmed the human rights of indigenous and tribal peoples to natural resources to sustain their way of life and livelihood.[20] The 1989 International Labour Organization Indigenous and Tribal Peoples' Convention (No. 169)[21] provides in Article 4(1) that special measures shall be adopted as appropriate to safeguard the property, cultures and environment of the indigenous and tribal peoples. The question is how to incorporate these parallel developments into the law of the sea in the context of human rights at sea.

While the working conditions of seafarers generally are protected by instruments concluded under the auspices of the International Labour Organization,[22] human rights of fishers in general are protected under Article 73 of UNCLOS. Article 73(2) of UNCLOS provides that arrested vessels and their crews shall be promptly released upon the posting of reasonable bond or other security. As of this writing, ITLOS has been seized of 33 cases, ten of which are requests for prompt release of arrested vessels and their crews and nine of them concern alleged violation of Article 73(2) by the respondent States.[23] Pursuant to Article 73(4), in cases of arrest or detention of foreign vessels the coastal State shall promptly notify the flag State, through appropriate channels, of the action taken and of any penalties subsequently imposed.

It is paragraph 3 of Article 73 of UNCLOS that has been widely breached. By virtue of this provision, coastal State penalties for violations of fisheries laws and regulations in the EEZ may not include imprisonment, in the absence of agreements to the contrary by the States concerned, or any other form of corporal punishment. To date, no State has ever concluded such an agreement with another State. Unfortunately, there are numerous instances of fishers being imprisoned around the world for unauthorised fishing in the EEZ of the imprisoning States. A question may be asked

---

[19] South China Sea Arbitration (The Republic of the Philippines v. The People's Republic of China), PCA Case No. 213-19, Award of 12 July 2016, para. 804.

[20] Saramaka People v. Suriname, Inter-American Court of Human Rights (2007) Series C, No 172, 28 November 2007; Centre for Minority Rights Development and Minority Rights Group International. *(on behalf of the Endorois Welfare Council) v. Kenya* [2010] African Commission on Human and Peoples' Rights, Communication 276/2003.

[21] 1650 UN Treaty Series 383.

[22] For example, the Maritime Labour Convention of 2006 sets minimum standards to ensure satisfactory conditions of employment for the world's seafarers, whereas the Work in Fishing Convention (No 188) sets safety and health standards to protect workers in the fishing sector.

[23] See Kriangsak Kittichaisaree, *The International Tribunal for the Law of the Sea* (Oxford: Oxford University Press 2021) Chap. 5.

as to why such violations of Article 73(3) of UNCLOS have not been brought before ITLOS against these States despite the fact that ITLOS has compulsory jurisdiction over disputes as regards violations of Article 73(3). Probably, fishers lack bargaining power to persuade the flag State, through their fishing vessel owners or charterers, to protect these fishers' rights.

States are the primary entities that have capacity to bring international claims and exercise diplomatic protection on behalf of their respective nationals as well as bear responsibility for every internationally wrongful act which is attributable to each of the States under international law and which constitutes a breach of an international obligation of the State. In *M/V "Virginia G"*[24] and *M/V "Norstar"*,[25] ITLOS reasons that UNCLOS considers a ship as a unit as regards the obligations of the flag State with respect to the ship and the right of the flag State to seek reparation for loss or damage caused to the ship amounting to a direct injury to the flag State itself by acts of another State irrespective of the nationalities of the persons on board the ship. Such right by the flag State under international law is different from the exercise of diplomatic protection by a State in respect of its nationals. Therefore, it may be deducted from ITLOS' aforesaid jurisprudence that the State of nationality of imprisoned fishers may exercise the right of diplomatic protection in respect of these fishers, provided that the State of nationality does not seek reparation or damage for the direct injury caused to the flag State by the arresting/imprisoning State. It is important to raise general awareness about this matter.

5 Challenges Caused by New Technologies and Grey Areas Under UNCLOS

In relation to military uses of the sea, there are on-going disputes between China and several developing States, on the one side, and maritime powers, on the other, regarding activities of warships in their respective maritime zones. The following are just a few examples. China asserts the right as a coastal State to request, in accordance with its laws and regulations, a foreign State to obtain advance approval from or give prior notification to the coastal State for the passage of its warships through its territorial sea. Bangladesh, Myanmar and Vietnam require foreign warships to get permission prior to entry into their territorial sea. India, Malaysia and Pakistan do not authorise other States to carry out in the EEZ and on the continental shelf military exercises or manoeuvres, in particular those involving the use of weapons or explosives without the consent of the coastal State concerned. Cabo Verde and Thailand declare that enjoyment of the freedom of navigation in the EEZ under UNCLOS excludes any non-peaceful use without the consent of the coastal State, in particular, military exercises or other activities which may affect the rights or interests

[24] M/V "Virginia G" (Panama/Guinea-Bissau), Judgment, ITLOS Reports 2014, p. 4 at p. 48.

[25] M/V "Norstar" (Panama v. Italy), Preliminary Objections, Judgment, ITLOS Reports 2016, p. 44 at p. 95 para. 230.

of the coastal State concerned. These positions and laws by the said developing States are opposed by such maritime powers as the United Kingdom, Germany, Italy, Netherlands and the USA, which is not a party to UNCLOS.[26]

This issue has become more complex with the advent of technological innovation and the use of unmanned craft/autonomous vessels/unmanned maritime vehicles belonging to a navy, the status of which has been subject to diverging interpretations among the States concerned. UNCLOS uses the terms "ship" and "vessel" interchangeably, without defining either. Yet, Article 29 UNCLOS defines "warship" as "a ship belonging to the armed forces of a State bearing the external marks distinguishing such ships of its nationality, under the command of an officer duly commissioned by the government of the State and whose name appears in the appropriate service list or its equivalent, and manned by a crew which is under regular armed forces discipline". Article 32 of UNCLOS recognises the immunities of warships and other government ships operated for non-commercial purposes. When these vessels travel in a submerged mode as unmanned underwater vehicles (UUVs) or new-generation military underwater robots,[27] for instance, conflicting interpretations of the law can give rise to international disputes. This happened in December 2016 when a Chinese warship removed from the water in the South China Sea a U.S. autonomously operating drone deployed by the U.S. Navy oceanographic surveillance ship, the *Bowditch.* The U.S. position was that the *Bowditch* and the UUV were carrying out scientific research in "international waters" and that it was a U.S. vessel with sovereign immune status. For China, its navy performed a duty of mariners by taking an "unidentified object" (i.e. not a ship)[28] out of the water in order to prevent the device from causing harm to the safety of navigation and personnel of passing vessels, and after verifying that the device belonged to the US Government, China returned it.[29]

There are some gaps in UNCLOS that need to be addressed for the sake of comprehensive ocean governance in the twenty-first century. For example, UNCLOS does not have any provision specifically imposes a duty to promptly notify the flag State in cases of arrest or detention of foreign vessels unrelated to the exercise of the sovereignty rights of the arresting coastal State over its EEZ; regulation of non-manganese nodule resources, including energy resources, beyond 200-n.m. EEZs

---

[26] Multilateral Treaties Deposited with the Secretary-General, Chapter XXI; Ying Yang, "The prior notification issue of military activities in EEZ" in *Maritime Order and the Law in East Asia*, eds. Gordon Houlden and Nong Hong (Abingdon: Routledge, 2018), 158.

[27] JR Wilson, "Unmanned submarines seen as key to dominating the world's oceans", *Military & Aerospace* (15 October 2019).

[28] For an argument that many unmanned maritime vehicles may not be considered to fall under the definition of "ship" so as to enjoy states' rights of navigation under UNCLOS, see Robert Veal, Michael Tsimplis and Andrew Serdy "The legal status and operation of unmanned maritime vehicles", *Ocean Development & International Law* 50 (2019): 23. Cf Henrik Ringbom and Felix Collin 'Terminology and concepts' in *Autonomous Ships and the Law*, eds. Henrik Ringbom, Erik Røsæg, and Trond Solvang (London/New York: Routledge 2021): 7–20.

[29] Mark Valencia, "U.S.-China Underwater Drone Incident: Legal Grey Areas", *The Diplomat*, 11 Jan 2017, https://thediplomat.com/2017/01/us-china-underwater-drone-incident-legal-grey-areas/.

and beyond continental margins; and regulation of a new generation of multi-purpose submarine cables.

6 Conclusion

UNCLOS will continue to play its omnipotent role in the law of the sea. For instance, on plastic pollution at sea which is being accorded priority by the international community, it has been argued that the existing regime under Part XII of UNCLOS appears to be adequate to deal with this challenge[30] although the Executive Director of the UN Environment Programme (UNEP) has convened an Intergovernmental Negotiating Committee (INC) to develop "the instrument", which is to be based on a comprehensive approach that addresses the full life cycle of plastic, including its production, design and disposal.[31]

By virtue of Article 20 of the Statute of ITLOS, ITLOS shall be open to States Parties as well as entities other than States Parties in any case expressly provided for in Part XI or in any case submitted pursuant to any other agreement conferring jurisdiction on ITLOS which is accepted by all the parties to that case. The standard formula used by these other agreements is that Part XV UNCLOS shall apply *mutatis mutandis* to any dispute between States Parties to these agreements concerning the interpretation or application of these agreements, whether or not they are also parties to UNCLOS.[32]

As regards advisory opinions, Article 48(7) of the 2023 Agreement under UNCLOS on the Conservation and Sustainable Use of Marine Biological Diversity of Areas beyond National Jurisdiction[33] provides that the Conference of the Parties to the Agreement may decide to request ITLOS to give an advisory opinion on a legal question on the conformity with this Agreement of a proposal before the Conference of the Parties to the Agreement on any matter within its competence.

These are some of the examples where UNCLOS can continue to apply in the light of the latest developments of conventional and customary international law to new and future law of the sea issues.

---

[30] Judith Schäli, The Mitigation of Marine Plastic Pollution in International Law: Facts, Policy and Legal Implications (Leiden/Boston: Brill, 2022) at 158–240.

[31] The INC started its work during the second half of 2022, with the aim of completing the negotiations by the end of 2024.

[32] For example, Article 30 of the 1995 Fish Stocks Agreement (n 1 *supra*) and Article 25 of the 2001 UNESCO Convention on the Protection of the Underwater Cultural Heritage ((2001) 41 *International Legal Materials* 37).

[33] C.N.203.2023.TREATIES-XXI.10.

Chapter 2
Legal Stability and Change in the Context of the South China Sea Dispute

Kentaro Nishimoto

1 Introduction

Treaties are products of their time. The United Nations Convention on the Law of the Sea (UNCLOS) was adopted more than 40 years ago based on circumstances at the time of its negotiation.[1] Many factors relevant to the operation of the convention, such as the international political landscape, scientific knowledge of the oceans, and the technology for utilizing ocean resources, have changed significantly over the years.[2] However, these changes have not rendered the convention obsolete. On the contrary, there continues to be a widespread conviction internationally that UNCLOS provides "the legal framework within which all activities in the oceans and seas must be carried out."[3]

[1] The convention is commonly described as a reconciliation of competing interests among States. See, for example, Tommy T. B. Koh, "Negotiating a New World Order for the Sea," *Virginia Journal of International Law* 24, no. 4 (1984): 768–780.

[2] On the role of scientific knowledge and technology in the development of the law of the sea, see Kentaro Nishimoto, "Kaiyoho no Hatten to Kagakuteki Chiken" [The Development of International Law and Scientific Knowledge], *Kokusaiho Gaikou Zasshi* [Journal of International Law and Diplomacy] 120, no. 3 (2021): 23–48 (in Japanese); James Kraska, "From the Age of Discovery to the Atomic Age: The Conflux of Marine Science, Seapower, and Oceans Governance," in *Science, Technology, and New Challenges to Ocean Law,* eds. Harry N. Scheiber et al. (Leiden: Brill, 2015): 27–62.

[3] This recognition is now regularly repeated in the annual "Oceans and the Law of the Sea" resolution adopted by the United Nations General Assembly. The latest example is in UNGA Resolution 78/69, UN Doc. A/RES/78/69, 2.

K. Nishimoto (✉)
Graduate School of Law, Tohoku University, 27-1 Kawauchi, Aoba-ku, Sendai, Miyagi, Japan
e-mail: nishimoto@tohoku.ac.jp

L. A. T. Nguyen and H. D. Vu (eds.), *Viability of UNCLOS amid Emerging Global Maritime Challenges*, https://doi.org/10.1007/978-981-97-5838-8_2

The overall success of UNCLOS in responding to change after its adoption has been a subject of academic interest in recent years.[4] In this context, UNCLOS has been referred to as a "living instrument" or a "living treaty" in that it is able to adapt to changing circumstances and address new challenges unforeseen at the time it was negotiated.[5] While oceans face new challenges, particularly concerning the marine environment and biodiversity, there is support for the understanding that these challenges must be addressed within the legal framework provided by UNCLOS instead of renegotiating UNCLOS itself.[6]

In the context of the South China Sea dispute, the People's Republic of China (PRC) has made the argument that "UNCLOS does not cover everything about the maritime order" and that "[s]ince its adoption in 1982, UNCLOS has continuously developed and improved."[7] In the abstract, these statements reflect commonly held understandings about UNCLOS. The recognition of UNCLOS as "the legal framework within which all activities in the oceans and seas must be carried out" does not mean that UNCLOS is an exclusive source of law of the law of the sea. It is widely accepted that UNCLOS does not contain rules on certain matters and that those remain "governed by the rules and principles of general international law."[8] Moreover, describing UNCLOS as having "continuously developed and improved" could be regarded as another way of describing the nature of UNCLOS as a "living treaty," which is not problematic in itself.

However, the arguments by the PRC regarding UNCLOS carry problematic implications in the context of the South China Sea, where the PRC continues to disregard the award in the *South China Sea Arbitration*. The award regarded PRC's claims to the waters within the so-called "nine-dash lines" inconsistent with UNCLOS. To justify non-compliance, in addition to arguments against the arbitral tribunal's jurisdiction, the PRC has made efforts to provide alternative justifications on the merits of its claims based on customary international law.[9] The reliance on customary international law, coupled with the emphasis on the changing nature of UNCLOS,

---

[4] Alex G. Oude Elferink, ed., *Stability and Change in the Law of the Sea: The Role of the LOS Convention* (Leiden: Martinus Nijhoff, 2005); Jill Barret and Richard Barnes, eds., *Law of the Sea: UNCLOS as a Living Treaty* (London: British Institute of International and Comparative Law, 2016); Rozemarijn J. Roland Holst, *Change in the Law of the Sea: Context, Mechanisms and Practice* (Leiden: Brill, 2022).

[5] Jill Barrett, "The UN Convention on the Law of the Sea: A 'Living' Treaty'," in *Law of the Sea: UNCLOS as a Living Treaty*, 4–5.

[6] See, for example, the report of the inquiry by the House of Lords (United Kingdom), which considered whether UNCLOS remains "fit for purpose" in the 21st Century. House of Lords, International Relations and Defence Committee, *UNCLOS: The Law of the Sea in the 21st Century* at https://committees.parliament.uk/publications/9005/documents/159002/default/, 19–22 (paras. 42–55).

[7] People's Republic of China, Note CML/63/2020 at https://www.un.org/depts/los/clcs_new/submissions_files/mys_12_12_2019/2020_09_18_CHN_NV_UN_009_e.pdf (accessed 1 March 2024).

[8] One example is the rules on the use of force in maritime law enforcement operations. See Cameron Moore, "The Use of Force," in *Routledge Handbook of Maritime Regulation and Enforcement*, eds. Robin Warner and Stuart Kaye (Oxon: Routledge, 2015), 27.

[9] See, for example, People's Republic of China, Note CML/32/2021 at https://www.un.org/depts/los/clcs_new/submissions_files/mys_12_12_2019/20210803NzNote.pdf (accessed 1 March 2024).

is a potentially dangerous argument with broad implications about the ability of UNCLOS to provide stable expectations about the legal regime of the oceans and standards for resolving disputes.

An unjustified assertion of customary international law for matters that are actually regulated by UNCLOS could be used as a "back door" for States to justify claims that cannot be made on the basis of the provisions of UNCLOS. Moreover, the emphasis on the need to "continuously develop and improve" the current legal regime could be used as a justification for non-compliance with the existing rules embodied in treaties. While the change of circumstances (*rebus sic stantibus*) can only justify a deviation from a treaty in limited circumstances as a matter of law,[10] States could always attempt to politically justify non-compliance by arguing that it is unreasonable to require compliance with an obsolete rule that is in need of updating. Such approaches to interpreting and applying the UNCLOS regime, if taken to extremes, would depict UNCLOS as an ever-changing body of rules that is unable to provide concrete outcomes for specific situations.

Given such implications, it is important to take the PRC's arguments seriously and consider whether they are justifiable as legal arguments. In this light, this chapter will focus on the PRC's arguments on the need to "develop and improve UNCLOS" and assess whether they have any real bearing on the legal situation of the South China Sea. In order to do so, the chapter first considers the PRC's arguments based on a *note verbale* dated September 18, 2020, in which the PRC clearly laid out its arguments on the need to "develop and improve UNCLOS" as a counter-argument against criticism by other States of its claims in the South China Sea. Next, the mechanisms identified in existing literature as the means through which UNCLOS has been able to change in response to changing circumstances are discussed to provide a background against which the question of whether the PRC's arguments are justified can be considered. This will be followed by a discussion of how the PRC's narratives focusing on the incompleteness of the UNCLOS regime and the need for improvement are relevant in the context of stability and change in the South China Sea. Finally, brief concluding observations are offered.

2 PRC's Arguments on the Need to "Develop and Improve" UNCLOS

A *note verbale* by the PRC in response to Malaysia's submission to the CLCS in 2019 sparked a chain of notes from other States, including those outside the region.[11] Although the specific legal issues addressed in the notes vary from State to State,

---

[10] Article 62, Vienna Convention on the Law of Treaties, 1155 UNTS 331

[11] The notes are available on the website of the Division for Ocean Affairs and the Law of the Sea (DOALOS), United Nations, at https://www.un.org/depts/los/clcs_new/submissions_files/submission_mys_12_12_2019.html (accessed 1 March 2024).

States outside the region emphasized the central role of UNCLOS in the international maritime order.[12] Their main concerns, expressed as parties to UNCLOS, were related to the integrity of UNCLOS rather than the immediate dispute in the South China Sea between the PRC and other coastal States in the region.

The response by the PRC to these concerns included two arguments concerning the role of UNCLOS. The first argument is that "UNCLOS does not cover everything about the maritime order." The second argument is that UNCLOS has continuously developed and improved. Interestingly, the PRC referred to the then-ongoing negotiation of the BBNJ Agreement to support both arguments. For example, in response to a *note verbale* by New Zealand, the PRC stated that

> [t]he States Parties to UNCLOS affirm that "matters not regulated by this Convention continue to be governed by the rules and principles of general international law." At present, an international instrument is under negotiation on marine biological diversity of areas beyond national jurisdiction. This also proves that UNCLOS cannot solve all maritime issues.[13]

In response to notes by France, Germany, and the United Kingdom, the PRC stated that

> [s]ince its adoption in 1982, UNCLOS has continuously developed and improved. The ongoing negotiation for an international instrument on the conservation and sustainable use of marine biodiversity in areas beyond national jurisdiction is an important effort for the development and improvement of UNCLOS. China is a firm supporter of UNCLOS and an active participant in the process of developing and improving UNCLOS.[14]

The first argument on the non-comprehensive character of UNCLOS can be regarded as intending to reinforce legal justifications for the PRC's jurisdictional claim to the waters within the so-called "nine-dash lines" in the South China Sea. The PRC notoriously justifies its claim based on historic rights despite a clear finding in the South China Sea award that such a claim is incompatible with the UNCLOS to the extent that it exceeds the limits of China's maritime zones as provided for by UNCLOS.[15] The understanding that there are instances where historic rights may be exercised on the basis of customary international law is in itself uncontroversial.[16] However, the South China Sea award considered that the requirements for the establishment of historic rights under customary international law are not met in regard to

---

[12] See, for example, the identical notes verbales from France, Germany, and the United Kingdom, "recall[ing] the universal and unified character of UNCLOS that sets out the legal framework within which all activities in the oceans and seas must be carried out." United Kingdom, Note UK NV No. 16/20 at https://www.un.org/depts/los/clcs_new/submissions_files/mys_12_12_2019/2020_09_16_GBR_NV_UN_001.pdf (accessed 1 March 2024).

[13] People's Republic of China, Note CML/32/2021.

[14] People's Republic of China, Note CML/63/2020.

[15] *South China Arbitration, Award of 12 July 2016, Reports of International Arbitral Awards* XXXIII (2020): 287 (para. 261).

[16] See generally, United Nations, Historic Bays: Memorandum by the Secretariat of the United Nations, UN Doc. A/CONF.13/1.

the PRC's claims in the South China Sea.[17] The PRC nevertheless continues to refer to its historic rights in the South China Sea.[18]

The rules of customary international law also play a role in the PRC's practice of drawing straight baselines enclosing offshore archipelagos.[19] The South China Sea arbitral award considered that the rules on baselines are comprehensively regulated under UNCLOS.[20] It reasoned that unless Article 7, which provides general rules on the drawing of straight baselines, together with Articles 46 and 47, which permits archipelagic States to draw archipelagic baselines subject to specific conditions, is read as excluding the possibility of employing straight baselines in other circumstances, the conditions in Articles 7 and 47 would be rendered meaningless.[21] However, the PRC government and Chinese authors continue to argue that this issue was left to be regulated under UNCLOS and that there is a rule of customary international law that supports the adoption of baselines that would be impermissible under the rules contained in UNCLOS.[22]

The second argument on "developing and improving UNCLOS" is difficult to understand in terms of its relevance to the overall argument in the *note verbale*. In the same paragraph where this argument appears, the PRC first declares that it "treats UNCLOS with a rigorous and responsible attitude and opposes using UNCLOS as a political tool to attack other countries" and expresses its position that "UNCLOS does not cover everything about the maritime order." Furthermore, it is argued that "the rules of international law of the sea, including UNCLOS" should be "faithfully, comprehensively and correctly" interpreted and applied and that "[a]ny partial interpretation and application of UNCLOS is unjust, illegal, and has an ulterior motive."

Thus, while the logic is not necessarily clear, the PRC appears to regard the fact that UNCLOS has continuously "developed and improved" as relevant to its interpretation of "the rules of international law of the sea, including UNCLOS," which it claims is an impartial one. It is also reasonable to understand that the PRC is accusing other States of adopting "a partial interpretation" that fails to take into account the development and improvement of UNCLOS after its adoption. If this is the case, how have these changes occurred? How is the BBNJ Agreement relevant in this context, where the PRC is seeking to justify its understanding of rules relating to maritime entitlement and jurisdiction under the international law of

---

17 *South China Sea arbitration*, 288–292 (paras. 263–275).

18 People's Republic of China, Note CML/63/2020, para. 2; Chinese Society of International Law, "The South China Sea Arbitration Awards: A Critical Study," *Chinese Journal of International Law* 17, no. 2 (2018): 421–449.

19 See Hua Zhang, "The Application of Straight Baselines to Mid-Ocean Archipelagos Belonging to Continental States: A Chinese Lawyer's Perspective," in *Implementation of the United Nations Convention on the Law of the Sea: State Practice of China and Japan*, eds. Dai Tamada and Keyuan Zou (Singapore: Springer, 2021), 115–131; Yurika Ishii, "A Critique Against the Concept of Mid-Ocean Archipelago" in *Implementation of UNCLOS*, 133–147.

20 *South China Sea arbitration*, 396 (para. 575).

21 *South China Sea arbitraiton*, 396 (para. 575).

22 Chinese Society of International Law, *Critical Study*, 508–510.

the sea? In considering these issues, it is useful to look at the overall picture regarding mechanisms for change in the law of the sea.

3 Mechanisms for Change in the Law of the Sea

Various mechanisms built into the design of UNCLOS have provided it with the resilience to remain relevant as a comprehensive legal regime for oceans amid changing circumstances. It appears unlikely that formal amendment procedures will ever be used.[23] Unlike recent multilateral environmental treaties, UNCLOS lacks a robust institutional mechanism to support its operation.[24] However, it has been able to respond to changing circumstances through other means, such as adopting implementing agreements, rule-making by bodies created under UNCLOS, incorporating generally accepted international rules and standards (GAIRS), shaping interpretation through subsequent practice, and developing the law through the dispute settlement mechanism.

3.1 Adoption of Implementing Agreements

In order to address issues not adequately covered by UNCLOS, implementing agreements have been concluded to provide further detail to the overall legal framework under UNCLOS. The Part XI Implementing Agreement was adopted because of particular circumstances after the adoption of UNCLOS but prior to its entry into force.[25] In contrast, the adoption of two additional implementing agreements, the

---

[23] David Freestone and Alex G. Oude Elferink, "Flexibility and Innovation in the Law of the Sea: Will the LOS Convention Amendment Procedures Ever be Used?," in *Stability and Change in the Law of the Sea*, 169–221.

[24] The Meeting of States Parties to UNCLOS (SPLOS) has played only a limited role in this context, reflecting the differences of views among parties on its competence. Alex G. Oude Elferink, "Reviewing the Implementation of the LOS Convention: the Role of the United Nations General Assembly and the Meeting of States Parties" in *Oceans Management in the 21st Century: Institutional Frameworks and Responses,* eds. Alex G. Oude Elferink and Donald R. Rothwell (Leiden: Martinus Nijhoff, 2004), 307–310; James Harrison, "The Law of the Sea Convention Institutions," in *The Oxford Handbook of the Law of the Sea,* eds. Donald R. Rothwell et al. (Oxford: Oxford University Press, 2015), 387–390.

[25] On the circumstances relating to the adoption of the Part XI Implementing Agreement, see Annick de Marffy-Mantuano, "The Procedural Framework of the Agreement Implementing the 1982 United Nations Convention on the Law of the Sea," *American Journal of International Law* 89, no. 4 (1995): 814–817. The Part XI Implementing Agreement is widely seen as a de facto amendment of UNCLOS. Alan Boyle and Christine Chinkin, *The Making of International Law* (Oxford: Oxford University Press, 2007), 243.

UN Fish Stocks Agreement[26] and the BBNJ Agreement,[27] reflect further efforts to fill gaps in the legal regime by providing content to the principles and rules contained in UNCLOS.

UNCLOS implementing agreements have undoubtedly added certain elements to UNCLOS. Hayashi has pointed out that the UN Fish Stocks Agreement significantly adds to UNCLOS in three ways: by helping States to implement UNCLOS by indicating specific measures, strengthening UNCLOS provisions by elaborating on general rules and expanding their application, and developing basic rules and principles in UNCLOS.[28] However, the underlying premise is that there is nothing in UNFSA that is inconsistent with UNCLOS. In this regard, Article 5(1) of UNFSA provides that "[n]othing in this Agreement shall prejudice the rights, jurisdiction and duties of States under [UNCLOS]. This Agreement shall be interpreted and applied in the context of and in a manner consistent with [UNCLOS]."

The same applies to the BBNJ Agreement that the PRC mentioned explicitly in its *note verbale*. From the beginning of the negotiations, it was agreed that the agreement would be an instrument "under UNCLOS," and would not undermine existing relevant legal instruments, including UNCLOS.[29] Article 5(1) of the BBNJ Agreement, mirroring some of the language in Article 4 of UNFSA, provides that "[t]his Agreement shall be interpreted and applied in the context of and in a manner consistent with [UNCLOS]. Nothing in this Agreement shall prejudice the rights, jurisdiction and duties of States under the Convention, including in respect of the exclusive economic zone and the continental shelf within and beyond 200 nautical miles." The rules and mechanisms for the conservation and sustainable use of biodiversity on the high seas and in the Area are regarded as providing details to the rules and principles already contained in UNCLOS. There is nothing in the BBNJ Agreement that overrides or is inconsistent with UNCLOS, and States were particularly careful to ensure that the jurisdictional framework under UNCLOS is not affected by the BBNJ Agreement.

[26] Agreement for the Implementation of the Provisions of the United Nations Convention on the Law of the Sea of 10 December 1982 relating to the Conservation and Management of Straddling Fish Stocks and Highly Migratory Fish Stocks, 2167 UNTS 3. For further details on developments after UNCLOS leading to the UN Fish Stocks Agreement, see José A. De Yturriaga, *The International Regime of Fisheries: From UNCLOS 1982 to the Presential Sea* (The Hague: Martinus Nijhoff, 1997), 173–227.

[27] Agreement under the United Nations Convention on the Law of the Sea on the Conservation and Sustainable Use of Marine Biological Diversity of Areas beyond National Jurisdiction at https://treaties.un.org/doc/Treaties/2023/06/20230620%2004-28%20PM/Ch_XXI_10.pdf (accessed 1 March 2024).

[28] Moritaka Hayashi, "The 1995 Agreement on the Conservation and Management of Straddling and Highly Migratory Fish Stocks: Significance for the Law of the Sea Convention," *Ocean and Coastal Management* 29, nos. 1–3 (1995): 51–69.

[29] UNGA Resolution 69/292, UN Doc. A/RES/69/292, paras. 1 and 3. In Resolution 72/249, which established the BBNJ Intergovernmental Conference, it was explicitly reaffirmed that "the work and results of the conference should be fully consistent with the provisions of [UNCLOS]." UN Doc. A/RES/72/249, para. 6.

3.2 Rule-Making by Bodies Created Under UNCLOS

In addition to creating the International Tribunal for the Law of the Sea (ITLOS) as a dispute settlement body, UNCLOS established two bodies: the Commission on the Limits of the Continental Shelf (CLCS) and the International Seabed Authority (ISA). While technical in nature, the CLCS has provided additional rules required to fulfill its role in delineating the outer limits of the continental shelf. The ISA has a broad mandate to adopt further rules and regulations concerning its functions, including setting detailed standards that govern the operations and activities in the Area.[30] The regulation of deep-seabed mining activities is currently a subject of increasing debate, with some States calling for a moratorium on mining in the Area until strict environmental rules are agreed upon.[31] This development is an important change from when UNCLOS and the Part XI Implementing Agreement were negotiated, reflecting the development of international environmental law and advancements in scientific knowledge concerning the environment of the deep seabed. The existence of the ISA as an institution with competence under UNCLOS to address these issues would allow decisions to be made that reflect changes in circumstances after UNCLOS.

3.3 Incorporation of Generally Accepted International Rules and Standards

Using the rules of reference in UNCLOS is another way in which the UNCLOS framework may consider recent circumstances. Part XII of UNCLOS on the protection and preservation of the marine environment makes extensive use of reference clauses, which refer to GAIRS. The provisions in Part XII on different sources of marine pollution provide rules for the allocation of jurisdiction among flag, coastal, and port States.[32] The reference to GAIRS creates a dynamic system for specifying the extent of the powers and obligations of States, where the technical rules and standards to be followed may be updated by "competent international organizations," such as the International Maritime Organization.[33] This system has allowed for responses to new threats to the marine environment, such as the issue of invasive species under the Ballast Water Management Convention and greenhouse gas emissions by ships

---

[30] James Harrison, *Making the Law of the Sea: A Study in the Development of International Law* (Cambridge: Cambridge University Press, 2011), 117–118.

[31] Nanaia Mahuta, "NZ Backs Conditional Moratorium on Seabed Mining in International Waters," at https://www.beehive.govt.nz/release/nz-backs-conditional-moratorium-seabed-mining-international-waters (accessed 1 March 2024).

[32] For an overview of this aspect of Part XII, see Daniel Bodansky, "Protecting the Marine Environment from Vessel-Source Pollution: UNCLOS III and Beyond," *Ecology Law Quarterly* 18 (1991): 719–777.

[33] Holst, *Change in the Law of the Sea*, 153; Rudiger Wolfrum, "IMO Interface with the Law of the Sea Convention," in *Current Maritime Issues and the International Maritime Organization*, eds. Myron H. Nordquist and John Norton Moore (The Hague: Martinus Nijhoff, 1999), 229.

through Annex VI of the MARPOL Convention. Part XII also recognizes the roles of global and regional bodies in the implementation of UNCLOS rules, which allows these bodies to adopt measures for new developments.

3.4 *Subsequent Practice of the Parties*

A treaty regime can take into account new circumstances after its adoption through a shift in how its provisions are interpreted. One way this can occur is through the influence of the practice of the parties.[34] The most direct effect of State practice on treaty interpretation is through Article 31(3)(b) of the Vienna Convention on the Law of Treaties (VCLT), which provides that "any subsequent practice in the application of the treaty which establishes the agreement of the parties regarding its interpretation" shall be taken into account in interpreting a treaty, together with the context. However, a change in interpretation in this form is not easily realized.

In the *South China Sea Arbitration*, the arbitral tribunal recognized that State practice may have the effect of modifying a provision of a treaty. However, regarding Article 31(3)(b) of the VCLT, the arbitral award considered that "the Parties must have acquiesced in such practice so that one can speak of an agreement reached concerning the interpretation of the provision in question" and adopted a high threshold that is consistent with international jurisprudence on this point.[35] In addition, the award considered the relevance of State practice apart from Article 31(3)(b) of the VCLT when it considered the possibility that the PRC had established exceptional rights or jurisdiction after the adoption of UNCLOS based on State practice. The award stated that for such a case to be made, there must be an "assertion by a State of a right at variance with the Convention, acquiescence therein by the other States Parties, and the passage of sufficient time to establish beyond doubt the existence of both the right and a general acquiescence."[36]

Notwithstanding the high threshold and exceptional circumstances that must exist for State practice to effect a change in the law, there is an emerging issue on which State practice may play a significant role. Due to concerns about the impact of sea-level rise caused by climate change on coastal States' maritime entitlements, small island States in the Pacific are adopting the practice of notifying their maritime zones to the Secretary-General of the United Nations and taking the position that the maritime zones will be preserved notwithstanding any physical changes connected to climate-change related sea-level rise.[37] This interpretation is not universally shared at

[34] Holst, *Change in the Law of the Sea*, 237–240.

[35] *South China Sea arbitration*, 390–391 (para. 552).

[36] *South China Sea arbitration*, 292 (para. 275).

[37] Declaration on Preserving Maritime Zones in the Face of Climate Change-Related Sea-Level Rise adopted by the Pacific Islands Form (PIF), at https://www.forumsec.org/wp-content/uploads/2021/08/Declaration-on-Preserving-Maritime.pdf. For an overview of related State practice, see Davor Vidas and David Freestone, "Legal Certainty and Stability in the Face of Sea Level Rise:

present.[38] However, the fact that some States are starting to accept it may be signaling a move toward subsequent practice which establishes an agreement between the parties.[39] While the legal justifications for the "freezing" of baselines and the preservation of maritime zones continue to be discussed, including in the International Law Commission, it is worth noting that the discussion is framed as an issue relating to the possible interpretation of existing provisions and not as the emergence of a new rule of customary international law.[40]

3.5 Development of the Law by International Courts and Tribunals

The UNCLOS dispute settlement mechanism is commonly associated with the need to preserve the integrity of the "package deal" reflected in UNCLOS.[41] In regard to issues concerning the allocation of jurisdiction under UNCLOS, international courts and tribunals have provided clarity regarding the extent of the powers that States have under UNCLOS through the interpretation and application of its provisions. In the *MV "Saiga" (No. 2)* and *MV "Virginia G"* cases, the ITLOS provided important guidance on the jurisdiction of coastal States over bunkering activities in the exclusive economic zone (EEZ), which is not explicitly provided for in UNCLOS.[42] The ITLOS also made an important, although somewhat controversial, finding with

---

Trends in the Development of State Practice and International Law Scholarship on Maritime Limits and Boundaries," *International Journal of Marine and Coastal Law* 37, no. 4 (2022): 30–35.

[38] See discussions in International Law Association, "Baselines Under the International Law of the Sea," *International Law Association Reports of Conferences* 75 (2012), 413; Tim Stephens, "Warming Waters and Souring Seas: Climate Change and Ocean Acidification" in *Oxford Handbook of the Law of the Sea*, 789; Rosemary Rayfuse, "Sea Level Rise and Maritime Zones: Preserving the Maritime Entitlements of "Disappearing" States," in *Threatened Island Nations: Legal Implications of Rising Seas and a Changing Climate,* eds. Michael B. Gerrard and Gregory E. Wannier (Cambridge: Cambridge University Press, 2013), 172–173.

[39] Japan, for example, has expressed its position that "it is permissible to preserve the existing baselines and maritime zones established in accordance with [UNCLOS], notwithstanding the regression of coastlines." Ministry of Foreign Affairs of Japan, "Foreign Minister Hayashi's Meeting with the Delegation of the Pacific Islands Forum (PIF)" at https://www.mofa.go.jp/press/release/press1e_000369.html (accessed 1 March 2024).

[40] International Law Commission, Sea-level Rise in Relation to International Law: Additional paper to the first issues paper (2020), by Bogdan Aurescu and Nilüfer Oral, Co-Chairs of the Study Group on sea-level rise in relation to international law, UN Doc. A/CN.4/761, 39–40 (paras. 95–96).

[41] Alan E. Boyle, "Dispute Settlement and the Law of the Sea Convention: Problems of Fragmentation and Jurisdiction," *International and Comparative Law Quarterly* 46 (1997): 38–39; Natalie Klein, *Dispute Settlement in the UN Convention on the Law of the Sea* (Cambridge: Cambridge University Press, 2004), 367.

[42] *MV "SAIGA" (No. 2) (Saint Vincent and the Grenadines v. Guinea), Judgment, ITLOS Reports 1999*, 54–55 (paras. 126–131); *M/V "Virginia G" (Panama/Guinea-Bissau), Judgment, ITLOS Reports 2014*, 66–71 (paras. 206–224).

respect to legislative jurisdiction over ships on the high seas.[43] These cases have more implications for the stability of the UNCLOS regime rather than its development.

However, judgments and awards by international courts and tribunals have also contributed to the further development of the law in response to changing circumstances. Recent decisions have shown that judicial processes can reinforce environmental obligations under the law of the sea.[44] For example, in contrast to the focus on marine pollution in Part XII of UNCLOS, which reflects the framing of the issues at the time it was negotiated, the jurisprudence of international courts and tribunals now affirms that the conservation of ecosystems and biodiversity is included within the scope of Part XII.[45] In the *South China Sea Arbitration*, the arbitral tribunal considered that the content of the general obligation to protect and preserve the marine environment in Article 192 is "informed by the other provisions of Part XII and other applicable rules of international law."[46] Such an approach would allow for the further development of principles and rules related to the protection of the marine environment and biodiversity.

The use of advisory proceedings to seek clarification of the law is another approach that has been increasingly utilized in recent years. In the *SRFC Advisory Opinion*, ITLOS confirmed its jurisdiction to issue advisory opinions where an agreement confers jurisdiction on ITLOS.[47] The advisory opinion issued by ITLOS, in that case, contributed to the development of the law by clarifying issues such as the obligation of flag States for IUU activities in the EEZs of third States.[48] Some States, including the PRC, maintain reservations regarding the power of ITLOS, apart from the seabed dispute chamber, to give advisory opinions.[49] However, there appears to be a trend in States' positions toward accepting the power of ITLOS to do so.[50] ITLOS will likely reconfirm its powers in answering the request for an advisory opinion by

---

[43] For a critical analysis of the Judgment, see, for example, Arron N. Honniball, Freedom of Navigation Following the MV "Norstar" case, JCLOS Blog, https://site.uit.no/nclos/2019/06/04/freedom-of-navigation-following-the-m-v-norstar-case/ (accessed 1 March 2024).

[44] Joanna Mossop, "Can We Make the Oceans Greener? The Successes and Failures of UNCLOS as an Environmental Treaty," *Victoria University of Wellington Law Review* 49 (2018): 587–590.

[45] Award in the Arbitration regarding the Chagos Marine Protected Area between Mauritius and the United Kingdom of Great Britain and Northern Ireland, Award of 18 March 2015, *Reports of International Arbitral Awards* XXXI (2018): 499–500 (para. 320) (citing Article 194(5) and noting that "[w]hile the control of pollution is certainly an important aspect of environmental protection, it is by no means the only one.").

[46] *South China Sea arbitration*, 519 (para. 941).

[47] *Request for Advisory Opinion submitted by the Sub-Regional Fisheries Commission, Advisory Opinion, 2 April 2015, ITLOS Reports 2015*, 21 (para. 56).

[48] *SRFC Advisory Opinion*, 63–68 (para. 218).

[49] See, for example, the submission of the PRC on request for an advisory opinion submitted by COSIS at https://www.itlos.org/fileadmin/itlos/documents/cases/31/written_statements/1/C31-WS-1-8-China__transmission_ltr._.pdf (accessed 1 March 2014), 2–11.

[50] For example, the BBNJ Agreement allows its Conference of the Parties to seek advisory opinions to ITLOS (Article 47(7)). Although the questions on which advisory opinions may be requested are narrowly prescribed ("legal question on the conformity with this Agreement of a proposal before the Conference of the Parties on any matter within its competence"), it is significant that States

the Commission of Small Island States on Climate Change and International Law (COSIS).[51]

4 Stability and Change in the Context of the South China Sea

The South China Sea is often considered an area of instability. An important question from the perspective of international law is whether this instability derives from the state of the law. Where the rules of international law are unclear or have become inadequate due to changing circumstances, international relations may remain unstable until the change of circumstances is reflected in the law. As mapped in the previous section, there are various ways in which the law develops in the law of the sea. However, the reason for instability in the South China Sea is completely different from situations where the law of the sea has seen development in response to changing circumstances. Even though States continue to take different views on their territorial and maritime entitlements in the South China Sea, the applicable rules can be regarded as fairly clear.

Although territorial or maritime boundary disputes may create uncertainties regarding the extent of coastal States' entitlements, these are not exceptional or unforeseen circumstances. On the contrary, Articles 74 and 83 of UNCLOS on maritime boundary delimitation envisage that States may be unable to agree on a maritime boundary for a certain period. Articles 74(2) and 83(2) oblige States to "resort to procedures in Part XV" if no agreement can be reached within a reasonable period of time.[52] In addition, Articles 74(3) and 73(3) require the States concerned to make every effort to enter into provisional arrangements and not to jeopardize or hamper the reaching of the final agreement. Although the exact scope of this obligation has been subject to discussion, it is significant that UNCLOS provides a legal framework that regulates the conduct of States even where they have different views regarding the extent of their maritime entitlements.[53]

agreed on a text which is premised on the understanding that ITLOS has the jurisdiction to give advisory opinions to the extent such jurisdiction is conferred to it through the BBNJ Agreement.

[51] Commission of Small Island States on Climate Change and International Law, Request for Advisory Opinion at https://www.itlos.org/fileadmin/itlos/documents/cases/31/Request_for_Advisory_Opinion_COSIS_12.12.22.pdf (accessed 1 March 2024).

[52] However, this obligation is limited by optional exceptions to the compulsory dispute settlement procedure in Article 298. The PRC declared that it would not be bound by the compulsory dispute settlement procedures for all categories of disputes listed in Article 298. The People's Republic of China, Declaration under Article 298, 25 August 2006, *Law of the Sea Bulletin* 62 (2006): 14.

[53] On this issue, see British Institute of International and Comparative Law, *Report on the Obligations of States under Articles 74(3) and 83(3) of UNCLOS in Respect of Undelimited Maritime Areas* (London: British Institute of International and Comparative Law, 2016); Kentaro Nishimoto, "The Obligation of Self-Restraint in Undelimited Maritime Areas," *Japan Review* 3, no. 1 (2019): 28–38.

The legal situation of the South China Sea is unique because, unlike typical maritime delimitation disputes in which entitlements based on UNCLOS overlap, the PRC's claim to historic rights within the "nine-dash lines" calls into question the existence of an overlapping entitlement to begin with. The validity of such claims, while subject to significant skepticism by experts outside the PRC,[54] might initially have been seen as a genuine issue regarding the interpretation of UNCLOS.[55] However, the Philippines sought to clarify whether the assertion of historic rights based on rules external to UNCLOS is justified, using the dispute settlement procedure. The award in the *South China Sea Arbitration* provided legal clarity by declaring that China's claims within the "nine-dash line" are "contrary to the Convention and without lawful effect to the extent that they exceed the geographic and substantive limits of China's maritime entitlements under [UNCLOS]."[56] Thus, the main source of continued instability in the South China Sea is not a result of any ambiguity or shortcoming in the legal regime itself but rather an issue of a State unwilling to adhere to the rules and mechanisms contained in UNCLOS.

The PRC's argument on the need to "develop and improve" creates the impression that there may be certain aspects of UNCLOS relevant to the South China Sea that need to be "developed and improved." However, the negotiation and adoption of the BBNJ Agreement that is cited in the PRC's notes were done in a different context and do not support what the PRC appears to be intending to establish. First, the BBNJ Agreement is a good indication that the development of the law of the sea occurs with the consent of States, which is a fundamental principle of international law. The BBNJ Agreement was adopted by consensus[57] and will be subject to ratification by States. The other mechanisms for change in the law of the sea are also based on consent to UNCLOS, through which States agreed to confer certain powers to bodies, incorporate GAIRS, and enter into a system of compulsory dispute settlement.

---

[54] Florian Dupuy and Pierre-Marie Dupuy, "A Legal Analysis of China's Historic Rights Claims in the South China Sea," *American Journal of International Law* 107, no. 1 (2013): 124–141; Robert Beckman, "The UN Convention on the Law of the Sea and the Maritime Disputes in the South China Sea," *American Journal of International Law* 107, no. 1 (2013): 142–163; Kentaro Nishimoto, "Minami-Shina Kai ni okeru Chugoku no Shucho to Kokusaiho jyo no Hyouka" [Chinese Claims in the South China Sea and their Validity under International law], *Hogaku* [Legal Studies] 78, no. 3 (2014): 225–259 (in Japanese).

[55] *South China arbitration*, 438 (para. 704) (stating that "Tribunal accepts that China has asserted its claim to rights in the waters within 200 nautical miles of the Philippines baselines in good faith. That the Tribunal disagrees with China's understanding of its rights and considers that there is no possible legal basis for China's claimed rights does not mean that China's understanding has not been genuinely held").

[56] *South China Sea arbitration*, 612 (para. 1203).

[57] Report of the Intergovernmental Conference on an International Legally Binding Instrument under the United Nations Convention on the Law of the Sea on the Conservation and Sustainable Use of Marine Biological Diversity of Areas beyond National Jurisdiction at its Fifth Session, UN Doc. A/CONF.232/2023/5, 9 (para 29 and note 1), https://undocs.org/Home/Mobile?FinalSymbol=a%2Fconf.232%2F2023%2F5 (accessed 1 March 2024). However, the Russian Federation expressed its intent to dissociate itself from consensus after the Agreement was adopted.

A unilateral assertion of the need to "develop and improve" the law will not result in a change of the law unless other States accept it.

Second, the BBNJ Agreement does not fill a gap in the sense of a complete lacuna in the law but provides detailed rules that were missing in UNCLOS and are now required due to new concerns of the international community. The newly introduced rules are based on rules and principles already contained in UNCLOS. Therefore, it is a mischaracterization of the adoption of the BBNJ Agreement to refer to it as an indication of the incompleteness of the UNCLOS regime. Moreover, the fact that UNCLOS has undergone certain improvements does not necessarily mean that the original rules were substituted with new rules, which allows arguments contrary to UNCLOS to be made. As different mechanisms for change in the law of the sea illustrate, with the exception of the Part XI Implementing Agreement, the UNCLOS regime has developed in a manner that is consistent with the original agreement.

Third, the adoption of the BBNJ Agreement is representative of the fact that the development of the law of the sea has mainly occurred in relation to ocean sustainability issues. The response to change through various mechanisms for change also paints the same picture. The arguments that the PRC is seeking to buttress by referring to the need to "develop and improve" UNCLOS does not fall within this category. In regard to rules on maritime entitlements and jurisdiction, States have adhered to the regime under UNCLOS that is generally considered to provide a comprehensive set of rules on this matter. With the possible exception of the effect of sea-level rise, there has not been any widely supported initiative for the modification of rules under UNCLOS that define States' maritime entitlements and jurisdiction.

5 Conclusion

Although UNCLOS faces challenges concerning the need to protect the marine environment, conserve marine biodiversity, and respond to the effects of climate change, solutions are still being sought within the existing legal framework. While considerable efforts may be required to address these sustainability challenges, it is important that the need to respond to such difficulties is not exploited by States seeking to challenge the existing legal framework. The discussion of the need for change necessarily requires a distinction between what needs to be changed and what needs to remain as it is. Apart from the possible exception of the ongoing discussions on the effect of sea-level rise on baselines, there is little to suggest that the basic legal framework under UNCLOS per se requires modification or "improvement." It is expected that States will continue to act under the UNCLOS framework, where necessary, utilizing various mechanisms that have provided UNCLOS with its resilience to remain relevant.

Chapter 3
Potential of the International Dispute Settlement Mechanisms as Established Under UNCLOS: Options for Improvement

Rüdiger Wolfrum

1 Introduction

One of the major achievements of UNCLOS—there are many—is the establishment of a mandatory system for the settlement of maritime disputes. Since we are celebrating UNCLOS let me briefly mention some of the important issues, which distinguishes this regime from previous ones.

As I said the dispute settlement system is mandatory. Whoever ratifies is automatically committed to Part XV. As emphasized by the then President of UNCLOS III Professor Tommy Koh this avoids cherry picking. No State can take advantage of the benefits UNCLOS offers, such as the participation in deep seabed mining or the claim to an extended continental shelf without being committed to the dispute settlement mechanism. Sure some may argue that most of UNCLOS was or has been developed by now into customary international law. True but the extended continental shelf, the deep seabed mining regime and the regime on the peaceful settlement of disputes have not acquired that status.

This commitment to a mandatory dispute settlement system theoretically constitutes an infringement into the sovereignty of an individual State. Such an infringement is compensated by various means which I will list only in a telegraphic style.

Being party to the dispute settlement mechanism means not only that a State may be faced with a dispute with the consequence that it has to follow the procedural rules—which means to cooperate with the other party to the dispute as well as the court or tribunal concerned—but it can also initiate a claim itself or a counter-claim as the case may be.

R. Wolfrum (✉)
Mühltalstrasse 129 B, 69121 Heidelberg, Germany
e-mail: wolfrum@mpfpr.de

L. A. T. Nguyen and H. D. Vu (eds.), *Viability of UNCLOS amid Emerging Global Maritime Challenges*, https://doi.org/10.1007/978-981-97-5838-8_3

Additionally, UNCLOS provides certain restrictions—they may be qualified as sovereignty induced restrictions—before a particular court or tribunal can be approached. These are matters of jurisdiction and admissibility to put it technically. These restrictions are contained in section I of Part XV. They all are meant to ensure that the parties may solve a legal dispute according to means of their own choice. So far individual State sovereignty prevails. However, this choice concerning the procedure to be followed has to reflect the will of both parties to the legal dispute concerned; this choice cannot be dictated by one party alone. This is crucial, otherwise the more powerful of the parties could enforce its will on other States. In that respect, the provisions referred to have an equalizing effect. Apart from that it has already been ruled by international Courts and Tribunals that negotiations—one of the non-judicial means of dispute settlement may not last forever.

A central provision in this respect is Article 283 UNCLOS, a frequently misunderstood provision. The jurisprudence of ITLOS was in the past not always coherent. Only on 11 June 2022 an Arbitral Tribunal has rendered a remarkable judgment on Article 283 UNCLOS.

[1]It has stated that it is necessary to overcome the threshold of Article 283 UNCLOS that the parties to the dispute—in this case Ukraine and the Russian Federation—must exchange views on the potential means how to solve the dispute. In this case, such an exchange of views had not taken place. Nevertheless, the Tribunal decided that, given the particular situation of the Ukrainian sailors and servicemen, justified the Ukrainian application without having exhausted Article 283 UNCLOS. This somewhat sounds like a decision ex aequo and bono but it is better than just disregarding the wording of Article 283 UNCLOS.

Further sovereignty saving clauses are that the courts and tribunals acting under Part XV UNCLOS do not have the jurisdiction to decide on the issue of sovereignty over the land or islands, unless both parties so agree. Law of the sea disputes concerning ITLOS and arbitral tribunals are only those on the interpretation or application of UNCLOS (Articles 286 and 288). In this context also the possibility should be mentioned to choose between several means of dispute settlement (ITLOS, ICJ, and Arbitration). Parties frequently prefer arbitration or -as in the case between Mauritius and the Maldives a special chamber of ITLOS. The recourse to arbitration and special chambers is definitely guided by the desire to have some influence concerning the selection of arbitrators—again an issue, which may be qualified as a sovereignty concern. Finally, let me mention as a strong sovereignty saving clause Article 298, para.1 lit. a and b UNCLOS through which it is possible to exclude certain disputes from the generally mandatory dispute settlement mechanism. The sovereignty relevance was emphasized when this provision was negotiated.

---

[1] PCA case No. 2019–28, In the Matter of an Arbitration before an Arbitral Tribunal Constituted under Annex VII to the 1982 Convention on the Law of the Sea, *Ukraine v. the Russian Federation*, Award on Preliminary Objections, of 27 June 2022, at para. 74 et seq.

In particular, Article 298 (1) b UNCLOS has been invoked several times already. The Arbitral Tribunal referred to has now clarified the scope and the meaning of the terms "military activities" albeit several questions have been left open to be decided on the merits. The Arbitral Tribunal deviates from an Order of ITLOS touching upon an identical issue.

Let me conclude this first introductory part of my presentation with a positive note. UNCLOS has adopted in 1982 a modern dispute settlement system, which was well tailored to the needs of an efficient ocean governance as it was seen 40 years ago. Compared to the then traditional mechanisms the UNCLOS dispute settlement mechanism as set out in Part XV was innovative and it featured a well-balanced equilibrium between a settlement system serving the dogma of peaceful international relations while ensuring the sovereignty of States in respect of certain issues.

However, 40 years have gone by; public international law underwent significant changes and it is facing challenges not thought of 40 years ago. May I just mention sea-level rise due to global warming, the increasing pollution of the sea, increasing over-fishing and the lack of coordination of marine economic activities at a moment where these activities increase and are becoming more complex.

A sustainable government of the ocean space is in the interest of the international community. And accordingly, UNCLOS belongs to the permanently growing typology of international treaties serving community interests.[2] To invoke these treaties before international court or tribunal with the view of their implementation and enforcement entails particular procedural challenges. The question is whether the dispute settlement regime under UNCLOS is adequately tailored to meet these challenges. To put it into a nutshell the main challenge is whether individual States may be considered as legitimate agents of the international community and therefore my initiate claims not serving their individual interests but the one of the international community?

To illustrate the challenges international as well as national juridical bodies are facing let me briefly address the decision of the ICJ indicating whether the Courts realized the challenge so far indicated and how it overcame it. Unfortunately, I cannot have recourse to ITLOS or awards of arbitral tribunals established under Annex VII. Therefore must have recourse to an Order of the ICJ of 23 January 2020 in the case *The Gambia v. Myanmar.*[3]

---

[2] For further details see Rüdiger Wolfrum, Solidarity and Community Interests: Driving Forcesfor the Interpretation and Development of International Law, General Course on Public International Law, RdC vol. 416p. 12 at 179 et seq.

[3] Application of the Convention on the Prevention and Punishment of the Crime of Genocide (*The Gambia v. Myanmar)*, Provisional Measures, Order of 23 January 2020, I.C.J. Reports 2020, p. 3, 17 (paras. 39 et seq.).

1.1 *ICJ Order of 23 January, 2020 in the Case the Gambia V. Myanmar*

In this case, The Gambia argued that Myanmar had committed genocide against the Rohingya, a Muslim minority in that country, and submitted an application to the ICJ with the objective to have the measures taken against the Rohingya to be ended. The ICJ in its Order of 23 January 2020 *prima facie*[4] accepted the standing of The Gambia, while having recourse to its previous jurisprudence.[5]

Other cases where the same problem arose were the Case Duarte Agostinho and Others v. Portugal and 32 States before the European Human Rights Court, the People's Climate case before the European Court of Justice and several national court decisions. However, it should be mentioned that in the Whaling case (Australia v. Japan) the ICJ avoided to decide whether the abolition of whaling was demanded by the international community—represented by Australia.

1.2 *The Jurisprudence of the ICJ, Concerning Standing in Disputes Touching on Erga Omnes Obligations—A Preliminary Analysis*

What was the mechanism used by the ICJ in *The Gambia v. Myanmar* case? The ICJ distinguished in a first step between the right invoked by the applicant—a question to be decided on the merits—and the procedural question of standing. In a second step, the Court established that the applicant could invoke an individual right guaranteed by the treaty in question serving community interests. The step to establish the procedural right of the applicant's standing was based upon the pragmatic argument of the ICJ that otherwise no State may invoke the responsibility of another State party.[6] At exactly at this point Mme XU Vice-President of the ICJ disagreed. Although I agree to the result of the Court, I am of the opinion that the reasoning could have been improved by invoking Article 48 of the ILC Articles on Responsibility of States for Internationally Wrongful Acts.[7] This would have had the advantage that this would underline the claim for cessation of the wrongful act and assurances and guarantees of non-repetition whereas a claim for reparation would be limited.

---

[4] See note 3.

[5] Advisory Opinion on Reservations to the Convention on the Prevention and Punishment of the Crime of Genocide, I.C.J. Reports 1951, p. 23.

[6] Questions relating to the Obligation to Prosecute or Extradite (*Belgium v. Senegal*) ICJ Reports 2012, 450 at para. 69.

[7] The reasoning of Jean-Marc Thouvenin, La saisine de la Cour international de Justice en cas de violation des règeles fondamentales de l'ordre juridique international, in The Fundamental Rules of the International Legal Order, Jus Cogens and Obligations *Erga Omnes,* Christian Tomuschat and Jean-Marc Thouvenin, 2006, 311 (327/8).

One may add a further endorsing consideration. Based upon the Mavrommatis clause[8] it is traditionally requested that the applicant claims an individual right opposed by the one of the respondent. In fact, in the context of regimes serving community interests the applicant may claim its interest in upholding the integrity of the regime concerned or—to put it into different terms—that the commitments of the applicant to the international community or a particular community are not devalued by the violations committed by the respondent belonging to the same community.

To summarize on the question who may act as claimant in judicial proceedings in upholding regimes serving community interests, the jurisprudence of the ICJ has demonstrated a high degree of responsiveness to modern challenges of international law. It has not only accepted that regimes serving community interests have a place in international law but—to be effective—deserve adjustments as far as judicial review procedures are concerned. The progressive development in this respect is best demonstrated by comparing the statements in the South-West Africa case with the one in the case *Questions relating to the Obligation to Prosecute or Extradite.* Whereas the former denies rights individual States may have in a regime, which is qualified as serving community interests (the reference is to a "sacred trust") the latter clearly acknowledges "… that any State party to the Convention may invoke the responsibility of another State party with a view to ascertaining the alleged failure to comply with its obligations *erga omnes partes* … and to bring that failure to an end."[9]

The particularity of the cases The Gambia v. Myanmar or the Case Questions relating to the Obligation to Prosecute or to Extradite before the ICJ are that applicants and respondents are States and as such both members of the international community. Therefore, it is a matter of consequence that the applicant can act as a trustee of that community. The international community mostly acts through international Conferences such as the Rio Conference system or the UN General Assembly. The principles these conferences develop are included into the international normative order.[10] So far, I have referred to human rights cases—however it should be more than evident that claims resulting from human rights violations may be an equally fertile ground for international claims. In particular, the Paris Agreement can serve as a basis.

[8] See R. Ueprpman-Wittzack, The Mavromatis Concessions Cases, Max-Planck-Encyclopedia of Public International Law, voll. VIIp. 28 et seq.

[9] On that Christian J. Tams, Enforcing Obligations *Erga Omnes* in Internationa Law, CUP, Cambridge, 2005, at 99; in respect of the European Court foe Human Rights, see Angelika Nußberger, The concept of "jurisdiction" in the Jurisprudence of the European Court of Human Rights, Current Legal Problems, vol. 65 (2012), 241–268.

[10] For details see Rüdiger Wolfrum, Solidarity and Community Interests (note 2), p. 280 -297.

1.2.1 Who is Bound by a Judgment or Award on Disputes Touching upon Community Interests: Is There a Possible Impact Different from Being Legally Binding?

This question rarely brought up is nevertheless essential as to whether international or national courts constitute a decisive element in enforcing community interests. According to Article 59 of the ICJ Statute, judgments (decisions) of the ICJ are binding only upon the parties and in respect to the legal dispute concerned. Article 33(2) Annex VI to UNCLOS (Statute of ITLOS) repeats this wording. This clause is, with alterations, common in other statutes of dispute settlement institutions. Taken literally, this clause does not seem to be adequate for deciding on disputes related to community interest driven regimes. It rather reflects the traditional bi-focal nature of legal disputes. A more differentiated ascertainment of the dogmatic basis of this clause and the relevant judicial practice of international courts and tribunals allows a more lenient approach thereto.

According to Article 38(1)(d) ICJ Statute, judicial decisions are "subsidiary means for the detection of rules of law". They are not promulgating rights and obligations of States but "documentary sources" indicating where a court or tribunal can find evidence of the existence of the rules it is to apply.[11] Although it is commonly emphasized that international courts and tribunals do not exercise legislative functions, international judicial decisions may, de facto, modify or supplement the international normative order. The dividing line between norm interpretation and the modification of existing norms or their normative supplementation is thin. Therefore one could possibly argue that international courts or tribunals when interpreting a norm should not only take into account the interpretation of a relevant norm by a judicial forum—which they actually mostly do—but to accept such interpretation if they have no convincing reason not to do so. In the award Bangladesh v. India, one may find a cautious wording to the extent that international courts and arbitral tribunals have de facto a norm establishing function.

2 Summary and Tentative Suggestions for an Adjustment of National as well as International Adjudicative Systems

The perusal of some recent cases decided at the international, regional, and at the national level have shown that the present system concerning dispute settlement is procedurally not ideally tailored to deal with claims by States or individuals, which on their face protect individual interests but in reality fostering community oriented regimes. Although the option of an *actio popularis* is being denied some courts found means to deal with the issue on the merits after having circumvented the procedural aspect of standing.

[11] Alain Pellet, Article 38, in: The Statute of the International Court of Justice: A Commentary MN 299.

Critically one may say that this jurisprudence which very much focuses on environmental law—in particular on environmental damage—may push the courts or tribunals into the situation to decide on issues for which the national executive is better equipped or to say it otherwise to become legislators. The principle of the separation of powers constitutes an important element within the principle of the rule of law equally relevant at the international as well as the national level. A rather unknown example illustrating this issue is to be found in Article 189 UNCLOS according to which the Seabed Disputes Chamber has no jurisdiction "with regard to the exercise by the Authority of its discretionary powers."

If the existing rules, concerning the settlement of disputes on community oriented treaties is not satisfactory it is recommendable to consider solutions de *lege ferenda.* It may be advisable to design a regime in which disputes may be solved via advisory opinions. Is it really adequate to say that conflicts may be solved via advisory opinions?

In fact, it is, advisory opinions state the content of the applicable law or rather norms. It is for the addressees to implement such statement, and this can even been done by a subsequent decision of an international court or tribunal as ITLOS has demonstrated in the case between Mauritius and Maldives.[12]

What are the advantages of Advisory opinions?

- Concentrating on law rather on facts;
- Avoidance of a bi-polar focus;
- Participation of many States and even international organizations in hearings;
- Recourse not only to treaty law and customary law but also to non-judicially binding international norms.

What are the disadvantages? It may be said that recommendations or findings of an advisory 0pinion are not binding—is this really a disadvantage? Sure, judgments of international courts and arbitral awards are legally binding. However, they are in practice hardly enforceable. Their implementation and their impact on public international law rests upon how they are reasoned. The same apply to advisory opinions.

To highlight the difference between an advisory opinion concerning environmental responsibility of industrial States concerning sea-level rise initiated by Pacific island States and a claim of one or more of these States against one or the other industrialized States. I believe you most will agree with me that an advisory opinion would be the most appropriate mechanism to clarify the relationship between climate change and sea level rise and which—if any—concrete conclusion may be drawn therefrom in respect of State responsibility.

[12] Case No. 28, Judgment of 28 January 2021, Preliminary Objects, paras. 176 -192.

Part II
UNCLOS and Emerging Global Maritime Challenges

Chapter 4
Marine Data Collection Outside the MSR Regime

James Kraska

1 Introduction

Part XIII of the United Nations Convention on the Law of the Sea (UNCLOS) governs marine scientific research (MSR). The rules on MSR were designed to give coastal states greater control over the right to consent or withhold consent from foreign research activities in their exclusive economic zone (EEZ) and on the continental shelf. This approach was initially opposed by the United States and other maritime powers, which sought a liberal order of the oceans where the right to conduct MSR in the EEZ and on the continental shelf were high seas freedoms. However, there are other types of marine data collection that are regulated either through other parts of the treaty or are not addressed by it.[1]

This chapter explores the rules governing MSR and considers 9 other types of marine data collection that fall outside the MSR regime. Flag states have jurisdiction over MSR conducted from their vessels but this authority or competence may be concurrent with coastal state jurisdiction in littoral waters. Coastal states have sovereignty over the territorial sea, archipelagic waters, and straits used for international navigation. MSR within these waters is subject to coastal state prior consent.[2] The regulation of MSR in these areas falls within specific provisions in UNCLOS. Coastal states have legal competence over MSR in the EEZ and on the continental shelf through Part XIII. This regime reflects sovereign rights and jurisdiction over

[1] United Nations Convention on the Law of the Sea, art. 246, 1833 U.N.T.S. 397, 21 I.L.M. 1261 (1982) [Hereinafter "UNCLOS").

[2] Coastal state sovereignty also includes archipelagic waters and straits used for international navigation.

J. Kraska (✉)
Stockton Center for International Law, U.S. Naval War College, 686 Cushing Rd, Newport, RI 02841, United States
e-mail: James.Kraska@usnwc.edu

L. A. T. Nguyen and H. D. Vu (eds.), *Viability of UNCLOS amid Emerging Global Maritime Challenges*, https://doi.org/10.1007/978-981-97-5838-8_5

in situ activities designed to advance the state of knowledge of the marine environment. As scientific methods have progressed, marine data may be collected pursuant to other provisions of UNCLOS, such as hydrographic surveys. These activities are governed by sources of law lying entirely outside of Part XIII. Exceptions to Part XIII generally fall within 9 different categories and are subject to separate rules.

This chapter mainly focuses on exceptions to the general regime of MSR in Part XIII of UNCLOS. Part I unpacks the basic rules governing MSR in UNCLOS. While it was envisioned as a liberal regime to enable MSR, the regime governing marine science is subject to coastal state control over activities in the territorial sea, the EEZ and on the continental shelf. Therefore, only MSR conducted beyond national jurisdiction is done pursuant to high seas freedom of navigation. Furthermore, the MSR regime only covers specific classical MSR expeditionary science, generally conducted aboard a research vessel. There are, however, a numerous methods used to collect information about the marine environment that do not fall within Part XIII. Part 2 turns to the first of these methodologies—operational oceanography. Operational oceanography includes data collected from routine ship transits. The data is typically used to ensure the safety of normal ship operations. While it may be stored and later combined with other data to help better understand the marine environment, it is not MSR per se and not regulated by Part XIII. Part 3 addresses the use of remote sensing of the oceans from outer space, which is also not regulated by Part XIII. Remote sensing uses satellites and aircraft to collect data about the marine environment from beyond the jurisdictional reach of the coastal state. Because the activity occurs well beyond national jurisdiction, coastal states have no authority to regulate it.

Part 4 looks at the rules regarding exploration for natural resources either in the EEZ of a coastal state and subject to Article 56 of Part V or in the International Seabed Area, subject to the rules of Part XI on deep seabed mining. Part 5 focuses on hydrographic surveys, which may be conducted on the high seas or near a coastal state. There are separate rules in UNCLOS for the conduct of hydrographic surveys in coastal state zones. In the EEZ, for example, coastal states may regulate hydrographic surveys related to their exclusive sovereign rights and jurisdiction over living and non-living resources because survey work typically is done to locate oil and natural gas in the seabed. Part 6 turns to underwater cultural heritage, which also is not an activity classified as MSR. The traditional approach, which remains customary law, is that shipwrecks and man-made objects on the seabed are not "natural resources," and therefore are subject neither to the regime of the EEZ or continental shelf when within areas of coastal state jurisdiction, or under the purview of the International Seabed Authority when lying on the deep seabed. There are about 3 million of shipwrecks worldwide and most of them are within the EEZ and on the continental shelf because historically ships powered by oar and sail traveled close to the shore.

Part 7 examines the right to conduct environmental monitoring and assessment of the oceans, including in a coastal state's EEZ. Part XII on the protection of the marine environment requires all states to be active participants in the protection of the marine environment, including the requirement to conduct environmental impact assessments for activities that may affect the quality of the marine environment. States are called on to "observe, measure, evaluate and analyze" the effects of pollution on the marine environment.[3] These activities involve collecting information about the marine environment, but they are not MSR. Likewise, Part 8 explores military and intelligence activities, which are also not MSR. Warships, military aircraft, spy satellites, and other national technical means may collect information about the marine environment, including in coastal state EEZs and on their continental shelves. These activities are not for the purpose of advancing marine science and therefore are not regulated through the MSR regime in Part XIII, even if they use similar or sometimes identical means of MSR. Parts 9 and 10 conclude with two other methods of collecting information about the marine environment that fall outside the regime of MSR. In part 9, bio-logging involves tagging marine organisms and wildlife to study them and their surroundings. These animals follow natural and unpredictable courses on the surface of the ocean, through the water column and (with birds) airspace of coastal states, relaying data to scientists along the way through electronic signals. Although the data is collected for the purpose of advancing marine science, the unpredictable path of the animals makes it impractical to regulate before the data are collected. Part 10 concludes with the recent phenomenon of citizen science, in which citizens are enlisted through technology applications, such as on the iPhone, to report activity about the marine environment. This crowd sources information that later may be analyzed and used by scientists to study the marine environment. Because of the distributed method of data collection and the impracticality of regulation by the coastal state, this method lies outside of the regime in Part XIII.

The chapter concludes with some thoughts on what to expect going forward. Just as the Internet has bypassed state sovereignty in many ways, the MSR regime in Part XIII is challenged by technological methods that bypass the cumbersome rules and exclusive control coastal states have traditionally exercised over MSR in their EEZ and on their continental shelves.

2 Marine Scientific Research

Marine scientific research is subject to a specific governance regime set forth in Part XIII of UNCLOS. All states are entitled to conduct MSR. There is a general duty among states and competent international organizations to "promote and facilitate" MSR in accordance with UNCLOS. MSR is subject to four principles. First, it shall be conducted exclusively for peaceful purposes. Second, MSR shall be conducted with "appropriate scientific methods and means." Third, MSR shall not "unjustifiably interfere with other legitimate uses of the sea." These uses include shipping navigation and military operations. Fourth, MSR shall be conducted in compliance with UNCLOS, including the rules in Part XII on the protection of the marine environment.[4]

[3] UNCLOS, art. 204.

[4] UNCLOS, art. 240.

Coastal states should cooperate and create favorable conditions for the conduct of MSR in the marine environment, but in reality they often impose expenses and requirements that impede marine science in their EEZ and on their continental shelf.[5] Coastal states have exclusive authority to regulate MSR in their territorial sea.[6] In the EEZ, and on the continental shelf, however, coastal states shall in "normal circumstances" grant their consent for MSR projects by other States and competent international organizations.[7] States may at their discretion withhold consent to conduct MSR if the project is of "direct significance" for the exploration and exploitation of natural resources, involves drilling on the continental shelf or the use of explosives, involves construction, operation, or use of artificial islands installations and structures, or is conveyed with a proposal that contains information which is inaccurate.[8] States conducting MSR in the EEZ and on the continental shelf may rely upon the implied consent of the coastal state if the coastal state has not communicated a decision to withhold consent.[9] One final and dispositive key is essential for understanding the extent and limit of coastal state jurisdiction over MSR in the EEZ and on the continental shelf. MSR shall be conducted exclusively for peaceful purposes and "in order to increase scientific knowledge of the marine environment for the benefit of all mankind."[10] The stipulation that the purpose of MSR is to benefit all mankind means that information collected for exclusive purposes and that does not inure benefits to mankind as a whole is not MSR. Consequently, marine data collected for restricted purposes, such as commercial enterprises or for military or intelligence activities, and that will not be shared with the global scientific community for the benefit of all mankind, are not MSR. That is not to say, that all such activities that fall outside of MSR are unregulated by the coastal state, although in the case of military activities, the coastal state may never assert jurisdiction over foreign warships and sovereign immune vessels and aircraft.

3 Operational Oceanography

Data to support operational oceanography is collected for weather forecasting and operational necessity, rather than MSR. Operational oceanography involves the routine collection of data at sea, such as pressure, temperature, current, salinity, and wind, and the rapid interpretation and dissemination of the data. This mission encompasses a wide variety of activities to form estimates of physical and biogeochemical variables and properties for the past, present, and future ocean. Data is collected from ships, such as through expendable bathythermographic instruments

---

[5] UNCLOS, art 243.

[6] UNCLOS, art. 245.

[7] UNCLOS, art. 246.

[8] UNCLOS, art. 246(5).

[9] UNCLOS, art. 252.

[10] UNCLOS, art. 246(3).

(XBTs) and other devices placed into the water. Vessels collect operational data in the water column, on the sea surface of the water, and in the atmosphere above the water to monitor and forecast weather and ocean state, such as surface currents and waves. The immediate dissemination of data is characterized as "nowcasts" and supports the safety of navigation. The data also supports continuous forecasts of future conditions as well as hindcast modelling integration to assemble long-term data sets that describe past events in a time series that shows trends over time.

Operational oceanography provides input to data centers that use numerical forecasting models to produce output that can warn against storms, coastal floods, ice and storm damage, and harmful algal blooms. End users include industry and government. Data are added to electronic charts to optimize ships' routing, predict seasonal or annual events, and identify ocean currents and ocean climate variability. The collection of this data is not only driven by the operational necessity for the protection of life but is also a legal requirement embedded in the Safety of Life at Sea Convention.

During the negotiations for UNCLOS, the World Meteorological Organization (WMO) expressed concern that the rules for MSR do not unduly limit theobservations needed for the timely issuance of weather forecasts and storm warnings.[11] After completion of the negotiations at the Ninth Session of the Third UN Conference on the Law of the Sea, the Chairman of the Third Committee stated that he agreed with the sense of the WMO, which had been expressed in a resolution:

> [T]he provisions on marine scientific research would not create any difficulties and obstacles hindering adequate meteorological coverage from ocean areas, including areas within the exclusive economic zone, carried out both within the framework of existing international programs and by all vessels, since such activities had already been recognized as routine observations and data collecting which were not covered by Part XIII of the negotiating text. Furthermore, they were in the common interest of all countries and had undoubted universal significance.[12]

Consequently, although operational oceanography collects data that may be used in the pursuit of knowledge to benefit all mankind, it is primarily employed for real-time weather forecasting to ensure the safety of maritime navigation. Hence, the MSR process would be too cumbersome and such data collection is not regulated by it.

4 Remote Sensing

Remote sensing is an observational technique to acquire data without physically measuring at location, thereby sidestepping sovereignty and jurisdictional limitations. Sensors on satellites and aircraft can capture electromagnetic radiation either from the sun or emitted from the platform. The variable intensity of radiation and

[11] WMO Res. 16(Cg-VIII), United Nations Conference on the Law of the Sea, March 1979, Doc. A/CONF.62/80, Aug. 9, 1979, XII Official Records 56 (1979).

[12] Statement of Mr. Yankov, XIV Official Records 103, para. 5.

specific wavelength windows permit retrieval of a spectral signature for each location. The physical and chemical state of the surface of the water affects the emissivity and reflectance within the spectrum, linking the signals to physical properties of the ocean without having to be on site.[13] Thermal infrared radiometry from satellites may be used to measure sea surface temperature and optical satellites like Sentinel-2 or active radiometers like Sentinel-3 and MODIS can capture the reflection of the ocean surface to locate algal blooms. Similarly, satellite RADAR altimetry is used to determine sea surface height. Because the satellites and aircraft are observing at a distance, they have optimal spatial coverage that can measure the changing dynamic of the ocean along a temporal scale. Active remote sensing instruments can also measure the two-way travel time of the signal, which can be used to determine the distance between the sensor and the imaged surface.

Beyond the territorial sea, including over the EEZ and continental shelf and high seas, aircraft may collect data as they fly with due regard for the rights and duties of the coastal state, as enumerated in UNCLOS.[14] Satellites are inviolable and as objects in outer space, orbital craft are beyond the jurisdiction of coastal states and their regulatory competence over MSR in the EEZ. Space objects that are positioned beyond the atmosphere may freely range over any part of the globe, including the territorial sea and land area of a state. Nonetheless, remote sensing is free from coastal state regulation or control. Customary international law has long supported the proposition that satellites operating beyond the vertical limit of the territorial airspace are free from foreign regulation.

There is no international consensus on the issue of where airspace ends, and outer space begins. The Kármán Line is a line based on a technical/scientific criterion that has received some support in state practice. There seems to be more support for the proposition that the limit of state airspace (possibly) ends where low earth orbit satellites are found. Many satellites orbit as low as 80 km above the sea, and orbits of 90–120 km above the sea are common.[15]

5 Prospecting for Natural Resources in the EEZ and Area

In the EEZ and on the continental shelf, the coastal state exercises sovereign rights and jurisdiction over the living and non-living resources.[16] The coastal state's sovereign rights and jurisdiction in this regard are exclusive and are not subject to encroachment by any other state. In particular, the 2016 South China Sea arbitration held that the coastal state's exclusive sovereign rights over resources in its EEZ and on

[13] Ranganath Navalgund, Comprehensive Remote Sensing, Volume 9: Applications for Societal Benefits, Current Science. 115 (5): 988. (2018-09-01).

[14] UNCLOS, art. 56.

[15] See e.g., Ilias I. Kuskuvelis, 'La légalité coutumière de l'observation spatiale militaire' (1990) 176 Revue Française de Droit Aérien et Spatial at 297.

[16] UNCLOS, art. 56.

its continental shelf are incompatible with another State having historic rights to the same resources.[17] The tribunal held that the construction of the EEZ "supersedes any earlier rights and agreements."[18] During the negotiations for UNCLOS, distant water fishing states such as Japan and the USSR offered a proposal for preferential historic fishing rights to remain in newly created EEZs of foreign states, but the idea was rejected by the conference.[19] During this time China was a particularly ardent supporter of the exclusive jurisdiction of the coastal state in its own EEZ.[20]

In the deep seabed beyond the continental shelf of coastal states, the International Seabed Authority (ISA) has the competence to regulate "activities in the Area," which are defined as the "exploration for and exploitation of, the solid, liquid, and gaseous resources in situ in the deep seabed.[21] It is uncertain whether prospecting lies outside the remit of the ISA, although the Authority has preempted challenges in this regard and covered prospecting in its regulations. MSR in the Area is a separate activity from mineral exploration or prospecting and instead is a high-seas freedom.[22]

States, state enterprises, and other entities may apply for prospecting, exploration, and exploitation in the Area. Annex III of UNCLOS, which expands on Article 153, sets forth the procedures for these activities, including plans of work for exploration and exploitation. These rules are further modified by the rules adopted by the Council of the ISA pursuant to its authority.[23]

The Council is the executive organ of the ISA, and it supervises and coordinates the implementation of Part XI on all matters within the competence of the Authority.[24] The Council has the power to approve plans of work for the exploration and exploitation of seabed resources which is not subject to further action by the Assembly of the ISA. The Assembly of the ISA, however, approves the rules relating to prospecting, exploration, and exploitation of mineral resources in the international seabed area.

The ISA has adopted three sets of regulations that address the prospecting and exploration of mineral resources in the Area. In 2000, the first set of Regulations were adopted. These apply to prospecting and exploration of polymetallic nodules. In 2010, the Regulations for polymetallic sulfides were released. The Regulations for cobalt-rich crusts were produced in 2012.[25] Together, these three sets of regulations implement prospecting and exploration of mineral development under Part XI

---

[17] South China Sea Arbitration (Phil. v. China), Case No. 2013–19, Award, ¶¶ 243–244 (Perm. Ct. Arb. 2016), https://pcacases.com/web/sendAttach/2086.

[18] Id., ¶¶ 246–47.

[19] Id., ¶ 250.

[20] Id., ¶ 251–252.

[21] UNCLOS, art. 1(3).

[22] UNCLOS, arts. 143, 256.

[23] UNCLOS, art 162.

[24] UNCLOS, art. 162(2)(a).

[25] International Seabed Authority, Regulations on Prospecting and Exploration for Polymetallic Nodules in the Area (13 July 2000). The official text of the Regulations was published as Doc No ISBA/6/A/18 (13 July 2000) Annex, and reproduced in International Seabed Authority, The Law of the Sea: Compendium of Basic Documents (International Seabed Authority/The Caribbean Law Publishing Company Jamaica 2001) 226.

and Annex III of UNCLOS, as revised by the 1994 Implementing Agreement. The Regulations define "prospecting" as the "search for deposits of minerals including estimation of the sizes and distribution of mineral deposits and their economic values, without any exclusive rights." The definition covers general searches for mineral deposits rather than pre-production survey—and it is difficult to distinguish between them and MSR.[26]

6 Hydrographic Surveys

Hydrographic surveys are synonymous with maritime cartography and involve activities that measure and describe features that affect uses in the ocean, such as maritime navigation, dredging, offshore oil exploration, and other activities. For millennia, this was accomplished with lead lines, which have given way to sonar beginning in World War I. Today, multibeam echosounders can map a large path through the ocean.

Survey data may be used to create navigation charts and digital terrain models. The science of hydrographic surveys accounts for shorelines, tides, currents, and seabed and submerged features. Hydrographic surveys generally are conducted by ships with a sounding or echo into the seabed. In shallow-water areas, lidar (light detection and ranging) onboard aircraft may be used.

Coastal states exercise full control over hydrographic surveys in the territorial sea, in straits used for international navigation, and in archipelagic waters.[27] Coastal states have a duty to adopt laws to regulate hydrographic surveys in the territorial sea.[28] These laws shall not apply to the construction, design, equipping, and manning of foreign ships unless they give effect to internationally accepted standards.[29] Once the laws and regulations are adopted, the coastal state shall give them "due publicity," and foreign ships have a duty to comply with them.[30]

Surveys are inconsistent with the right of innocent passage in the territorial sea.[31] These rules also apply to innocent passage through certain straits used for international navigation when the regime of innocent passage is applicable, and to vessels in innocent passage in archipelagic waters. Likewise, during transit passage through straits, ships, and aircraft may not conduct MSR or survey activities without the

---

[26] Michael W. Lodge, International Seabed Authority's Regulations on Prospecting and Exploration for Polymetallic Nodules in the Area, Journal of Energy and Natural Resources Law 270; 20(3) (2002).

[27] UNCLOS, arts. 19(2)(j).

[28] UNCLOS, art. 21(1)(g).

[29] UNCLOS, art. 21(2).

[30] UNCLOS, art. 21(3), (4).

[31] UNCLOS, art. 206.

prior authorization of the coastal state.[32] This rule also applies in archipelagic sea lanes passage.[33]

Foreign states may conduct hydrographic surveys in the EEZ that are unrelated to the resource rights of the coastal state. For example, military surveys are not within reach of coastal state jurisdiction, while the coastal state may regulate commercial hydrographic surveys to search for oil and gas beneath the seabed. The majority view is that military surveys are an element of high seas freedoms and other internationally lawful uses of the sea associated with the operation of ships and aircraft.[34] China represents a minority view on this matter, and it claims that marine survey and mapping activities in the EEZ by foreign-flagged ships require its approval. For example, Chinese ships have interfered with US Navy military surveys in its EEZ, most notably in the incident involving the USNS *Impeccable* in 2009, in which five Chinese vessels surrounded the USNS ship as it was tracking a towed Surveillance Towed Array Sensor System (SURTASS) array behind it.[35] The towed sonar is used by USNS special mission ships and includes both active and passive components to detect submarines at great distances.[36] While regulation of civilian marine scientific research is indeed under the competence of the coastal State, military and hydrographic surveys are not MSR.[37] China conflates these terms. In Chinese law, the conduct of marine surveys, both military and hydrographic, in the EEZ without the consent of China constitutes a criminal offense and is considered as a violation of the regime of marine scientific research. Violators may be fined, ordered to leave the area, or subjected to criminal prosecution. Yet, China's attempts to assert coastal state criminal jurisdiction over sovereign immune warships and naval auxiliaries is a violation of general international law and UNCLOS.[38]

7 Underwater Cultural Heritage

All States share a duty to protect underwater cultural heritage (UCH) and shall cooperate for that purpose.[39] This obligation applies to all archaeological and historical objects wherever they are found at sea. UCH is not categorized as a natural resource, and therefore it is not part of the coastal state's competence within the

[32] UNCLOS, art. 40.

[33] UNCLOS, art. 54.

[34] UNCLOS, art. 58(1).

[35] Raul Pedrozo, Close encounters at sea: the USNS Impeccable incident, 62 *Naval War College Review* 101-11 (2009); David Morgan, 'U.S. says Chinese vessels harassed Navy ship', *Reuters*, 9 March 2009, www.reuters.com/article/us-usa-china-navy/u-s-says-chinese-vessels-harassed-navy-ship-idUSTRE52845A20090309.

[36] SURTASS LFA Supplemental Environmental Impact Statement, U.S. Navy, https://www.nepa.navy.mil/surtass-lfa/systems-description/.

[37] UNCLOS, Art. 246.

[38] UNCLOS, Arts. 32 and 95.

[39] UNCLOS, art. 303.

EEZ or on the continental shelf (living and non-living resources). In the contiguous zone, coastal states may prevent the "removal from the seabed" of shipwrecks and objects of archaeological and historical interest pursuant to articles 33 and 303(2) of UNCLOS. Yet this provision does not entitle coastal states to extend sovereign rights and jurisdiction in shipwrecks beyond the territorial sea or contiguous zone. The regime of the EEZ only includes sovereign rights and jurisdiction over the living and non-living resources, meaning natural resources and not man-made objects or relics, such as archaeological finds.

In the territorial sea, coastal states can regulate activity that affects UCH. In the contiguous zone, the coastal state has authority over the removal of "objects of an archeological and historical nature."[40] In the Area, archeological and historical objects "shall be preserved or disposed of for the benefit of mankind as a whole," although "particular regard" is paid to the "preferential rights" of the state of origin.[41]

There are two basic approaches to underwater cultural heritage among states. Most states regulate access to underwater cultural heritage, such as archaeological and cultural properties including shipwrecks, through a ministry at the national level. In Italy, for example, the Ministry of Cultural Heritage and Activities and Tourism, also known by the acronym MIBACT (Ministero dei beni e delle attività culturali e del turismo) is positioned to authorize access to shipwrecks. The removal and taking into custody of any of these properties may be done only with the explicit consent of the ministry. The properties offshore found by anyone in the seabed or subsoil belong to the state demesne. The finder may be entitled to a reward. Other states that adhere to the common law tradition apply classic admiralty law, and the law of salvage and fines to underwater cultural heritage. For example, The United States applies the law of admiralty and finds to ancient sunken ships as part of the "well-known and well-developed venerable law of the sea."[42]

Heritage in the international seabed area "shall be preserved or disposed of for the benefit of mankind as a whole."[43] The state or country of historical or cultural origin enjoys preferential rights to such shipwrecks. There exists the perception of a lacuna between the coastal state's right to enforce access to shipwrecks in the contiguous zone and the preservation of shipwrecks in the international seabed area. The region in between these two areas is the EEZ, which covers only natural objects and not man-made objects such as underwater cultural heritage. Under the theory of freedom of the seas, any person appears entitled to explore for shipwrecks on the EEZ and on the continental shelf of a coastal state. Consequently, a number of states negotiated the Convention on the Protection of Underwater Cultural Heritage, which was adopted in Paris in 2001 and entered into force in 2009. The conventional applies to "all traces of human existence having cultural, historical or archaeological character which have been partially or totally underwater, periodically or continuously, for at least

[40] UNCLOS, art. 33.

[41] UNCLOS, art. 149.

[42] RMS Titanic v. Haver, 171 F.3d 943, 960 (4th Cir. 1999); United States v. W. M. Webb, Inc., 397 U.S. 179, 191 (1970).

[43] UNCLOS, art. 149.

100 years."[44] The UCH Convention states that underwater cultural heritage shall not be commercially exploited, eliminating the traditional law of salvage from the equation.[45] The treaty has 77 states party. Most states during the negotiations wanted to extend the jurisdiction of the coastal state to underwater cultural heritage but a minority of states declined to do so out of concern that it would unduly empower coastal states and at the expense of the freedom of the seas enjoyed by other states.

8 Environmental Monitoring and Assessment

Section 4 of Part XII focuses on monitoring and environmental assessment of pollution in the marine environment. States are required to "observe, measure, evaluate and analyze, by recognized scientific methods," the risks or effects of marine environmental pollution.[46] States are also required to monitor and surveil the effects of certain activities to ensure they do not pollute the marine environment.[47] Article 205 requires states to publish reports of the monitoring and surveillance. States are also required to assess activities when they "have reasonable grounds for believing that planned activities under their jurisdiction or control may cause substantial pollution of or significant and harmful changes to the marine environment…" Consequently, states are required to collect observations and oceanographic data to assess the impact of their activities and fulfill their duty to protect the marine environment. This type of data collection does not constitute MSR.

Monitoring is becoming more important as states are developing means to fulfill their obligations under UNCLOS. The 2023 High Seas Biodiversity Treaty requires states to conduct environmental impact assessments (EIAs) for their activities at sea in areas beyond their national jurisdiction.[48] This obligation will be supported through sufficiently detailed marine data to inform the EIAs and be uploaded to the Clearing-House Mechanism established in the treaty. Parties shall promote the use of EIAs using the "best available science and scientific information and, where available, relevant traditional knowledge of Indigenous Peoples and local communities."[49] Furthermore, parties to the High Seas Treaty shall ensure that the environmental information is combined with other associated impacts, such as economic, social, cultural, and human health impacts, further expanding the scope of the collection necessary to collect the marine environment.[50]

[44] The Convention on the Protection of the Underwater Cultural Heritage, 2562 U.N.T.S. 3 (2012), art. 1(1)(a).

[45] Id., art. 2(7).

[46] UNCLOS, art. 204(1).

[47] UNCLOS, art. 204(2).

[48] BBNJ, art. 28.

[49] BBNJ, art. 31.

[50] BBNJ, art. 31(b).

9 Military Surveys and Intelligence Collection

Military surveys may be indistinguishable in their operations from hydrographic surveys, yet they are not regulated by the terms of MSR in Part XIII of UNCLOS. Military activities, including military surveys by warships with sovereign immunity, do not constitute MSR because military survey data is classified and does not meet the description in Article 246 of information that is collected and published "for the benefit of all mankind."

Although foreign warships may exercise high-seas freedoms in the EEZ, their operations must have due regard for the rights of the coastal state.[51] A minority of states do not accept that high-seas freedoms of navigation and overflight and other internationally lawful uses of the sea apply in the EEZ. Article 58(1) of UNCLOS states that the high-seas freedoms in Article 87 of the high seas also apply in the EEZ. Pakistan, however, has rejected this text and protested the operation of U.S. military survey ships in its EEZ. In response to the Pakistani demarche over the transit of the USNS *Invincible* in Pakistan's EEZ, the United States responded:

> The United States notes that, as stated in Article 56 of the Convention, a coastal State's rights and jurisdiction within its exclusive economic zone are subject to the rights and duties of other states as provided for in international law. The rights specifically preserved for ships and aircrafts of all States in the exclusive economic zone include the freedom of navigation and overflight, and other internationally lawful uses of the sea related to those freedoms, without requirement to provide prior notification to or obtain prior permission from the coastal State. These include military surveys, exercises and maneuvers.
>
> The United States does not accept the view that a coastal state may require its prior notification or consent. As reflected in the Convention, the United States considers that all States have the right to conduct military activities within the EEZ, subject to an obligation to have due regard to coastal State resource and other rights as well as the rights of other States as set forth in the Convention. It is the duty of the flag State, not the right of the coastal State, to enforce this due regard obligation. The United States has the honor to inform the Ministry of Foreign Affairs that the USNS INVINCIBLE conducted its activities with due regard to the rights and duties referenced in Article 58 of the Convention.[52]

China has also attempted to stretch the "due regard" standard in Articles 56 and 58 to include a requirement to observe impinging on any conceivable coastal state interest, such as a security or political interest. China believes, for example, that foreign military aircraft and warships in the EEZ "shall be appropriately considerate of the security interests of the coastal state."[53] That interpretation is inconsistent with UNCLOS and state practice—including the state practice of the PLA Navy, which operates in the EEZ of the United States off the coast of Hawaii, Guam, and Alaska.[54]

---

[51] UNCLOS, arts. 56, 58.

[52] Freedom of Navigation—Pakistan, February 17, 2012, *in* Digest of US Practice in International Law 420–421 (CarrieLyn D. Guymon, ed. 2012).

[53] Shen Dingli, The US Military's Hegemonic Logic for Administering Close-In Reconnaissance (20 December 2013), reprinted at Fortuna's Corner (7 January 2014).

[54] James Kraska & Raul Pedrozo, Disruptive Technology and the Law of the Sea 36 (2022).

China claims that marine survey and mapping activities by foreign-flagged ships require its approval. In Chinese law, the conduct of marine surveys in the EEZ without the consent of China constitutes a criminal offense. Violators may be fined, ordered to leave the area, or be subject to criminal prosecution. Chinese ships have interfered with U.S. Navy military surveys in its EEZ, most notably in the incident involving the USNS *Impeccable* in 2009, in which five Chinese vessels surrounded the U.S. ship as it was tracking a towed array behind it. Yet Chinese warships routinely conduct military surveys off the coast of numerous states, including those in the South China Sea and in the EEZ of Japan and Australia.

10 Bio-logging

The use of advanced and remote data collection technologies attached to marine migratory species raises fundamental questions about the scope of authority of coastal states to regulate MSR in waters under their jurisdiction. Bio-logging involves the attachment of devices to marine animals that collect and transmit data about their movements and aspects of the local marine environment. This method is routinely used by marine scientists to support conservation programs and augment oceanographic data collection. Tagged marine life, including seabirds, marine mammals, sea turtles, and pelagic fishes, interact unpredictably with the territorial seas and EEZs of numerous coastal states.

As they move unpredictably from the high seas into areas under national jurisdiction, marine animals collect and transmit data to scientists. This practice is done outside of the regime of MSR. When bio-logging is initiated outside a coastal state's jurisdiction it is the exercise of a high sea freedom. This status does not change if the tagged animal later enters the territorial sea or EEZ of a coastal state because the location is a wild event and not under the control of the scientists.[55]

Part XIII in UNCLOS was established so the coastal state could regulate research conducted from boats or aircrafts, not for research using tagged animals that swim or fly uncontrolled by human action. Tracking animals through bio-logging techniques allows researchers to learn about the movement, behavior, and abundance of a variety of marine animals including turtles, fish, mammals, and birds. The power of bio-logging stems from its ability to collect data remotely, but it provides no certainty about where animals will go. It is essentially unknowable where tagged animals are going to go before you start tracking them. You can tag two turtles of the same species found in a single location in the Indian Ocean, and one may swim to South Africa while the other swims to Yemen.

Even if it were possible to predict where the tagged animals would go, waiting for consent from some coastal nations before collecting data in their waters via tagging is impractical. A researcher could spend years trying to gain consent from

[55] James Kraska, et. al, Bio-logging of Marine Migratory Species in the Law of the Sea, Marine Policy 51 (2015), 394–400.

some nations, while the tagged species go their own way, often into waters under the jurisdiction of other coastal states. In the meantime, the moment would be lost and with it the ability to learn about the life and conservation of marine resources. While nations have the right to regulate traditional marine scientific research in their coastal waters, research using bio-logging techniques can be regulated only by the nation with jurisdiction over the water where the tagging occurs. Nations whose water the animal traverses after being tagged do not enjoy this right. The randomness of the course of bio-logged animals is somewhat analogous to that of floaters and gliders that are not programmed or under the control of marine scientists and are carried by the currents and wind. This situation is like the release of a weather balloon over a nation's territory that happens to stray unguided into the airspace of a neighboring state. The state releasing the weather balloon is not violating the second state's airspace unless it has a reasonable belief that the balloon would indeed travel into the neighbor's airspace. Weather, ocean currents and wind patterns, however, provide greater predictability than animals, which move with greater individual volition.

11 Collaborative Organizations and Citizen Science

Citizen science involves networked individuals collecting and sharing observations and data on the natural environment. This approach to understanding the marine environment relies on numerous volunteers who partner with scientists to collect data to address real-world questions. The volunteers may help identify research questions, collect, and analyze data, interpret results, and contribute to making new discoveries. One example might be to report via a cellphone application the presence of flora or fauna, such as observing whale migration or the presence of birds from the shoreline and reporting it in the application. Crowdsourcing this information capitalizes on the willingness of individuals to contribute to our understanding of the marine environment. The information is then analyzed byscientists and amateur naturalists.

In the United States, for example, the Stellwagen Bank National Marine Sanctuary relies on volunteers to assist research staff by gathering data that fills specific gaps. Experienced birders who can identify migratory sea birds and operate on the open water can report the presence of certain species. Pleasure boat and yacht enthusiasts can be enlisted to help track the movement of humpback whales between their North Atlantic feeding grounds and their breeding grounds in the Caribbean Sea. By taking photographs of the tail fluke of individual whales, amateur scientists can aid in tracking the migration of megafauna. Similarly, the smartphone application (whale alert) helps mariners report the presence of whales, thus decreasing the risk to whales of injury or death from ship strikes. Pleasure divers at the Flower Garden Banks National Marine Sanctuary can photograph or video the underside of manta rays, helping the National Oceanic and Atmospheric Administration compare it to other images and reports. This data helps to identify individual manta rays by the characteristic spot patterns on their bellies. Scientists may utilize social media and the

Internet to reach citizen science populations in other countries, bypassing officials. In many ways, this is symptomatic of the Internet more generally, which permits users to interact with online information and foreign scientists. This type of distributed activity was not contemplated in the negotiations for Part XIII of UNCLOS, and today it might be seen as weakening the coastal state's authority to render or withhold consent over MSR. Citizen science is just one more dilemma introduced by the virtual and connected world and the horizontal expansion and democratization of information to discrete communities.

12 Conclusion

This chapter explored the legal regime for the conduct of marine scientific research in UNCLOS. MSR is a high seas freedom that may be exercised by all flag states in areas beyond national jurisdiction. Although research vessels are subject to exclusive flag state jurisdiction, they have a duty to observe certain coastal state control or oversight when operating in the territorial sea, archipelagic waters, the EEZ and in conducting MSR on the continental shelf. In internal waters and the territorial sea of coastal state, vessels conducting MSR are subject to the rules for MSR that flow from the sovereignty of the coastal state, which may exercise concurrent jurisdiction with the flag state. Under Article 246 of UNCLOS, Coastal states also may exercise oversight over ships conducting MSR in the EEZ and on the continental shelf. MSR activities in these areas may be conducted only subject to the explicit (or implied) consent of the coastal state.

The MSR regime was designed for ship-based research by non-military expeditions, the primary method for studying the ocean in the post-World War II era. Even as UNCLOS was being negotiated and entering into force, however, new methods for data collection, and new purposes for the data, were already emerging. Some of these, such as prospecting for seabed minerals, were incorporated into UNCLOS but outside of Part XIII. Other methods to collect data about the ocean were completely ignored and have even greater salience today. For example, vessels of all flag states may collect marine data or operational oceanography to aid the safe transit of their vessel. These include activities such as XBTs, which may be deployed in the water to take salinity and temperature readings.

Remote sensing using satellites positioned in outer space may collect information on the marine environment, and they also do so outside of the regime of MSR in UNCLOS. Even though satellite remote sensing existed during the period of the negotiations of UNCLOS, the collection of oceanographic information from outer space is not regulated by the treaty. This lacuna in the law is much like the lack of regulation over the collection of information by crowdsourcing and citizen science. There are other methods for collecting marine data that are regulated by UNCLOS but do not constitute MSR. For example, prospecting for natural resources in the EEZ, on the continental shelf may be regulated by the coastal state under separate legal authorities, including Parts V, VI of UNCLOS. Data collection in the Area may be governed by Part XI of the Convention if it relates to seabed minerals. Likewise, hydrographic surveys are subject to coastal state control in the territorial sea, archipelagic waters, and straits used for international navigation. If hydrographic surveys are for a purpose other than economic purposes, however, they may not be regulated by the coastal state in its EEZ or on its continental shelf. Military surveys, for example, constitute a lawful exercise of high-seas freedoms and other internationally lawful uses of the sea associated with the operation of ships and aircraft in the EEZ. Warships and military aircraft may conduct surveys pursuant to national security or intelligence missions. These operations lie beyond the jurisdiction of the coastal state and furthermore are protected by the sovereign immune status of military aircrafts and naval vessels.

Exploring or finding underwater cultural heritage, such as shipwrecks, also does not constitute MSR. This activity may be regulated by the coastal state to the outer breadth of the contiguous zone but not the EEZ. Those states that have joined the Underwater Cultural Heritage Convention have agreed to expand the jurisdiction of coastal states over shipwrecks in the EEZ. The treaty does not bind other states. With the increased focus on the collection of marine data for environmental purposes, states are authorized to collect information in areas subject to coastal state sovereign rights and jurisdiction for the purposes of fulfilling their obligations to monitor and assess human impacts on the marine environment. This environmental loophole in the MSR regime will only grow larger as the EIA provisions of the BBNJ Treaty enter into widespread practice. Bio-logging or attaching sensors to biological organisms ranging in size from small turtles to large whales is also not subject to regulation by the coastal state when the animals are tagged in areas beyond the national jurisdiction of the coastal state. Even if a tagged animal enters an area within the jurisdiction of the coastal state and relays information to scientists via satellite communications who are located on another continent that activity may not be regulated by the coastal state because the course of the animal is unpredictable.

These nine exceptions to the regime of MSR in UNCLOS provide additional nuance and context when thinking about the rules applicable to marine scientific research. Each of these exceptions has either a separate legal regime that applies to it or exists in a position that lacks any controlling legal authority that would render it subject to foreign coastal state regulation. Some of these technologies, such as remote sensing, bio-logging, and citizen science, are helping to fulfill the liberal vision of MSR that was originally proposed during the UNCLOS negotiations even as they are not subject to Part XIII.

James Kraska is Charles H. Stockton Chair of International Maritime Law and Chairman of the Stockton Center for International Law at the United States Naval War College and Visiting Professor of Law and John Harvey Gregory Lecturer on World Organization at Harvard Law School. The views presented are those of the author and do not reflect the official policy or position of the U.S. Navy or the Department of Defense or Harvard Law School.

Chapter 5
Sea Level Rise: Implications for Baselines, Limits and Boundaries

Clive Schofield

1 Introduction

Global mean sea levels are rising and the rate of this rise is accelerating. This has significant implications for coastal States, especially those with long stretches of low-elevation coasts or which are wholly or partially comprise of low-elevation islands. This Chapter outlines the causes and projections for sea level rise before considering how coastal State baselines along the coast are defined and claimed, the outer limits of zones of maritime jurisdiction are delineated and international maritime boundaries are delimited. The discussion then turns to the potential implications of sea-level rise for baselines, limits and boundaries. Potential response options are then briefly explored before some concluding thoughts are offered.

2 Global Sea Level Rise

Global sea level has fluctuated substantially over millions of years in keeping with cycles of ice-sheet growth and decay. Indeed, the geological record indicates that sea levels were over 5 m higher than present levels during periods when global mean temperature was up to 2 °C warmer than pre-industrial levels.[1] However, there is now clear recognition in the scientific community, as evidenced by successive Assessment Reports of the Intergovernmental Panel on Climate Change (IPCC) that global mean

[1] Intergovernmental Panel on Climate Change (IPCC) (2013) Climate Change 2013: The Physical Science Basis, Contribution of Working Group I, Fifth Assessment Report of the Intergovernmental Panel on Climate Change, Cambridge University Press, Cambridge and New York, p. 1139.

C. Schofield (✉)
Australian National Centre for Ocean Resources and Security (ANCORS), University of Wollongong, Wollongong, NSW 2522, Australia
e-mail: chs@wmu.se

L. A. T. Nguyen and H. D. Vu (eds.), *Viability of UNCLOS amid Emerging Global Maritime Challenges*, https://doi.org/10.1007/978-981-97-5838-8_7

sea level (GMSL) is rising and, further, that human influence is considered "very likely" to be the main driver for these changes.[2] Moreover, there is strong evidence that the rate of sea level rise is accelerating.

Projections of GMSL rise have tended to increase over time as scientific understanding of this complex phenomenon has improved. The IPCC in its 5th Assessment Report of 2013 indicated that sea level was projected to rise up to 98 cm by 2100.[3] This compares with a projection of up to 59cm above 1990 levels by 2100 under the IPCC's previous Assessment Report 4 (AR4) of 2007.[4] Further, in its 2019 Special Report on the *Ocean and Cryosphere in a Changing Climate* the Intergovernmental Panel on Climate Change (IPCC) suggests that global mean sea-level rise in the period 2006–2015 has been two and a half times the rate for the period 1901–1990, a rate of sea-level rise stated with high confidence to be "unprecedented over the last century."[5]

Here is important to recognize that the oceans serve as the Earth's primary heat sink and as the oceans warm they expand leading to rising sea levels. This represents the primary cause of sea level rise is thermal expansion of the ocean which it is estimated will account for 33–55% of GMSL rise in the twenty-first century.[6] A further key driver for global sea level rise is contributions from the cryosphere. That is, the role of melting land-based or grounded ice in changing sea levels. The possibility of the melting of major land-based ice sheets, resulting in massive and abrupt sea level rise has been appropriately termed as one of the major climate "wild cards" with the potential to cause "massive, abrupt sea level rise" of the order of several metres.[7] Thankfully, complete disintegration and melting of the enormous volumes of ice held in the Antarctic and Greenland and ice sheets is considered unlikely but even moderately increased melting of such huge bodies of ice could

---

[2] IPCC, Climate Change 2021: The Physical Science Basis, Contribution of Working Group I to the Sixth Assessment Report (AR6) of the IPCC (6 August 2021), p. TS-44.

[3] The IPCC 2013 AR5 medium confidence-level projection is for global mean sea level rise of 0.52–0.98 under its representative concentration pathways (RCP) 8.5 scenario which envisages continued very high greenhouse gas emissions and a resulting increase in global mean temperature likely to exceed 2 °C. See, *Ibid.*, pp. 20, 25 and 1140.

[4] The IPCC's 2007 AR4 model-based range of sea level rise under its A1FI scenario was 0.26–0.59 m excluding future rapid dynamical changes in ice flow. See, IPCC, 4th Assessment Report 2007, Synthesis Report, Section 3.2.1, twenty-first century global changes, p. 45. The IPCC's A1FI scenario envisages, under the A1 storyline and scenario family, very rapid economic growth, global population that peaks mid-century and declines thereafter and with the rapid introduction of new and more efficient technologies coupled with the use of fossil fuel intensive (FI) energy sources. Regarding IPCC scenarios see, IPCC, Special Report on Emission Scenarios, 2000, available at, https://www.ipcc.ch/report/emissions-scenarios/.

[5] Intergovernmental Panel on Climate Change (IPCC), Special Report on the Ocean and Cryosphere in a Changing Climate, approved at its 51st Session held from 20–23 September 2019, available online: https://www.ipcc.ch/srocc/home/.

[6] IPCC, Climate Change 2013: The Physical Science Basis, p. 25.

[7] See, Walker G and King, D (2008) The Hot Topic: How to Tackle Global Warming and Still Keep the Lights On, Bloomsbury, London, pp. 75–80.

significantly influence the pace and scale of global sea level rise thus impacting on relative sea level, that is, sea level experienced at a particular part of the coast.

These findings have been reinforced in the IPCC's, at the time of writing, latest, Sixth Assessment Report (AR6).[8] In particular, the IPCC concluded that the average rate of sea-level rise had increased almost three-fold from 1.3mm/year over the period 1901–1971 to 3.7 mmm/year over 2006–2018.[9] Moreover, the IPCC indicated that under continued high emissions scenarios, radically higher sea level rise approaching 2 m by 2100 and 5 m by 2150 "cannot be ruled out due to deep uncertainty in ice sheet processes."[10] The IPCC also found that that not only is it 'virtually certain' that, with high confidence, global mean sea level will continue to rise over the twenty-first century, but that 'sea level is committed to rise for centuries to millennia … and that it will remain elevated for thousands of years'.[11]

3 Sea Level Rise and the International Law of the Sea

The development of the modern international law of the sea coincided with a period of general stability in sea level. Accordingly, while it was understood at the time of the negotiation of the UN Convention on the Law of the Sea (UNCLOS) that coastlines were dynamic and subject to change in response to natural processes of deposition and erosion, "there was no widespread recognition of the possible problems of sea level rise."[12] UNCLOS established a clear framework for the limits of coastal State claims to maritime jurisdiction. These maritime zones are predominantly defined by maximum breadth limits, such as 12 nautical miles (M) for the territorial sea and 200 M for the exclusive economic zone (EEZ), measured from baselines along the coast.[13] The exception in this context relates to the outer limits of the continental shelf (see below). Nonetheless, although the delineation of the outer limits of the continental shelf largely depends on complex geophysical factors, distance measurements from baselines, specifically the 200 M and 350 M limits, remain important (see Fig. 1). Consequently, baselines are critical to defining the limits of national claims to maritime jurisdiction.

---

[8] IPCC, Climate Change 2021: The Physical Science Basis, Working Group I contribution to the Sixth Assessment Report of the Intergovernmental Panel on Climate Change, 7 August 2021, available at https://www.ipcc.ch/report/ar6/wg1/.

[9] Ibid., at TS-44.

[10] Ibid.

[11] Ibid.

[12] See Freestone D (1991) International Law and Sea Level Rise. In: Churchill, RR and Freestone, D (eds) International Law and Global Climate Change, Graham and Trotman/Martinus Nijhoff, London/Dordrecht, pp. 109–125 at p. 114.

[13] LOSC, Arts. 3 and 4 re Territorial Sea and Art. 57 re the EEZ. While the delineation of the outer limits of the continental shelf largely depends on complex geophysical factors, distance measurements from baselines, specifically the 200-nm and 350-nm limits, remain important. LOSC, Article 76.

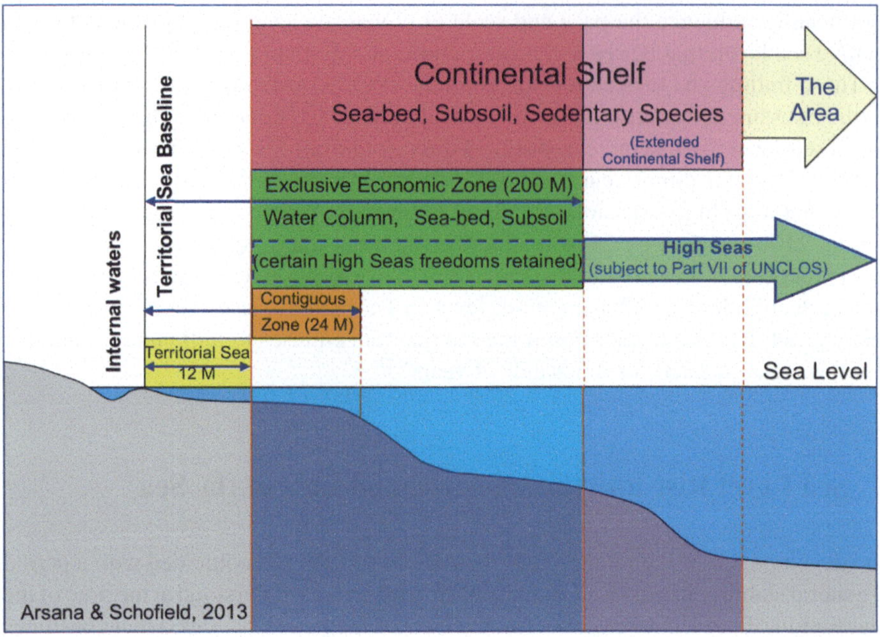

Fig. 1 Schematic of baselines and maritime claims of a coastal State. *Source* Clive Schofield and I Made Andi Arsana[14]

4 Defining Baselines

Baselines along the coast under UNCLOS can be broadly divided into natural and artificial baselines. Natural baselines relate to those that are coincident with the low-water line. Thus, "normal" baselines are defined under Article 5 of UNCLOS as being "the low-water line along the coast as marked on large-scale charts officially recognized by the coastal State."[15] Similarly, Article 6 of UNCLOS indicates that where islands occur on reefs or where fringing reefs exist, the "seaward low-water line of the reef" should constitute the baseline.

Such baselines represent a coastal State's "default" baselines in that they require no formal declaration or due publicity. The absence of a reference to a particular low-water line in Article 5 of UNCLOS implies that this choice is left up to the coastal State. The level of the low-water line forming the normal baseline is dependent on the choice of vertical datum, that is, the level of reference for the measurement of depths and elevations. In this context, many States have tended to opt for a particularly

[14] International Hydrographic Organization (2014) A Manual on Technical Aspects of the United Nations Convention on the Law of the Sea, Special Publication no. 51, International Hydrographic Bureau, Monaco, Chap. 5, p. 3 (hereafter TALOS Manual).

[15] LOSC, Article 5.

low vertical datum, such as lowest astronomical tide (LAT),[16] and thus low normal baselines. This choice of such a low interpretation of the low-water line is preferable in the context of nautical charting with a view to ensuring the safety of navigation, since it provides for any potential hazard to a vessel being shown on the chart. It is worth noting here from a law of the sea perspective that the use of a particularly low vertical datum such as LAT has the advantage of advancing the low-water line further seawards, thereby expanding and maximizing the coastal State's land territory and simultaneously potentially enhancing the scope of its claims to maritime jurisdiction by advancing the starting point for measuring its maritime claims.

UNCLOS also provides for several types of artificial baselines consisting of straight lines to address aspects of coastal complexity. These include straight baselines (UNCLOS, Article 7), river closing lines (Article 9), bay closing lines (Article 10) and in respect of archipelagic states (Article 47). However, such straight line types of artificial baselines are still fundamentally dependent on the location of normal baselines. This is because they need to connect or be anchored to the low-water line along the coast. On this issue, the United Nations Group of Experts report on baselines was clear in finding that a system of artificial baselines "must start and finish on or above the low water line", such that each system of baselines is "closed."[17]

It has long been recognized that the coast is dynamic and susceptible to change over time. This can occur because of a range of natural processes including deposition along the coast. For example, deposition along the coast and thus advance in the location seawards can occur due to sediment transport down river systems and along the coast as a consequence of currents. Coastlines may also incrementally advance thanks to isostatic (or post-glacial) rebound whereby the continental crust is gradually rising following the removal of the enormous weight of major ice-sheets, some several kilometres thick, with the onset of the present inter-glacial period.[18] Similarly, volcanic or tectonic activity can also lead to the emergence of additional land territory, and therefore coasts, above the surface of the sea.

For example, the island of Surtsey, located approximately 17 M (32 km) south of Iceland, emerged as a result of volcanic eruptions between 1963 and 1967.[19] Coastlines may also retreat as a consequence of erosion. For instance, the volcanic activity that led to the creation of Surtsey Island resulted in the formation of two

[16] LAT is defined as, "The lowest tide level which can be predicted to occur under average meteorological conditions and under any combination of astronomical conditions." TALOS Manual, Chap. 2, p. 18.

[17] See, United Nations (1989) Baselines: An Examination of the Relevant Provisions of the United Nations Convention on the Law of the Sea, United Nations Division of Ocean Affairs and the Law of the Sea (DOALOS), New York, p. 23.

[18] See, for example, Johansson, JM Davis, JL, Scherneck, H-G et al. (2002), Continuous GPS measurements of postglacial adjustment in Fennoscandia. 1 Geodetic results. 107 *Journal of Geophysical Research* B8.

[19] The island has been protected since it was formed and has been included in the United Nations Educational, Scientific and Cultural Organization (UNESCO) World Heritage List since 2008. See. UNESCO, Surtsey, World Heritage List, available at, https://whc.unesco.org/en/list/1267/.

other above-surface "satellite islands" which subsequently eroded such that they now lie 20–40 m below the ocean surface.[20] Indeed, depositional and erosional forces can occur cyclically on particular coasts. This occurs on Bangladesh's coast on the delta of the Ganges–Brahmaputra river systems where the enormous sediment load transported down these rivers leads to the coast advancing and the formation of islands, only for coastal erosion to trim the coast back and lead to the disappearance of insular features on a seasonal basis.[21]

5 Delineating the Outer Limits to Maritime Zones

As noted above, UNCLOS sets clear maximum limits for the territorial sea, contiguous zone and EEZ of 12, 24 and 200 M, respectively. The delineation of the outer limits of these zones is generally achieved through the construction of the "envelope of arcs" at the required distance measured from baselines. As a consequence of complexities in the coastline, by no means all of the baseline along the coast necessarily contribute to the delineation of the outer limits of maritime claims through this method. Instead, only the most seaward or protuberant parts of the coast, such as headlands, provide controlling or critical base points (see Fig. 2).

The exception to the rule in terms of maritime zones based solely on distance measurement from baselines along the coast is the continental shelf. Although in many areas continental shelf limits will be coincident with 200 M EEZ limits, for States located on broad continental margins, their continental shelf rights may be located substantially seaward of 200 M from baselines. UNCLOS, Article 76 establishes a complex series of entitlement formulae and cut-off lines which require the gathering of information on the geology, morphology and bathymetry of the continental margin. However, distance measurements from baselines, notably the 200 and 350 M limits, remain an integral part of determining the outer limits of the continental shelf.

6 Delimiting International Maritime Boundaries

In relation to the delimitation of the territorial sea, Article 15 of UNCLOS applies and offers a clear preference for the use of an equidistance or median line. This does not apply, however, if the states concerned agree to the contrary or there exists

[20] See, Friðriksson, S. (1975) Surtsey: Evolution of Life on a Volcanic Island, Butterworth, London, pp. 29–30.

[21] Schofield, CH (2009) Shifting Limits?: Sea Level Rise and Options to Secure Maritime Jurisdictional Claims, 4 Carbon and Climate Law Review, pp. 405–416, at p. 409; Symmons, CR (1995) Some Problems Relating to the Definition of Insular Features in International Law, Maritime Briefing, 1(5) (International Boundaries Research Unit, Durham, pp. 25–26.

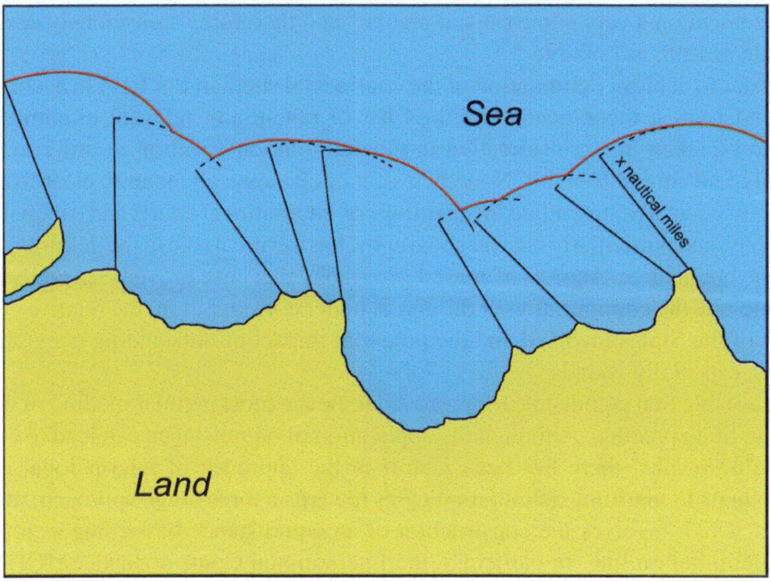

Fig. 2 Delineating the outer limits of maritime zones through an envelope of arcs. *Source* Clive Schofield and I Made Andi Arsana[22]

an "historic title or other special circumstances" in the area to be delimited which justifies a departure from the equidistance line.

Under the 1958 Convention on the Continental Shelf delimitation was also to be effected by the use of median lines unless, similarly, an agreement to the contrary or "special circumstances" existed that justified an alternative approach.[23] However, the relevant provisions of UNCLOS, Articles 74 and 83 dealing with the delimitation of the continental shelf and EEZ respectively, merely provide, in identical general terms, that agreements should be reached on the basis of international law in order to achieve "an equitable solution" with no preferred method of delimitation indicated.

While these provisions provide for substantial flexibility in ocean boundary-making, the lack of guidance offered by the provisions of the UNCLOS dealing with EEZ and continental shelf boundary delimitation also affords great scope for conflicting interpretation and dispute. Here it can be observed that the delimitation provisions of the UNCLOS were among the last elements of the 'package deal' to be agreed on and the general wording used was a means to overcome disagreement on a contentious issue. Indeed, as the Arbitral Tribunal in the Eritrea-Yemen Arbitration noted in reference to the drafting of Article 83, this was "a last minute endeavour…to

[22] TALOS Manual, Chap. 5, p. 6.

[23] Convention on the Continental Shelf, opened for signature 29 April 1958, 499 UNTS 311 (entered into force 10 June 1964).

get agreement on a very controversial matter," and therefore, "consciously designed to decide as little as possible."[24]

In order to achieve delimitation of the continental shelf and/or EEZ in accordance with UNCLOS a theoretically limitless list of potentially relevant circumstances needs to be taken into consideration in the delimitation equation in order to reach the goal of an equitable result. Nonetheless, it has become abundantly clear from the practice of coastal States, allied to the rulings of international courts and tribunals that geography, and particularly coastal geography, has a critical role in the delimitation of maritime boundaries. Aspects of coastal geography that have proved especially influential include the configuration of the coasts under consideration, the relative coastal lengths of the States involved and the potential impact of outstanding geographical features, especially islands.[25]

It is notable that equidistance has proved to be the most popular method of delimitation in State practice. Although the application of equidistance can lead to clearly inequitable results, there has been a shift in the approach of international courts and tribunals in maritime delimitation cases towards a three-stage approach, the first stage of which involves the construction of an equidistance-based line as a provisional delimitation line. In particular, the International Court of Justice (ICJ) in its 2009 ruling in the Black Sea Case[26] between Romania and Ukraine found that, at the first stage, a provisional delimitation line should be established using geometrically objective methods "unless there are compelling reasons that make this unfeasible in the particular case,"[27] at the second stage assessment is to be made as to "whether there are factors calling for the adjustment or shifting of the provisional equidistance line in order to achieve an equitable result,"[28] and at the third stage verification of the resulting potential delimitation line is undertaken through what the Court termed a "disproportionality test."[29] All subsequent international cases involving maritime boundary delimitation have similarly applied this three-stage approach to maritime delimitation.

The construction of an equidistance line between opposite coasts is illustrated (see Fig. 3). It is notable, however, that no international court or tribunal has applied a strict equidistance line at the first stage. Instead, international courts and tribunals

---

[24] Sovereignty and Maritime Delimitation in the Red Sea (Eritrea v. Yemen), Case No. 1996–04, Award in the Second Stage, 116 (Permanent Court of Arbitration. 1999).

[25] Prescott, JRV and Schofield, CH (2005) The Maritime Political Boundaries of the World, Leiden/Boston: Martinus Nijhoff Publishers, pp. 238–39; and, Legault, L and Hankey, B (1993) Method, Oppositeness and Adjacency, and Proportionality in Maritime Boundary Delimitation. In Charney, JI and Alexander, LM (eds), International Maritime Boundaries, Vol.1, pp. 203, 214, 221–22 (Dordrecht, London, Boston, Martius Nijhoff).

[26] Maritime Delimitation in the Black Sea (Romania v. Ukraine), Judgment, 2009 I.C.J. Rep. 61 (Feb. 3).

[27] Ibid., para.116.

[28] Ibid., para.120. At this point the Court cited its earlier Judgment in the Cameroon/Nigeria Case in support of its ruling. See, Land and Maritime Boundary between Cameroon and Nigeria (Cameroon v. Nigeria; Equatorial Guinea intervening), 2002 I.C.J. Rep. 303, at para.288.

[29] ICJ, Black Sea Case, para.122 and 210–216.

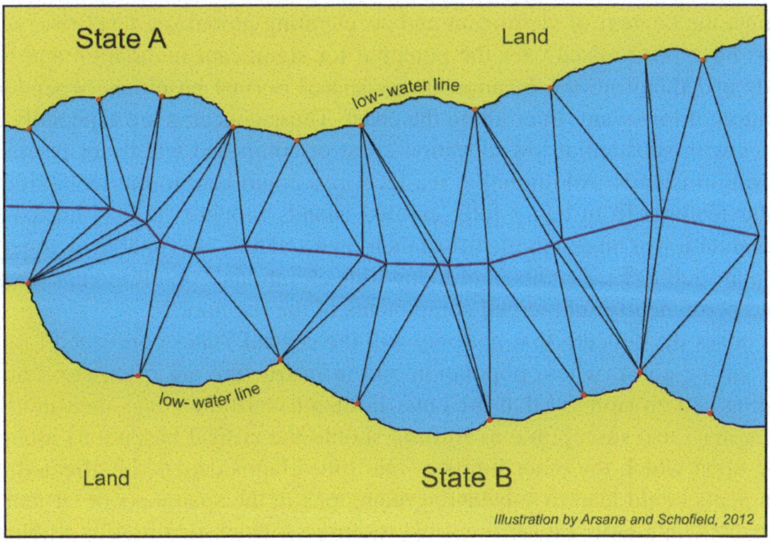

Fig. 3 Construction of an equidistance line between opposite coasts. *Source* Clive Schofield and I Made Andi Arsana[30]

have opted to select basepoints for the construction of the provisional line at the first stage of the three-stage approach. This makes it hazardous to attempt to predict the outcome of a case and arguably undermines the objectivity of this approach.

7 Implications of Sea Level Rise for Baselines, Limits and Boundaries

As noted above, coasts are dynamic. Accordingly, so too, inevitably, the location of the low-water line will also fluctuate and change. The traditional interpretation of Article 5 of UNCLOS is that as the low-water line along the coast fluctuates in location, so normal baselines also change or "ambulate" over time.[31] Indeed, the International Law Association (ILA) Committee on Baselines concluded in 2018 that "the normal baseline is ambulatory."[32] The direct relationship between the position of baselines and the limits of maritime jurisdiction is potentially and increasingly problematic, however.

[30] TALOS Manual, Chap. 6, at 5.

[31] Reed, MW (2000) Shore and sea boundaries: the development of international maritime boundary principles through United States practice (Washington, U.S. Government Printing Office), p. 185.

[32] Coalter G. Lathrop, J. Ashley Roach & Donald R. Rothwell (eds), *Baselines under the International Law of the Sea: Reports of the International Law Association Committee on Baselines under the International Law of the Sea*, in (2019) 2 Brill Research Perspectives in the Law of the Sea 1, 126–62, 58.

Against the context of significant and accelerating global sea level rise, serious concerns have been raised over the potential for significant inundation and retreat of coasts and therefore the location of associated normal baselines dependent on the location of low-water lines along the coast. These concerns are especially acute for States with substantial low-elevation coast or composed wholly or partially of low-elevation islands. Additionally, sea-level rise could lead to the reclassification of insular features from being fully entitled islands to mere "rocks" incapable of human habitation or an economic life of their own and thus not capable of generating continental shelf or EEZ rights,[33] or to low-tide elevations[34] or, ultimately simply to fully and permanently submerged components of the sea floor.[35]

This raises the concern that not only will the coastal States concerned lose land territory at the coast, where population and infrastructure are often concentrated, to flooding and erosion but that the outer limits of maritime zones measured from baselines may also susceptible to shifting should the critical basepoints along that baseline upon which the outer limits of maritime claims depend be affected. Such developments could lead to substantial reductions in the spatial scope of maritime entitlements containing valuable marine resources, which is a highly problematic one for many coastal States. This is particularly the case for small-island States, for whom global sea-level rise appears to be an existential threat.

Changes in the location of baselines along the coast also have potentially crucial implications for the delimitation of maritime boundaries. This is primarily because, as noted above, equidistance lines, that is geometric mid-lines, measured between the baselines on neighbouring coastal States coastlines where their maritime claims overlap with one another, have proved to be the most popular method of maritime boundary delimitation.[36] Clearly, if sea-level rise leads to changes in the location of baselines along the coast, this will potentially have impacts on the construction of an equidistance line that may be used in the negotiation of a maritime boundary or, alternatively, on the first stage of the three-stage process in the international judicial settlement of a maritime boundary dispute. This scenario suggests that coastal States, especially those in possession of low-elevation coasts and islands vulnerable to sea-level rise would be well advised to expedite the delimitation of their maritime boundaries.

This is particularly the case as international boundaries have a privileged status in the international law of treaties and are not subject to change even in the case of "subsequent fundamental change of circumstances".[37] This status applies to both land and maritime boundaries as was made plain in the ruling of the arbitral tribunal in the

---

[33] See, UNCLOS, Article 121.

[34] That is, features that are submerged at high tide but exposed at low-tide. See, UNCLOS, Article 13.

[35] For a more detailed discussion of the Regime of Islands by the present author see, Schofield, CH (2021) The Regime of Islands Reframed: Developments in the Definition of Islands and their Role in the Delimitation of Maritime Boundaries under the International Law of the Sea, *Brill Research Perspectives in the Law of the Sea*, 3(1–2): 1–126.

[36] See, for example, Prescott and Schofield, Maritime Political Boundaries of the World, p. 217.

[37] Vienna Convention on the Law of Treaties art. 62(2), May 23, 1969, 1155 U.N.T.S. 331.

maritime delimitation case between Bangladesh and India which stated that "maritime delimitations, like land boundaries, must be stable and definitive to ensure a peaceful relationship between the States concerned in the long term."[38] This strongly suggests that maritime boundaries, once established, will not be subject to change in the future. It remains to be seen, however, whether a maritime boundary delimited between two States where one or more critical basepoints on one side of the line become invalid as a result of sea-level rise, will remain unchallenged in the future.

8 Response Options

Traditional responses to coastal change, especially erosion to valuable coasts where population and coastal infrastructure are concentrated, have tended to feature efforts to stabilize the position of the coast through the construction of coastal defences of various types in what has been termed a "bulkhead" policy.[39] There are a wide range of options in terms of defending or protecting the coast, from minimal technical interventions to so-called "soft engineering" solutions to "hard" defences or even land reclamation.

Hard engineering options such as the construction of sea walls, groynes and wave reduction structures, notably revetments, offshore breakwaters, rock armour and gabions are generally designed to stabilize the location of the coast and protect key infrastructure located in the coastal zone.[40] Such interventions are, however, expensive to build and maintain and also run the risk of disrupting natural systems, for example interrupting sediment flow regimes, and as a result, potentially causing erosion elsewhere along the coast or compromising the capacity of coral islands to naturally adapt to sea-level rise.[41] Increasingly, therefore, efforts to work with nature and natural systems are being adopted as are hybrid approaches, for instance blending hard and soft engineering features.

An alternative response from a law of the sea perspective that is of increasing relevance to coastal States threatened by sea-level rise is declaring, fixing and thus stabilizing baselines limits as well as the delimitation of maritime boundaries. This approach has in large part been pioneered by the Pacific Island States. Following the

---

[38] PCA, In the Matter of the Bay of Bengal Maritime Boundary Arbitration between the People's Republic of Bangladesh and the Republic of India, Award, 7 July 2014, available online: https://pca-cpa.org/en/cases/18/., para. 216.

[39] Freestone, International Law and Sea Level Rise, pp. 117–119.

[40] Schofield, Shifting limits?, p. 411.

[41] See Kenchington, R. (2009) Maintaining coastal and lagoonal ecosystems and productivity. In: Terashima, H (ed.), Proceedings of the International Symposium of Islands and Oceans, Tokyo: Ocean Policy Research Foundation, pp. 1–11, p. 4. See also, Kench, P. (2009) Understanding Small Island Dynamics: A Basis to Underpin Island Management. In: Terashima, H (ed.), Proceedings of the International Symposium of Islands and Oceans, Tokyo: Ocean Policy Research Foundation, *Proceedings of the International Symposium of Islands and Oceans*, pp. 22–24.

adoption of the Framework for a Pacific Oceanscape,[42] regional practice has emerged regarding the fixing of maritime baselines, limits and boundaries. This regional ocean governance strategy includes a call for Pacific Island States and territories to deposit coordinates and charts delineating their maritime zones with the United Nations with a view to determining their maritime jurisdictions explicitly so that they "could not be challenged and reduced due to climate change and sea-level rise."

Multiple declarations have emerged from Pacific islands leaders consistent with this theme, notably the Taputapuātea Declaration on Climate Change of 2015, Delap Commitment on Securing Our Common Wealth of Oceans of 2018 and the 2018 Boe Declaration on Regional Security and the unanimous Communique of the 2019 Meeting of the Pacific Islands Forum. Of particular note was the Statement of the Pacific Islands Forum Leaders Ocean of 2021 where, under the heading "Securing the Blue Pacific", Pacific island leaders declared their intent to conclude outstanding maritime boundaries and indicated a commitment to:

> …develop international law, with that aim of ensuring that once a Forum Member's maritime zones are delineated in accordance with the 1982 UN Convention on the Law of the Sea, the Member's maritime zones cannot be challenged or reduced as a result of sea-level rise and climate change.[43]

This developing State practice arguably aligns with developments in relevant international law. For example, in 2018 the International Law Association (ILA) Committee on International Law and Sea Level Rise proposed a Resolution adopted by the ILA that:

> …on the grounds of legal certainty and stability, provided that the baselines and the outer limits of maritime zones of a coastal or an archipelagic State have been properly determined in accordance with the 1982 Law of the Sea Convention, these baselines and limits should not be required to be recalculated should sea level change affect the geographical reality of the coastline.

This finding was subsequently reiterated through the ILA's 2024 Resolution on this issue.[44] Further, in 2019 the International Law Commission (ILC) established a Study Group on Sea-level rise in relation to international law. The inclusion of this topic in the ILC's long-term programme of work was supported by nearly 120 UN Member States. Discussions on the implications of sea-level rise for the law of the sea have taken place from 2019 in the Sixth Committee of the UN General Assembly

---

[42] Pratt, C and Govan,, H. (2010) Our Sea of Islands, Our Livelihoods, Our Oceania. Framework for A Pacific Oceanscape: A Catalyst for Implementation of Ocean Policy, Pacific Islands Forum Secretariat, available at, http://www.forumsec.org/wp-content/uploads/2018/03/Framework-for-a-Pacific-Oceanscape-2010.pdf.

[43] Pacific Islands Forum (PIF), 2021. Leaders Ocean Statement 2021, available online: https://www.forumsec.org/2021/03/22/pacific-islands-forum-leaders-ocean-statement-2020-21/.

[44] See both 2018 and 2021 Resolutions of the ILA Committee on International Law and Sea Level Rise, available online: https://www.ila-hq.org/en_GB/committees/international-law-and-sea-level-rise.

with several States proving to be supportive of an approach to ensure certainty and stability under the LOSC.[45]

9 Concluding Considerations

The IPCC has made it abundantly clear that the sea level is rising and that this is directly caused by anthropogenically-induced climate change and that, further, the Earth is already committed to continued sea level rise for hundreds of years and probably millennia.[46] There is also little doubt that global sea-level rise poses significant issues for the definition of baselines along the coast, the delineation of the outer limits of maritime claims and the delimitation of maritime boundaries.

While coastal States have and no doubt will continue to make physical interventions along the coast to try and defend valuable parts of the coast there are problems and limitations associated with these efforts. However, from a law of the sea perspective, there are increasing signs of a move away from ambulatory to fixed baselines, limits and boundaries. These approaches have been pioneered by a sustained regional effort on the part of the Pacific Islands States, not only in terms of the delimitation of maritime delimitation but also to declare and try to fix these baselines and the outer limits of maritime claims with a view to preserving the spatial extent of their maritime entitlements. Additionally, the ILA and ILC are engaged with this issue such that it is arguably reasonable to suggest that this is an area of the international law of the sea that is in the process of evolution.

Ultimately, it remains to be seen whether the international community will accept this potential evolution in the interpretation of the law of the sea such that declared baselines, limits and boundaries will prove to be opposable to other States in the face of the threat posed by sea-level rise. Likewise, although the stability of international boundaries is clearly vital from the perspective of international peace and security, it remains to be seen whether an international maritime boundary can persist where critical basepoints on one side of the line change location radically or even disappear entirely.

[45] See reports of the Study Group on Sea-level rise in relation to international law, available online: https://legal.un.org/ilc/guide/8_9.shtml.

[46] IPCC, *Climate Change 2023*, SPM, C.1.3, p. 25.

Chapter 6
The Way Forward is not Fast-Forward: Sea-Level Rise, Maritime Zones and Back to Basics

Vincent Cogliati-Bantz

1 Introduction

For a large part, the law of the sea is based on a tension between sovereignty and freedom. Sovereignty projected out to sea is, in essence, the claim by coastal States to extend their exclusive control over the adjacent sea. Freedom, on the other hand, means the recognition and preservation of the equal rights of all States in relation to the sea as a common pool (navigation, fishing, overflight, etc.). If freedom triumphed with limited exceptions from the late seventeenth century, the second part of the twentieth century witnessed material restrictions and regulation of freedom.[1] It also witnessed unprecedented geographical limitations thereof; beginning as varied coastal States' claims, these, once acknowledged, recognized, defined, controlled and restrained, later became part of the substantive result achieved by the United Convention on the Law of the Sea (UNCLOS).[2] The causes include a lack of credible alternatives to coastal ambitions over off-shore resources, the dangers and cost of resisting these ambitions, the desire to exclude competitors, the belief in sound

[1] Due for a large part to a reaction to increasing risks to safety, security, harm to the marine environment, over-exploitation of resources (tragedy of the commons), in order to preserve the rights of all States; but also in response to demands of fairness and distributive justice in terms of access to resources: see UN Doc. A/C.1/PV. 1515 (1 November 1967), speech by Arvid Pardo of Malta.

[2] Opened for signature 10 December 1982, 1833 UNTS 3 (entered into force 16 November 1994). The preceding achievements of the 1958 Geneva conventions left a number of crucial issues unresolved.

This chapter was originally written for the 7th Ocean Dialogue in 2021; it has been expanded and updated (current as at 10 April 2024).

V. Cogliati-Bantz (✉)
Faculty of Law, University of Auckland, 17 Eden Crescent, Auckland 1010, New Zealand
e-mail: v.cogliati-bantz@auckland.ac.nz

L. A. T. Nguyen and H. D. Vu (eds.), *Viability of UNCLOS amid Emerging Global Maritime Challenges*, https://doi.org/10.1007/978-981-97-5838-8_6

coastal management.[3] The result is a system of maritime zones recognizing not only coastal sovereignty[4] but also coastal sovereign rights and jurisdiction in vast zones of functional competence.[5]

Communal concerns are best accommodated by multilateral processes leading to acceptable legal norms, institutions that sustain these norms and robust dispute settlement procedures that enforce them. In the UNCLOS, coastal gains necessarily redefined the thorny relationship between exclusive and inclusive interests, the balancing effort in the legal protection of which being itself of communal concern.[6] History (claims and practices) shows that coastal States are often more active than static when it comes to their entitlements, and often seek to expand them. Creeping green jurisdiction has not been unnoticed and collective initiatives are not immune from those trends.[7] Yet, recent history also shows that preserving entitlements in the face of climate change is no less controversial. The issue raises essential questions of substance and process, and of the long-term stability of the rule of law for the oceans that the UNCLOS established.

2 Climate Change, Sea-Level Rise (SLR) and Adverse Consequences

Loss of territory and of maritime zones have recently attracted attention because of the aggravation of SLR, a phenomenon the existence of which is widely supported by scientific evidence. An International Panel on Climate Change (IPCC) Working Group indicated in 2021 that the global mean sea level (GMSL) increased on average by 1.9mm/year between 1971 and 2006, and 3.7mm/year between 2006 and 2018.[8] Recent figures indicate that GMSL increased to 4.5 ± 0.6 mm/year during the period between 2011 and 2020.[9] SLR can be influenced by factors such as winds and ocean

---

[3] See Cogliati-Bantz V (2018) Freedom (?) of the high seas: some preliminary remarks on a venerable old concept. Australian International Law Journal 25:63–79, pp. 69–72; Oxman B H (2006) Territorial temptation: a siren song at sea. American Journal of International Law 100:830–851, pp. 834–835.

[4] Territorial sea, archipelagic waters (including the airspace): Articles 2 and 49 of UNCLOS.

[5] Most importantly, the exclusive economic zone (EEZ) and the continental shelf: articles 55–75 and 76–85 of UNCLOS.

[6] On this, see notably McDougal M S, Burke, W T (1962) The public order of the oceans, Yale University Press, New Haven and London, pp. 9–28.

[7] Cogliati-Bantz, n 3, p. 77. These trends do not exclusively concern coastal States but they are historically particularly acute with coastal States.

[8] Working Group I (physical science basis of climate change) contribution to the Sixth Assessment Report of the IPCC, Summary for Policymakers (2021), A.1.7. The Working Group found this with a high degree of confidence.

[9] World Meteorological Organization (2023) The global climate 2011–2020 (WMO-No. 1338), p. 15. Since 1993, the acceleration of the GMSL rise has been estimated at 0.11 ± 0.06 mm/year: ibid.

currents, vertical movements of the land, isostatic adjustment of the levels of land and coastal erosion.[10] Human influence is very likely the main driver of GMSL increases since at least 1971 and the main causes of human-induced SLR are ocean warming (thermal expansion) and ice melt (Greenland and Antarctic ice sheets and glaciers mass loss).[11] The likely GMSL will continue to rise due to continuing warming and ice melt.[12] These, in turn, are a consequence of global warming; the latter is unequivocally caused by human activities, principally through greenhouse gases emissions.[13] Ocean warming adversely affects food production in some regions; increased impacts include water-borne diseases, flooding, loss of ecosystems and their services with long-term impacts on people.[14] SLR is among the many negative consequences of climate change on the oceans.[15]

SLR varies regionally.[16] However, risk related to SLR is expected to significantly increase by the end of this century along all low-lying coasts.[17] The UN Secretary-General recalled that negative effects are likely to result in adverse social, cultural and economic ramifications for various communities.[18] This includes forced migration.[19]

---

[10] UN Doc. A/70/112, Summary of the first global integrated marine assessment (22 July, 2015), p. 16, para 48.

[11] It is highly likely that less than 50% of the SLR observed in the twentieth century would have occurred in the absence of global warming: Kopp R et al. (2016) Temperature-driven global sea-level variability in the common era. Proceedings of the National Academy of Sciences of the United States of America (113)(11):E1434-E1441, p. E1438.

[12] N 8, B.5.4.

[13] IPCC (2023) Sixth assessment report. Summary for policymakers, A.1. It is virtually certain that the global ocean has warmed unabated since 1970 and has taken up more than 90% of the excess heat in the climate system (high confidence). Since 1993, the rate of ocean warming has more than doubled (likely): IPCC (2019) Special report on the ocean and cryosphere in a changing climate. Summary for policymakers, A.2.

[14] UN Doc A/78/339, Report of the Secretary-General: oceans and the law of the sea (1 September 2023), para 37.

[15] Among which, ocean acidification due to increased uptake of atmospheric CO_2, loss of oxygen in the ocean and ocean stratification. In many regions, declines in the abundance of fish and shellfish stocks due to direct and indirect effects of global warming and biogeochemical changes have already contributed to reduced fisheries catches (high confidence). Coastal ecosystems are also affected by ocean warming, acidification, loss of oxygen, salinity intrusion and SLR: IPCC (2019), n 13, A.5, A.6.

[16] Rapid vertical land movements, including those caused by local anthropogenic factors such as groundwater extraction, is currently the most important cause of relative SLR change in many delta regions: IPCC (2019) Special report on the ocean and cryosphere in a changing climate, p. 324.

[17] Ibid.

[18] UN Doc A/75/70, Report of the Secretary-General: oceans and the law of the sea (16 March 2020), para 14. For some of these effects, see ibid, para 13–14.

[19] It is projected that losses in land due to erosion associated with SLR could lead to the significant displacement of people and loss of life. Displacement may occur both within and across States; it can be voluntary or forced, temporary or permanent: ibid, paras 15, 26.

The vulnerability of small island developing States (SIDS) has been recalled many times and in different fora.[20] Older official proposals, however, so far as can be ascertained, focused on management measures, impact studies and climate change negotiations.[21] The preservation of the function of land formations threatened with disappearance escaped wide-ranging legal scrutiny when material measures of protection rendered legal enquiries on baselines unnecessary.[22] Physical measures, however, have two main limitations; firstly, coastal protection is not without detrimental impacts: 'hard' measures like seawalls and sediment-based measures can disrupt ecosystems and alter hydrodynamic and morphodynamic patterns.[23] They can also impact reef growth, tourism and contribute to beach erosion. Ecosystem-based measures often require more land and can increase flooding.[24] Secondly, these measures are expensive; some coastal nations, particularly small island States, are confronted with adaptation costs amounting to several percent of GDP.[25] Yet, SIDS are expected to face very high impacts, as at least 11–15% of their population live on land with an elevation of 5 m or lower, and they provide few or no possibilities of retreat.[26] It has been emphasized that certain regions like the Pacific experience faster and higher rates of SLR than others, and that the low-lying small island States in the Pacific would have a shorter period to adapt.[27]

[20] E.g. UN Doc. A/RES/72/217 (20 December 2017), para 4. For earlier documents, see e.g. UN Doc. A/CONF.151/26/Rev, vol 1, Resolutions, Agenda 21 (1992), paras 17.123 et seq; UN Doc. A/CONF.167/9, Global Conference on the Sustainable Development of SIDS, Resolution 1, Annex 1: Declaration of Barbados (1994); UN Doc. A/CONF.207/11, International Meeting to Review the Implementation of the Programme of Action for the Sustainable Development of SIDS, Annex II: Mauritius Strategy, para 16 (2005); UN Doc A/RES/65/2, Outcome document of the review Meeting on the implementation of the Mauritius Strategy, para 6 (2010); UN Doc. A/CONF.216/16, Conference on Sustainable Development, resolution 1: 'The Future We Want', para 178 (2012); UN Doc. A/CONF.223/10, Third International Conference on SIDS, Resolution 1: Samoa Pathway, para 44(b) (2014).

[21] See the Male Declaration of 18 November 1989: text in Doc. OIC/OPC-IV/Inf.2, Fourth session of the OIC Committee on Ocean Processes and Climate (Paris, 27 February-1 March 1991); Holdgate M W et al. (1989) Climate change—meeting the challenge. Report by a Commonwealth group of experts (Commonwealth Secretariat, London), p. 95, paras 4.28–4.29; Agenda 21 (n 20), chapter 17.

[22] The Commonwealth Secretariat Report (ibid) recommended several low-cost adaptation mechanisms that could provide a viable option 'unless the more extreme forecasts are realised'.

[23] N 16, p. 389.

[24] Ibid, p. 392.

[25] E.g. Diaz D B (2016) Estimating global damages from sea level rise with the coastal impact and adaptation model (CIAM). 137:143–156.

[26] UN Doc. A/72/70, Report of the Secretary-General: oceans and the law of the sea (6 March 2017), para 20. Small island States in the Caribbean and South Pacific are disproportionately affected relative to their small population size: IPCC (2023) (n 13), A.2.5.

[27] UN Doc A/76/171, Report on the work of the United Nations open-ended informal consultative process on oceans and the law of the sea at its twenty-first meeting (16 July 2021), para 17.

3 SIDS and SLR: Impetus for Legal Change

The question of marine transgression in an age of anthropogenic SLR cannot be disconnected from causes that can be controlled; hence, emphasis has recently been put on the climate change regime and ongoing efforts and failures.[28] This includes ocean-related climate change initiatives.[29] However, the pace of progress led to increasing frustration.[30] Hence, attention turned, not only to potential disputes but also to dispute-settlement mechanisms. These include mechanisms under the UNCLOS and its environmental protection provisions, notably the sweeping duty in Article 192 to protect and preserve the marine environment and the definition of pollution in Article 1(1)(4).[31] In December 2022, the International Tribunal for the Law of the Sea (ITLOS) received a request for an advisory opinion submitted by the Commission of Small Island States on Climate Change and International Law (COSIS).[32] ITLOS is asked to determine what the obligations of the parties are to prevent pollution of, and to protect, the marine environment in relation to climate change, including through SLR. Despite the enthusiasm of some States Parties and

[28] Norway indicated: 'Our discussions about the legal consequences of sea-level rise must therefore be seen in tandem with, and not overshadow, our political determination to address climate change and its impacts'. Available at https://www.un.org/Depts/los/consultative_process/icp21/ICP21_item%203_Norway_English.pdf (2021). These initiatives include the 1992 United Nations Framework Convention on Climate Change, the 1997 Kyoto Protocol and the 2016 Paris Agreement, addressing emissions targets, mitigation and adaptation goals. The mitigation and adaptation mechanisms include the Warsaw Mechanism for Loss and Damage (2013), the Marrakech Partnership for Global Climate Action (2016) and the Sharm-El-Sheikh Adaptation Agenda (2022). At COP28 in December 2023, the first 'global stocktake' of the world's efforts to address climate change under the Paris Agreement was concluded. A decision was adopted to accelerate action across all areas by 2030, including financial and technical support to vulnerable nations: Doc FCCC/PA/CMA/2023/L.17, First global stocktake (13 December 2023).

[29] E.g. *Framework for Resilient Development in the Pacific: An Integrated Approach to Address Climate Change and Disaster Risk Management 2017–2030*, Suva, Pacific Community (2016); Ocean Pathways launched at the UNFCCC COP23 (2017), available at http://sdg.iisd.org/news/ocean-pathway-launched-at-cop-23/; Ocean and Climate Change Dialogue launched at COP25 (2020); 2030 Breakthrough Agenda (ocean and coastal zones) launched at COP 26 (2021); the 2022 United Nations Conference to Support the Implementation of Sustainable Development Goal 14 (UN Doc A/CONF.230/2022/14).

[30] The annual $100 billion goal enshrined in the Paris Agreement has not been reached, and the distribution of funds has not been equitable: https://www.un.org/en/climatechange/raising-ambition/climate-finance.

[31] E.g. Boyle A (2016) Climate change, ocean governance and UNCLOS. In: Barrett J, Barnes R (eds) Law of the sea: UNCLOS as a living treaty. The British Institute of International and Comparative Law, pp. 211–230; Sands P (2016) Climate change and the rule of law: adjudicating the future in international law. Journal of Environmental Law 28:19–35; Voight C (2023) Oceans and climate change: implications for UNCLOS and the UN climate regime. In: Platjouw F M, Pozdnakova A (eds) The environmental rule of law for oceans. Cambridge University Press, pp. 17–35.

[32] https://www.itlos.org/fileadmin/itlos/documents/cases/31/Request_for_Advisory_Opinion_COSIS_12.12.22.pdf. It was submitted under article 21 of the Statute and article 138 of the Rules. COSIS was created by treaty in 2021 and currently has eight members.

organizations in their written or oral statements, some urged the ITLOS to exercise caution in the way it exercises its jurisdiction and its discretion, as well as in the interpretation of the UNCLOS.[33] In April 2023, the International Court of Justice (ICJ) received a request from the UN General Assembly for an advisory opinion on the obligations of States to ensure the protection of the climate system and other parts of the environment from anthropogenic emissions of greenhouse gases, and on what the legal consequences are for States with respect to other States, including SIDS which are particularly vulnerable to climate change, and peoples and individuals of the present and future generations.[34] Such a request had been considered in the past.[35]

The advantage conferred on small island States by the UNCLOS seems disproportionate. Some have EEZs hundreds or thousands of times larger than their landmass.[36] That said, their maritime entitlements are often the source of a large portion of their GDP.[37] This includes planned resources from continental shelves exploitation.[38] The impact of SLR on maritime entitlements and the detriment to the coastal State's rights involved was officially noted in the past.[39] SLR and loss of territory may also result in disputes with neighbours over EEZs and, more broadly, over the sudden expansion of shared or un-demarcated resources.[40] Hence, while it is not surprising that some Pacific nations have been pressing for solutions to their potentially reduced or

---

[33] For instance, COSIS considers that the relevant provisions of Part XII, notably article 192, entail but also go beyond due diligence obligations. Many States, including the UK, Australia and France, opined that they are obligations of conduct not result. China considered that ITLOS does not have advisory jurisdiction.

[34] https://www.icj-cij.org/sites/default/files/case-related/187/187-20230412-app-01-00-en.pdf.

[35] In 2011, the President of Palau requested that the UN General Assembly seek an advisory opinion from the ICJ on the responsibility of States under international law to ensure that activities under their jurisdiction emitting greenhouse gases not damage other States: see https://www.un.org/press/en/2012/120203_ICJ.doc.htm. In 2002, Tuvalu threatened to sue the US and Australia before the ICJ: Janin H, Mandia S (2012) Rising sea levels. An introduction to cause and impact. McFarland Publishers, Jefferson, p. 86.

[36] Kiribati has an EEZ larger than that of Mexico, for a landmass about 2500 times smaller.

[37] The World Bank noted in 2022 that, on average, tuna fishing licenses represent more than 30 percent of government revenue excluding Papua New Guinea: https://www.worldbank.org/en/results/2022/08/10/supporting-a-path-to-more-ocean-based-livelihoods-through-more-sustainable-management-of-pacific-islands-fisheries. There are variations: Kiribati now receives fishing license revenues worth 66 percent of GDP on average per year. In Tuvalu, fishing licenses account for around 40 percent of Government revenue: https://pubdocs.worldbank.org/en/256961563917598074/mpo-cpi.pdf.

[38] E.g. the Pacific extended continental shelf project which assists some Pacific countries to gather scientific, legal and technical evidence necessary to support their extended continental shelf submissions: https://gem.spc.int/projects/pacific-extended-continental-shelf-project. On licensing and regulatory schemes see e.g. Ochoa C (2021) Contracts on the seabed. Yale Journal of International Law 46:103–153, pp. 126–130 (Vanuatu). On the Pacific maritime boundaries programme, see https://gem.spc.int/projects/pacific-maritime-boundaries-programme.

[39] See n 20, Gobal conference on the sustainable development of SIDS, p. 10, para 18: 'Inundation of outlying islands… may result in loss of exclusive economic rights over extensive areas'.

[40] UN Doc. A/64/350, Report of the Secretary-General: climate change and its possible security implications (11 September 2009), paras 17–18. This includes the possibility of exploiting

disappearing maritime zones, the impetus for a legal solution under the law of the sea seems to have originated in academia.[41] The question has since been precipitated by the fate of SIDS which perceive their whole existence as being under threat.

4 SLR, Maritime Zones and the Law of the Sea

The issues at stake involve some fundamental principles. In the law of the sea, it is a core principle that 'the land dominates the sea', that is, the coastal State's maritime zones depend on its sovereignty over the land.[42] While the expression is a judicial creation, the underlying principles are well-established in customary law. They are also enshrined in the UNCLOS, as maritime zones are predicated on the existence of some *terra firma.* Indeed, a State's title to maritime zones is based on the principle that the land dominates the sea through the projection of the coasts or the coastal fronts.[43] Maritime zones and their outer limits are measured or constructed from baselines.[44] These baselines (normal baselines, straight lines, straight baselines or archipelagic straight baselines) either follow the coastline's low-water line or join selected basepoints on the land's low-water line.[45] A partial exception applies to the outer limit of the continental shelf beyond 200 nautical miles from the baselines from

---

newly accessible natural resource deposits and transport routes through the Arctic: ibid para 18. On Tuvalu's concerns about the securitization of climate change, see UN Doc. S/PV.8144 (20 December 2017), 65. Brazil emphasized recently that legal certainty over SLR can be key in preventing disputes: UN Doc A/C.6/76/SR.21, sixth committee, summary record of the 21st meeting (29 October 2021), para 26.

[41] E.g. Caron D (1990) When law makes climate change worse: rethinking the law of baselines in light of rising sea level. Ecology Law Quarterly 17:621–653, p, 647; Soons A (1990) The effects of a rising sea level on maritime limits and boundaries. Netherlands International Law Review, 37:207–232, p. 225.

[42] See e.g. *Maritime Boundary Dispute between Norway and Sweden (Grisbadarna),* Award of 23 October 1909, Reports of International Arbitral Awards (IX):155–162, p. 159 (maritime territory as appurtenance to land territory); *North Sea Continental Shelf Cases (Federal Republic of Germany/ Denmark; Federal Republic of Germany/Netherlands), Judgment,* 1969 ICJ Rep, p. 51, para 96 (land dominates the sea); *Case Concerning the Continental Shelf (Libyan Arab Jamahiriya/Malta), Judgment,* 1985 ICJ Rep, p. 41, para 49; *Maritime Delimitation and Territorial Questions (Qatar v Bahrain (Merits), Judgment,* 2001 ICJ Rep, p. 97, para 185.

[43] *Maritime Delimitation in the Black Sea (Romania v. Ukraine), Judgment,* 2009 ICJ Rep, p. 89, para 77.

[44] See articles 4 (territorial sea), 33(2) (contiguous zone), 57 (EEZ); see article 48 on maritime zones measured from archipelagic baselines. For the limited exception in article 7(2), see n 98. Artificial structures do not generate maritime zones: article 60(8).

[45] See articles 5, 7, 9–13, 47. Apart from the express reference to the low-water line in these provisions, see also *Fisheries Case (United Kingdom v. Norway), Judgment*, 1951 ICJ Rep, pp. 129–130 (straight baselines). If there is no low-water line because there is little or no tidal range or where the coast is very steep, one uses the point of meeting between land and sea: International Hydrographic Bureau and International Association of Geodesy (2014) A manual on technical aspects of the United Nations Convention on the Law of the Sea 1982. Monaco, para 4.1.

which the breadth of the territorial sea is measured.[46] Baselines are thus 'ambulatory': they are affected by, and move along with, physical changes to the land; this is notably the case with SLR which, by definition, affects the low-water line. On that basis, the outer limits of maritime zones, which are generally defined by way of a specific distance from the baselines, are, logically, also ambulatory. The only permanent exception is the outer limit of the continental shelf. Beyond 200 nautical miles, the limits, established following a specified process, 'shall be final and binding' (UNCLOS Article 76(8)). Admittedly, this is explained by the high costs involved in the process, and the need for legal certainty of investors,[47] and of the Authority and contractors.[48] The final limits do not move with new geological surveys or changes to the coastline.[49] Similarly, whether or not the edge of the margin extends beyond 200 nautical miles, the outer limit is also 'permanently' described on charts, and relevant information is deposited with the UN and the Authority (UNCLOS articles 76(9) and 84(2)).

Regression of the coastline generally means regression of maritime zones and, hence, the high seas move landwards. Generally, there is no spatial loss to the coastal State's maritime zones: there is a geographical shift and, in absolute terms, the volume of high seas increases, which might be perceived as serving the common interest. The impact on baselines and outer limits with a slow phenomenon like SLR thus appears minimal. In some cases, basepoints could be changed and baselines redrawn; and outer limits may not be radically changed when the 'envelope-of-arcs' method only uses salient basepoints anyway.[50] However, things are not always that simple. SLR implies loss of land over time.[51] The most serious threat to baselines is the disappearance of the land, and would particularly affect small, low-lying island nations. Total submergence of the entire country may seem unlikely, but if an island or

[46] For the outer edge of the continental margin beyond 200 nautical miles, see article 76(4)–(6). The construction of the outer limit beyond 200 nautical miles uses the foot of the continental slope, not the baselines. However, the lines of constraint in article 76(5)–(6) take account of the baseline (for the 2500-m isobath, see UN Doc. CLCS/11, Scientific and technical guidelines of the commission of the limits of the continental shelf (13 May 1999), para 4.4). Whether the outer limit of the continental shelf is based on distance or outer edge of the continental margin, the existence of a legal continental shelf is predicated on sovereignty over emerged land territory.

[47] See Oxman B H (1981) The third United Nations conference on the law of the sea: the ninth session. American Journal of International Law 75:211–256, p. 230.

[48] The 'Area' is defined as the sea-bed and ocean floor and subsoil thereof, beyond the limits of national jurisdiction: UNCLOS article 1(1)(1).

[49] E.g. Commission on Marine Science, Engineering and Resources (1969) Our nation and the sea. A plan for national action. Government Printing Office, Washington, p. 145.

[50] Churchill R, Lowe A, Sander A (2022) The law of the sea, 3rd ed. Manchester University Press, p. 107.

[51] The question is not SLR per se, but SLR relative to land uplift or subsidence. Regional mean relative SLR will continue throughout the twenty-first century, except in a few regions with substantial geologic land uplift rates: above n 8, C.2.5. Island erosion may be balanced by progradation on other sectors of shorelines: Webb A, Kench P (2010) The dynamic response of reef islands to sea-level rise: evidence from multi-decadal analysis of island change in the Central Pacific. Global and Planetary Change 72:234–246, p. 234. Yet, displacement of people and infrastructures from one side of an island to the other is not easy, particularly in small territories.

part of an island disappears, the baseline disappears with it. Archipelagic States under Part IV of the UNCLOS may see the drawing of archipelagic baselines affected by the disappearance of some basepoints.[52] More generally, the disappearance of a low-tide elevation (LTE) means that the low-water line on that elevation may no longer be used as the baseline for measuring the breadth of the territorial sea[53]; this may have particular consequences for straight baselines (UNCLOS Article 7(4)) and straight archipelagic baselines (UNCLOS Article 47(1)). The disappearance of islands may also modify the configuration of a fringe of islands along the coast (UNCLOS Article 7(1)). Apart from the disappearance of territory, SLR could also affect the indentation of a bay or the distance between the low-water marks of its natural entrance points (UNCLOS Article 10), or the drawing of straight baselines under UNCLOS Article 7(1).[54] In addition, marine transgression may impact the legal status of some land features. A low-lying island turning into an LTE could affect the drawing of baselines under UNCLOS article 13; SLR could also negatively impact the State being able to rely on UNCLOS article 6[55] or on the land-to-water ratio in UNCLOS article 47(7).[56]

One can also conceive of SLR rendering an island uninhabitable, for instance through loss of land, saltwater intrusion and food security more generally. An island that is unable to sustain human habitation or economic life of its own (a 'rock' in UNCLOS) has no EEZ or continental shelf.[57] The tribunal in the *South China Sea* arbitration made it clear that an 'island' in its natural form must have the capability of sustaining human habitation or economic life.[58] However, some cases are more obvious than others. The fact that a feature is currently not inhabited does not prove that it is uninhabitable and the fact that it has no economic life does not prove that it cannot sustain an economic life; but if a feature was never inhabited and never sustained an economic life, this may be consistent with an explanation that it

[52] See articles 47(1)–(3). On Indonesian archipelagic baselines in a changing environment, see https://www.iho.int/mtg_docs/com_wg/ABLOS/ABLOS_Conf5/Presentations/Session6-Presentation2-Patmasari.pdf (17 October 2008).

[53] Article 13(1) of the UNCLOS. States are free to select any high-water datum that reasonably corresponds to the ordinary meaning of 'high tide': *South China Sea Arbitration (Philippines v People's Republic of China)*, Award of 12 July 2016, para 311.

[54] In which case, a spatial loss of internal waters may ensue.

[55] 'In the case of islands situated on atolls or of islands having fringing reefs, the baseline … is the seaward low-water line of the reef'.

[56] Under Article 47(7), land areas may include waters lying within fringing reefs of islands and atolls. Also, if a fringing reef is incomplete as a result of submersion in some places, the question might be asked to what extent gaps may be joined by straight lines: see United Nations (1989) Baselines: an examination of the relevant provisions of the United Nations Convention on the Law of the Sea. New York, p. 12, para 27 and p. 37, para 85.

[57] UNCLOS Article 121(3). See e.g. Bird E, Prescott V (1989) Rising global sea levels and maritime claims. Marine Policy Reports 1:177–196, p. 186. An even worse scenario is an island turned into an LTE or becoming completely submerged even at low tide.

[58] N 53, para 483.

is uninhabitable.[59] SLR would arguably make matters worse. Conversely, positive evidence that humans historically lived on a feature or that the feature was the site of economic activity could constitute relevant evidence of a feature's capacity.[60] The tribunal added that, in the absence of human habitation, it should be considered whether there is evidence that human habitation has been prevented or ended by forces that are separate from the intrinsic capacity of the feature; it alluded to intervening forces such as '[w]ar, pollution or environmental harm that could all lead to the depopulation, for a prolonged period, of a feature that, in its natural state, was capable of sustaining human habitation'.[61] But that does not mean that, if a feature was capable of sustaining human habitation or economic life, it will forever remain so. The tribunal was arguably referring to possible explanations for depopulation which may displace a presumption that an uninhabited island is, most likely, uninhabitable. There must be a distinction between, say, war and radical environmental harm. The former might not transform the intrinsic capacity of the feature; the latter might. Anthropogenic SLR could be considered environmental harm likely to be permanent, not just 'prolonged', and it would be very difficult to consider the state of a feature 'but for' the impact of SLR, a gradual phenomenon. Further, in the case of the continental shelf, while the outer limit is final and permanently described on charts, it could still be wondered whether the total disappearance of emerged land impacts the permanence of that outer limit.[62] Indeed, it is sovereignty over the emerged landmass that generates sovereign rights over the continental shelf. It has been suggested that the maintenance of maritime entitlements does not necessarily follow the same rule as their establishment. Thus, reinforcing a feature such as an LTE is allowed, but not necessary, to preserve entitlements.[63] This goes against State practice; the States that invested large sums of money to reinforce features against physical change

---

[59] Ibid, para 484. Economic activity derived from a possible EEZ or continental shelf is insufficient; similarly, there must be a link between the economic life and the feature itself, rather than merely its adjacent waters (territorial sea): ibid paras 502–503.

[60] Ibid, para 484.

[61] Ibid, para 549. SLR does not necessarily render an island uninhabitable. The line between habitability and uninhabitability is a question of degree and needs to be examined on a case-by-case basis. 'Humans have shown no shortage of ingenuity in establishing communities in the far reaches of the world, often in extremely difficult conditions': ibid.

[62] For the suggestion that it does not, see e.g. Hayashi M (2013) Sea level rise and the law of the sea: how can the affected states be better protected?. In: Kwon M S et al. (eds) Limits of maritime jurisdiction. Brill, Leiden, pp. 609–625, at pp. 613–614; Soons, n 41, 218–219.

[63] Purcell K (2019) Geographical change and the law of the sea. Oxford University Press, p. 247. Purcell refers to the use of an LTE shown on existing charts: ibid. Indeed, there must be some evidence that there was an LTE in the past, if it is now submerged. However, her argument is that the LTE may be used in the unilateral process of drawing maritime limits 'regardless of whether it in fact remains above water at low-tide at the time of delimitation': ibid. On the other hand, a feature permanently submerged 'may indeed preclude its use in the construction of a new maritime boundary' (unless by agreement): ibid. Since any delimitation has an international aspect, the rationale for the distinction may be questioned. A similar argument is made by Churchill, Lowe and Sander who claim that islands becoming LTEs could still be used as basepoints for straight baselines, even without a lighthouse or other installation on them, on the ground that they had legitimately served as basepoints: n 50, p. 107.

were admittedly convinced that they had to do so to preserve their entitlements.[64] Additionally, disputes over a feature's status and its reinforcement to preserve it may arguably be aggravated by its alleged continuation despite submergence.[65] More fundamentally, the exposition of what the rules on maintenance of maritime spaces are, leaves a number of questions unsettled.[66] At all events, the question of the continued existence of a State whose territory has disappeared through submergence is different from that of the continuing capacity to enjoy maritime spaces; a State is not necessarily a coastal State.

5 Options for Saving Entitlements: Reformation, Deformation or Affirmation?

Baselines and outer limits are marked on charts of an adequate scale or designated by geographical co-ordinates of points. Some of these must be deposited with the UN Secretary-General.[67] These are only a representation of reality, not the source of the State's entitlement to maritime spaces. The International Law Association (ILA) also concluded that, *de lege lata*, coastal States may not 'protect and preserve territory through...the legal fiction of a charted line that is unrepresentative of the

[64] Iceland (Kolbeinsey), Japan (Okinotori) and the Netherlands (coastal defense in the North Sea) all undertook such works.

[65] On protests against the status of Okinotori, see e.g. https://www.un.org/Depts/los/clcs_new/submissions_files/jpn08/chn_3aug11_e.pdf (China); https://www.un.org/Depts/los/clcs_new/submissions_files/jpn08/kor11aug11.pdf (Republic of Korea).

[66] Purcell argues that, when a condition for the continued existence of a right is not expressly stated to be the same as for the creation of the right, there must be a sound basis for applying the same condition: n 63, p. 230. That basis exists when territorial sovereignty over the coastal land generating entitlement to maritime space has been lost (ibid, p. 233), notably through abandonment or transfer of territory (ibid, pp. 236–238). However, in the case of islands or LTEs, the rules specifying the circumstances in which entitlement to particular maritime zones may be claimed, do not indicate that loss of entitlement will follow if these circumstances no longer obtain, notably because of the vagaries of nature: ibid, pp. 238–240. This is based on the view that States, when negotiating the UNCLOS, were not concerned with the continuation of entitlement to maritime space: ibid, p. 239. If an island can no longer sustain human habitation or economic life of its own, this does not impact on the continued existence on the maritime zones once generated by the island; the same argument goes for archipelagic waters and baselines (ibid, pp. 238–244) and, interestingly, appears to also apply to fully submerged features: ibid, pp. 238–239, 247. This is seemingly so because the sovereignty over the island/rock is preserved unless abandoned; the argument also seems to be rooted in some consideration of fairness to the State victim of unfortunate geographical change. Following that argument, one could claim that if, say, the island subsequently becomes an LTE, and while an LTE cannot be appropriated (see *Territorial and Maritime Dispute (Nicaragua v Colombia), Judgment*, 2012 ICJ Rep, p. 641, para 26), it could continue to generate the maritime zones it generated when it was an island (and, perhaps, State's sovereignty continues to obtain).

[67] E.g. UNCLOS articles 16, 47, 75.

actual low-water line'.[68] This stemmed from its conclusion that the normal baseline is ambulatory, though it left open the possible need to 'develop' the law on baselines in the light of SLR.[69] International cases also looked at contemporary physical reality when performing the task of delimitation.[70] Ambulation of baselines was also the expressed official view of several States[71] while others, such as Belize, favoured relying on official maritime charts (not the actual low-water line) as conclusive evidence of baselines[72] but very few writers supported that view in the past.[73]

Some States in the Pacific began advocating for change, both singly and, especially, collectively, towards the recognition of the possibility to 'freeze' or 'fix' baselines.[74] This arguably militates against the view that the permanence of baselines and, hence, maritime zones, may be legitimate as a matter of course without wide-ranging support. As is well known, the ILA explored the problem and its committee on sea-level rise proposed in 2018: 'States should accept that, once the baselines and the outer limits of the maritime zones ... have been properly determined in accordance with the detailed requirements of the [UNCLOS] that also reflect customary international law, these baselines and limits should not be required to be readjusted should sea level change affect the geographical reality of the coastline'.[75] Regrettably, the distinction between interpretation and progressive development (change) is not always made very clearly; but it is discernible. While the committee emphasized the *de lege ferenda* nature of some of its proposals, notably by referring to a 'change in the current interpretation' of the UNCLOS,[76] it also alluded to subsequent practice in the interpretation of the UNCLOS.[77] The development of new law has challenges. For instance, despite seeing in regional activities 'strong evidence of emerging State

---

[68] (2012) International Law Association Reports of Conferences. 75, p. 424. Some domestic laws elevate charts to the rank of determinative evidence of the baseline. While this is understandable for frequently updated charts, outdated charts may not be acceptable: ibid, p. 413. See also (1952-I) Yearbook of the International Law Commission, p. 178, para 52 (Mr Scelle).

[69] Ibid, pp. 385–386, 426,

[70] See *Delimitation of the Maritime Boundary between Guyana and Suriname,* Award of 16 September 2007, XXX RIAA, p. 110, paras 394–396; *Territorial and Maritime Dispute*, n 66, p. 644, paras 35–36.

[71] E.g. the UK, note of 10 January 2020, available at https://legal.un.org/ilc/sessions/72/pdfs/english/slr_uk.pdf: 'ambulatory baselines in accordance with the [UNCLOS]'; the U.S., note of 14 February 2020, available at https://legal.un.org/ilc/sessions/72/pdfs/english/slr_us.pdf ('baselines are generally ambulatory'); the Netherlands, note of 27 December 2019, available at https://legal.un.org/ilc/sessions/72/pdfs/english/slr_netherlands.pdf ('baselines are adjusted accordingly').

[72] UN Doc. A/C.6/74/SR.30 (9 December 2019), p. 12, para 70.

[73] But see Kapoor D, Kerr A (1986) A guide to maritime boundary delimitation. Carswell,Toronto, p. 31.

[74] See Cogliati-Bantz V P (2020) Sea-level rise and coastal states' maritime entitlements: a cautious approach. Journal of Territorial and Maritime Studies 7:86–110, pp. 93–94 (referring to declarations made between 2014 and 2018).

[75] (2018) International Law Association Reports of Conferences 78, p. 888.

[76] Ibid, p. 880.

[77] Ibid, p. 888. It also noted that its proposals could be influential in the contemporary interpretation of the UNCLOS: ibid.

practice in the Pacific region', the ILA committee was cautious enough to signal that the 'emergence of a new customary rule will require a pattern of State practice, as well as *opinio juris*'.[78] The present author reviewed the other options' difficulties.[79] The committee also indicated that it had recommended 'an interpretation of the 1982 LOSC which favoured preserving entitlements'.[80] The resolution adopted by the ILA conference, which endorses the committee's proposals, also differentiates between interpretation and progressive development.[81] The ILA's view in so far as concerns interpretation of the UNCLOS was 'significantly influenced by the strong evidence of an emerging State practice in the Pacific'[82]; such interpretation neutralises the ambulation of baselines, 'if, as a matter of international law', the baseline is, indeed, ambulatory.[83] Maintaining the baseline despite geographical change was, nevertheless, expressly recognized as a breach of the ambulatory rule.[84]

Since the issue is, clearly, the effect of SLR on baselines, ambulation is at the heart of the enquiry. The two Co-Chairs of the International Law Commission (ILC) Study Group on SLR made valuable contributions to the debate, although not without criticism.[85] They authored two papers, one in 2020 (first issues paper, FIP) and an additional paper in 2023 (AP).[86] One might see with some satisfaction that the possible identification of a rule of customary law, sometimes breathlessly advocated in academia, has been largely side-tracked. The FIP had concluded that there was practice, at least for the Pacific and South-East Asia region but that *opinio juris* 'is not that evident'.[87] Some statements could lead to uncertainties as to the scope of the putative rule.[88] Further, it is not always clear whether earlier statements tended

---

[78] Ibid, p. 887.

[79] N 74. This involves amendment of the UNCLOS, the adoption of a new agreement, a protocol to the UNFCCC, the intervention of the meeting of the States Parties.

[80] N 75, p. 891.

[81] Resolution 5/2018: https://www.ila-hq.org/en_GB/documents/conference-resolution-sydney-2018-english-2.

[82] N 75, p. 919.

[83] Ibid, p. 879.

[84] Ibid, p. 882. And keeping the baseline ambulatory but maintaining the outer limits of maritime zones would entail a breach of the rule on the acceptable breadth of these zones: ibid, p. 883.

[85] UN Doc A/76/10, Report of the ILC on its seventy-sixth session (26 April-4 June and 5 July-6 August 2021), p. 168, para 266.

[86] UN Doc. A/CN.4/740, First issues paper (28 February 2020); UN Doc A/CN.4/761, Additional paper to the first issues paper (13 February 2023). The Co-Chairs are Bogdan Aurescu and Nilüfer Oral.

[87] FIP, p. 43, para 104(i). A view was expressed at the ILC that the desire of States for 'stability' was not necessarily an 'indication' of *opinio juris*, as suggested by the FIP, to the extent that it was difficult to qualify the preference for stability as reflecting 'a sense of legal right or obligation': n 85, p. 169, para 266.

[88] Papua New Guinea referred to 'existing and emerging State practice, particularly in the Pacific region, indicating that *small island States* intended to maintain existing entitlements to maritime zones established in accordance with [the UNCLOS], notwithstanding sea-level rise': UN Doc. A/C.6/74/SR.30 (9 December 2019), 5, para 20 (emphasis added). The Secretary-General was arguably more cautious, referring to 'some practice by States in the Pacific region aimed at establishing

towards the formation of a rule of customary law, or a subsequent practice in the interpretation of the existing law.[89] Any attempt at establishing regional custom does not solve its opposability outside the region—that solution became largely discounted. More fundamentally, even a general customary rule poses a risk to the integrity and universality of the UNCLOS. It also raises the scope of the divergence between conventional and customary rule, and to what extent a pre-existing customary rule had been codified and subsequently modified.[90] The customary process of claims and counterclaims, characteristic of the 'old' law of the sea, is inherently unilateral and unstable; it entails risks of escalation. The AP makes it clear that States, in their subsequent submissions and statements, include very few references to the formation of customary law on the freezing of baselines and outer limits of maritime zones. In fact, both Micronesia and Papua New Guinea refuted attempts to establish a new rule of customary law.[91] The lack of customary rules on SLR, the preference against customary law and the dangers of fragmentation was evident to several States.[92] Yet, the customary route has not been abandoned.[93]

Most importantly, the Co-Chairs considered that the UNCLOS does not expressly indicate that coastal States must draw, recognize (article 5 on the normal baseline) or notify (article 16) new baselines, including straight baselines, when coastal conditions change.[94] They conclude: '[N]othing prevents Member States from depositing notifications, in accordance with the Convention, regarding the baselines and outer limits of maritime zones measured from the baselines and, after the negative effects of sea-level rise occur, to stop updating these notifications in order to preserve their

permanent baselines': UN Doc. A/75/70, above n 18, p. 10, para 31. The FIP's presentation of South Asian practice appears misleading, noting that States in the region favour geoengineering or land reclamation work to consolidate their fixed basepoints and maintain baselines and maritime zones. This is very different from the South Pacific claims to fix the baselines by simple proclamation. Yet, the FIP classifies both types of 'practice' in the same category of practice in relation to the maintenance of maritime zones: ibid p. 42, para 104(i), and p. 37, para 99.

[89] E.g. the Maldives referred to 'State practice in the Pacific [which] supports fixed maritime entitlements' (note of 31 December 2019, available at https://legal.un.org/ilc/sessions/72/pdfs/english/slr_maldives.pdf, 12); Antigua and Barbuda referred to 'its legal opinion, which is backed by its state practice—and by the legal practice of numerous other States' (available at https://legal.un.org/ilc/sessions/72/pdfs/english/slr_antigua_barbuda.pdf).

[90] See n 68 for the ILC in the 1950s. For the preparation of the 1930 Hague Codification conference, see Gidel G (1934) Le droit international public de la mer, vol III. Mellottee, Paris, p. 523 (cases where the real low-water line should replace the one on charts).

[91] AP, pp. 39–40, paras 95–96 (statements made in 2022 at the UN General Assembly's sixth committee).

[92] E.g. Israel, China: ibid, p. 40, para 96; and Germany in 2022 in its comments to the ILC: https://legal.un.org/ilc/sessions/74/pdfs/english/slr_germany.pdf.

[93] E.g. the EU: statement at the UN General Assembly's sixth committee in 2022, available at (https://www.un.org/en/ga/sixth/77/pdfs/statements/ilc/26mtg_eu_2.pdf, para 7. In the same document, the EU reaffirms its commitment to the integrity of the UNCLOS.

[94] FIP, p. 28, para 78. The normal baseline is marked on charts recognized by the coastal State under article 5. Article 16 concerns the duty to show other baselines or limits derived therefrom on charts or to record geographical coordinates on a list, and to deposit charts or lists with the UN Secretary-General (a similar obligation applies under articles 47, 75, 76 and 84).

entitlements'.[95] The authors were undoubtedly constrained by the ILC's earlier decision not to propose modifications to existing law, such as the UNCLOS.[96] They also assumed that the ILA's recommendation was *de lege ferenda*.[97] The FIP correctly concludes that relying on Article 7(2) of the UNCLOS (which applies to unstable coastlines because of the presence of a delta and other natural conditions) to justify keeping basepoints that may become submerged because of SLR, is not realistic.[98] The view that the UNCLOS does not require States to update their charts, limits derived from baselines or list of coordinates, is, in part, based on the view that the ambulatory theory is not the only way to interpret the UNCLOS, since there is no expressed duty in the UNCLOS to update charts or coordinates or their notification when notification is required.[99] This calls for certain comments:

Firstly, any *expressio unius* argument has to be cautiously approached.[100] Israel made the point explicitly.[101] Secondly, the Co-Chairs indicate that ambulation does not address the concerns of the States impacted by SLR; some statements are also replete with references to 'fairness' and 'equity'.[102] The Co-Chairs also consider that equity, as a method under international law for achieving justice, should be applied in favor of the preservation of existing maritime entitlements.[103] However, it is unclear

---

[95] ibid, p. 41, para 104(f).

[96] UN Doc. A/73/70, Report of the ILC on the work of its seventieth session (21 September 2018), p. 355, para 14 (inclusion of the topic on the agenda).

[97] FIP, p. 17, para 36. This does not appear to be entirely correct as argued earlier.

[98] Ibid, p. 29, para 79. Even if article 7(2) is read independently from, and not cumulatively with, article 7(1) and the conditions there (deeply indented coastline or fringe of islands), it is difficult to claim that the coastline is rendered 'highly unstable' by SLR, a very slow phenomenon. Hence, it matters not whether 'delta and other natural conditions' is read as 'delta or other natural conditions' (as in the Russian version of the Convention). Article 7(2) arguably does not allow for the selected basepoints and the baselines to remain in perpetuity. The baselines 'remain effective until changed by the coastal State *in accordance with this Convention*' (emphasis added). As the UNCLOS does not normally allow basepoints on water, it eventually requires the State to change its baselines, presumably when it is clear that the low-water line has significantly advanced or retreated: see Churchill, Lowe, Sander, n 50, p. 73; The Law of the Sea: Baselines, n 56, p. 24, para 49. This involves updating charts. One may find it surprising that France, in its comments to the ILC of 29 November 2022, relied on the Russian version to accommodate an interpretation of article 7(2) which could cater to SLR: https://legal.un.org/ilc/sessions/74/pdfs/english/slr_france.pdf. France also alludes to this possibility becoming the broadly accepted interpretation.

[99] FIP, p. 29, para 78.

[100] ITLOS recently confirmed that the exclusive jurisdiction of the flag State does not just operate 'on the high seas' as stated in article 92, but also in relation to port State jurisdiction in relation to a foreign ship's freedom of the high seas exercised on the high seas: see Cogliati-Bantz V (2020) Freedom of the high seas and extent of coastal state jurisdiction: reflections on the Norstar case. Cambridge Law Review 5:1–11.

[101] N 92.

[102] FIP, p. 30, para 80 and, e.g. Maldives (n 89); Pacific Islands Forum (submission of 30 December 2019, available at https://legal.un.org/ilc/sessions/72/pdfs/english/slr_pif.pdf); Micronesia (statement of 2021 at the UN General Assembly sixth committee, available at https://www.un.org/en/ga/sixth/76/summaries.shtml#21mtg).

[103] AP, p. 75, para 183(d).

why equity would be needed if the text supports the proposed interpretation, nor it is clear how equity is applied unless called for by a rule of law. Thirdly, if these, and parallel notions of predictability and stability, inspired the need to interpret the UNCLOS in that way, it is not detailed what motivated the interpretation in favor of ambulation. Since it was supported in writings and State practice, it clearly served a valuable purpose, be it safety, predictability and parallelism between facts and law.[104] Fourthly, not enough attention is paid to the difference in drafting between articles 5 and 16. The 'low-water line…as marked on…charts' in the former is different from the duty to show baselines or limits on charts in the latter. If the former could *textually* sustain an interpretation that the baseline is the one on the chart, the latter is more difficult.[105] In 2021, the UN Secretariat produced 'Guidelines on deposit with the Secretary-General of charts and lists of geographical coordinates'. These state: 'There are…no requirements as to the frequency of updates of the deposited information'.[106] Yet, this is different from saying that there is no requirement to update at all. Fifthly, the fundamental question is whether the UNCLOS allows States to retain zones or their limits to which they might otherwise not be entitled if they were constructed after geographical change. The retention of entitlements is seemingly based on the absence of a duty to update charts or lists, that is, to update baselines and limits. Limits on charts thus do not correspond to facts on the ground, which is arguably at odds with previous views.[107] If there is no duty to update, there is no legal ambulation, only change on the ground. In other words, the argument seems to be that the UNCLOS permits a legal fiction. It does so expressly in some cases.[108] But it is another thing to claim that it permits it in an area (the extent of maritime jurisdiction)

---

[104] Thus Singapore recommended 'to take into account the different equities that may apply in varying circumstances… [T]hese considerations may operate differently depending on the types of maritime zones and the rights exercisable within them, the types of baselines involved, whether the areas in question involve overlapping entitlements, and the extent to which the interests of third States and the freedom of navigation are engaged' (statement of 28 October 2021 at the UN General Assembly's sixth committee, available at https://www.un.org/en/ga/sixth/76/pdfs/statements/ilc/20mtg_singapore_2.pdf).

[105] Churchill, Lowe and Sander rely on the text of article 5 to conclude that there is no obligation of the coastal State to draw up a fresh chart, unless the presence of foreign navigation in the area calls for it for safety reasons: n 50, pp. 58–59. No such view was expressed in the previous edition: see Churchill R, Lowe, A (1999) The law of the sea, 3rd ed. Manchester university press, p. 53 (also noting that SLR is likely to cause States to redraw their baselines). The normal baseline is a line on the coast which exists regardless of its being marked on charts; charting is a supplementary requirement: see notably UN Doc. A/CONF.13/C.1/L.87 (29 March 1958), point (g): US proposal; United Nations (2000) Handbook on the delimitation of maritime boundaries. New York, p. 4, para 19: 'The low-water line along the coast is a fact irrespective of its representation on charts'.

[106] Available at https://www.un.org/Depts/los/doalos_publications/publicationstexts/DepositGuidelinesEnglish.pdf, p. 7, para 35. There are no time limits for deposits: para 33.

[107] N 68 and 90 and e.g. Lathrop C G (2015) Baselines. In: Rothwell D et al. (eds) The Law of the sea. Oxford University Press, pp. 77–78 (baselines may be fixed temporarily with an obligation of the coastal State to update in the event of significant geographic changes).

[108] E.g articles 7(2) and 303(2).

where the law is meant to represent geography.[109] Even if it does, it is one thing to claim that there is no duty to update charts, but another to assess the opposability of such a 'freeze'. In particular, due publicity does not imply the validity of the claim.[110] The ILA was careful to subject its recommendation to maritime jurisdiction being established in accordance with the UNCLOS.[111] In cases of controversy over the legality of the original baseline, no baseline or outer limit would be opposable if found originally unlawful, regardless of deposited charts.[112] If no original illegality is found, then does the proposed solution entail that charted lines and notified limits remain conclusive evidence of the coastal State's entitlement despite geographical change and opposable in all circumstances? How about the reluctance of courts to rely on charts that do not correspond to reality?[113] Is the source of entitlement the coast or basepoints as they existed at the moment of charting? Is it the chart itself?[114]

6 States' Support: Form and Scope

A growing number of States support the proposed interpretation of the UNCLOS in the FIP. It has notably been endorsed by some Pacific Island States and territories, supported by Australia and New Zealand in the context of the Pacific Islands Forum.[115] Views expressed earlier were less categorical and arguably not based on

---

[109] Representation allows for a degree of flexibility. Straight baselines for instance are precisely not meant to follow the coastline. However, there is a limit: see articles 7(3) and 47(3) and, generally, article 300. Germany was willing to endorse fictitious baselines: n 92. The limits of fiction were apparently obvious to those who raised concerns about the safety of mariners using outdated maps, to the point when the need was emphasized to distinguish between nautical charts used for navigation purposes and charts used for recording maritime zones: UN Doc A/78/10, Report of the ILC on its seventy-fourth session ((24 April-2 June and 3 July-4 August 2023), p. 104, para 218.

[110] UN Doc SPLOS/30/12, Practice of the Secretary-General in respect of the deposit of charts and/or lists of geographical coordinates (13 April 2020), para 8.

[111] N 81.

[112] Justiciability of the dispute may, however, be hampered by certain provisions like article 298(1)(a) of the UNCLOS.

[113] *Territorial and Maritime Dispute*, n 70; *Territorial and Maritime Dispute between Nicaragua and Honduras in the Caribbean Sea (Nicaragua v Honduras), Judgment*, 2007 ICJ Rep, p. 743, para 278 (basepoint as deposited 'is no longer in the mouth of the River Coco and cannot be properly used as a base point').

[114] Yet, maps never, in themselves, constitute a title: see *Frontier Dispute (Burkina Faso/Mali), Judgment,* 1986 ICJ Rep, p. 582, para. 54. They can, however, acquire such legal force if they are the physical expression of the will of States concerned (ibid). Is such a will to be found in the putative rule that deposited data need not be updated?

[115] Declaration on Preserving Maritime Zones in the Face of Climate Change-related Sea-Level Rise (6 August 2021), available at https://www.forumsec.org/wp-content/uploads/2021/08/Declaration-on-Preserving-Maritime.pdf. In it, the leaders of the Pacific Islands Forum affirm that the UNCLOS imposes no obligation to keep baselines and outer limits of maritime zones under review nor to update charts or lists of geographical coordinates once deposited with the UN Secretary-General, and that

interpretation but on the development of the law.[116] The 2021 Declaration might retrospectively clarify the intention of the relevant States when they defined, in their legislation, baselines and outer limits of maritime zones, since such intention was not expressed at the time and cannot be inferred from the mere existence of legislation establishing limits. Some notifications of new legislation now make such intention clear.[117] Such a view is clearly shared beyond the Pacific region, for instance by the thirty-nine members of the Alliance of Small Island Developing States in their declaration of 22 September 2021.[118] It is also shared by some non-island States.[119] That said, it cannot be said that that position is universal.

Three aspects, among others, can be highlighted here. Firstly, it is not fully clear whether the proposed interpretation gives States a general permission not to update, or whether it must be read in the context of SLR only, or possibly human-induced (climate change) SLR. The wording of the proposal suggests the latter.[120] This is

maintaining maritime zones established in accordance with the UNCLOS notwithstanding climate change-related SLR, is supported by both the UNCLOS and the legal principles underpinning it.

[116] E.g. Communiqué issued at the 50th Pacific Islands issued on 13–16 August 2019, para 26 (available at https://www.forumsec.org/wp-content/uploads/2019/08/50th-Pacific-Islands-Forum-Communique.pdf); Delap commitment signed on 2 March 2018 by eight Pacific island leaders, para 8 (available at https://www.pnatuna.com/sites/default/files/Delap%20Commitment_2nd%20PNA%20Leaders%20Summit.pdf); Taputapuātea Declaration on Climate Change signed on 16 July 2015 by eight Polynesian leaders, 3 (available at https://www.samoagovt.ws/wp-content/uploads/2015/07/The-Polynesian-P.A.C.T.pdf); Palau Declaration on 'The Ocean: Life and Future' made in August 2014 by Leaders of the Pacific Islands Forum, para 10 (available at https://www.forumsec.org/wp-content/uploads/2017/11/2014-Palau-Declaration-on-%E2%80%98The-Ocean-Life-and-Future%E2%80%99.pdf).

[117] See Cook Islands, deposit of 16 August 2021, available at https://www.un.org/Depts/los/LEGISLATIONANDTREATIES/PDFFILES/DEPOSIT/04ObservationsEng.pdf; Micronesia, deposit of 20 January 2020, available at https://www.un.org/Depts/los/LEGISLATIONANDTREATIES/PDFFILES/mzn_s/M.Z.N.151.2020.pdf.

[118] https://www.aosis.org/launch-of-the-alliance-of-small-island-states-leaders-declaration/, para 41.

[119] At the UN General Assembly's sixth committee in 2022: e.g. Bulgaria, Croatia, Cyprus, the EU, Romania, all available at https://www.un.org/en/ga/sixth/77/ilc.shtml; in 2023: Austria ('stability…though an interpretation of the Convention), Greece, Indonesia, Malta, all available at https://www.un.org/en/ga/sixth/78/ilc.shtml.

[120] N 94, para 78 ('so as to address those effects of sea-level rise on the baselines') and para 104(f) ('after the negative effects of sea-level rise occur, to stop updating these notifications').

also clear in some States' statements.[121] But not in others'.[122] Portugal raised the issue explicitly.[123] It thus appears essential to clarify the circumstances under which the rule operates. History shows that creeping jurisdiction wastes no time; baselines drawn on artificially extended land that is passed as coastal protection against SLR, may start appearing sooner rather than later.[124] Additionally, it is not clear when the charting/deposition/publicization must be made to preserve entitlements. Presumably, the State will want to communicate its baselines and limits as early as possible but it is odd to require that they do so 'prior to physical coastline changes brought about by [SLR]' as suggested by the ILA or 'after the negative effects of SLR occur', as suggested in the FIP.[125] Secondly, *if* the UNCLOS is indeed silent on whether baselines are ambulatory or fixed, an interpretation that the legal baselines may be fixed by notification and lack of updating also depends on the text and the purpose of all relevant provisions and the overall text and purpose of the UNCLOS, read in good faith.[126] The ILC's documents and debates, and some States' comments, mention the relevant States' statements and legislation as a possible subsequent practice in the interpretation of the UNCLOS.[127] However, it is difficult to claim at this stage that there is such a practice towards a common interpretation when States' views were expressed that: the importance of equity to the interpretation and application of the

---

[121] E.g. New Zealand (information of 30 June 2022 submitted to the ILC, available at https://legal.un.org/ilc/sessions/74/pdfs/english/slr_newzealand.pdf): 'In the event that New Zealand experiences coastal regression as a result of climate change related sea-level rise, New Zealand does not intend to update its notification of 8 March 2006'. That country had said earlier that 'coastal States' baselines and maritime boundaries should not have to change because of *human-induced* sea level rise': UN Doc. A/C.6/73/SR.22 (UN General Assembly's sixth committee, 3 December 2018), p. 2, para 5 (emphasis added); EU: statement at the UN General Assembly's sixth committee in 2022, available at https://www.un.org/en/ga/sixth/77/pdfs/statements/ilc/26mtg_eu_2.pdf: 'question of whether *in these circumstances* states are legally obliged to periodically review and update the charts' (emphasis added).

[122] E.g. France, n 98; Germany n 92.

[123] https://www.un.org/en/ga/sixth/78/pdfs/statements/ilc/24mtg_portugal_1.pdf.

[124] Malaysia made the point at the UN General Assembly's sixth committee in 2023, perhaps inspired by its neighbour's land-reclamation activities: https://www.un.org/en/ga/sixth/78/pdfs/statements/ilc/27mtg_malaysia_1.pdf.

[125] This implies knowing when SLR's effects appeared, which is difficult indeed. There is also an obvious difference between not updating data and 'freezing' baselines and limits; the latter seems to force the State in a certain situation but coastlines may in fact also extend seaward through accretion, a new island may appear, etc. and in these cases the State will presumably update the data.

[126] The debates at the ILC reveal that the question remains controversial: see UN Doc A/76/10, n 85, pp. 170–171; UN Doc A/78/10, n 109, pp. 92–93. Some members referred to a continuum of interpretation or to the need to focus on practical solutions.

[127] Subsequent practice needs to establish the agreement of the parties regarding such interpretation (article 31(3)(b) of the Vienna Convention on the Law of Treaties). It must establish 'the agreement of all the parties': UN Doc. A/73/10, Report of the International Law Commission Seventieth session (30 April-1 June and 2 July-10 August 2018), Draft conclusions on subsequent agreements and subsequent practice in relation to the interpretation of treaties, p. 31, para 16.

UNCLOS depends on context[128]; a more flexible approach is needed that takes into account the differing circumstances[129]; and practice must be sufficient and all voices need to be reflected.[130] Perhaps more importantly, some have cautioned against 'any deviation or *novel* interpretation of the...UNCLOS',[131] and 'the potential risks and unplanned consequences of any *change* in interpretation'.[132] There is a difference between new interpretation and interpretation that is possible because of silence or ambiguity in the law. The former emphasizes past consensus on a given interpretation, and the uncomfortable line between interpretation and modification.[133] Thirdly, it is clear that there is presently no consensus on the way to go about addressing the issue; some have suggested amendment rather than reinterpretation[134]; or a new agreement[135]; or a subsequent agreement or common understanding on interpretation.[136] In short, it is still unclear how long unilateral limits in conformity with the UNCLOS remain opposable to third States.

Opposability is also, surprisingly, generally absent from analyses on maritime delimitation agreements. The first question to examine is whether the agreement permanently fixes the delimitation line or allows for a movable line. The second

[128] Singapore, statement at the UN General Assembly's sixth committee in 2023: https://www.un.org/en/ga/sixth/78/pdfs/statements/ilc/23mtg_singapore_1.pdf.

[129] Republic of Korea, statement at the UN General Assembly's sixth committee in 2023: https://www.un.org/en/ga/sixth/78/pdfs/statements/ilc/28mtg_rok_1.pdf.

[130] Thailand, statement at the UN General Assembly's sixth committee in 2022: https://www.un.org/en/ga/sixth/77/pdfs/statements/ilc/28mtg_thailand_2.pdf. Subsequent practice by one or more, but not all, parties to a treaty is a supplementary means of interpretation under article 32 of the Vienna Convention. It has a lesser interpretative value than the practice of all parties: n 127, p. 36, para 33.

[131] Iceland's statement at the twenty-first meeting of the Open-ended Informal Consultative Process on Oceans and the Law of the Sea, 14–18 June 2021 (emphasis added), available at https://www.un.org/Depts/los/consultative_process/icp21/ICP21_item%203_Iceland_English.pdf.

[132] Statement of the UK at the UN general Assembly's sixth committee in 2023 (emphasis added), available at https://www.un.org/en/ga/sixth/78/pdfs/statements/ilc/23mtg_uk_1.pdf. The UK did not reject 'adaptive interpretations' but also urged caution when interpreting the silence of some States or the absence of protest against the FIP: ibid. In October 2021, the House of Lords launched an inquiry to consider the extent to which the UNCLOS is fit for purpose. The report recommends that 'baselines should remain fixed in their current position': https://committees.parliament.uk/publications/9005/documents/159002/default/, para 126 (1 March 2022). However, in response, the Government 'intends to take a cautious approach [and will] support adaptation and resilience in SIDS including through accessing finance': https://committees.parliament.uk/publications/22581/documents/168699/default/, pp. 19–20 (31 May 2022).

[133] '[T]he possibility of amending or modifying a treaty by subsequent practice of the parties has not been generally recognized': UN Doc. A/73/10, n 127, p. 51 (Conclusion 7(3)).

[134] See Albania's statement at the UN General Assembly's sixth committee in 2022, available at https://www.un.org/en/ga/sixth/77/pdfs/statements/ilc/27mtg_armenia_2.pdf.

[135] Côte d'Ivoire's statement at the UN General Assembly's sixth committee in 2023, available at https://www.un.org/en/ga/sixth/78/pdfs/statements/ilc/28mtg_cotedivore_1.pdf.

[136] See Germany, n 92 (possibly expressed and endorsed by the States Parties at a meeting of the Parties or by UN member States in a General Assembly resolution); Ireland's statement at the UN General Assembly's sixth committee in 2023: https://www.un.org/en/ga/sixth/78/pdfs/statements/ilc/25mtg_ireland_1.pdf.

question is whether a fundamental change has occurred, whether it was, or was not, foreseen by the parties and radically transforms the extent of obligations to be performed. Strong arguments have been made, in the ILA's recommendation, the FIP, the AP, States' statements and academic commentaries, against the applicability of the *clausula rebus sic stantibus* in this case, either on the basis of a need for stability, an analogy with land boundaries, or both.[137] Yet, other grounds to terminate or withdraw from a delimitation agreement have been explored.[138] Regardless of their merit, these solutions can only concern relations *inter se*, as only the parties may terminate or withdraw from the treaty.[139] While official statements and analyses are replete with references to the stability a maritime delimitation agreement achieves (indeed, how could it be otherwise?),[140] and while States may wish to preserve the way they delimited their overlapping entitlements, a decisive argument needs to be made on why these agreements would be an exception to the *pacta tertiis* rule, and why States could maintain by agreement what they may longer have under general law. No fully convincing argument has been made that delimitation agreements constitute an 'objective regime'.[141] In fact, one suggestion was made at the ILC to explore options for third States who could have an interest in the termination of delimitation treaties owing to SLR.[142]

7 Some Concluding Remarks

The concerns of affected States, especially the SIDS, are real, and pressing. The rates of SLR in the eastern Indian Ocean, western tropical Pacific and south and north mid-latitude Pacific are higher than the global mean.[143] Such rhetoric can strategically

[137] See article 62 of the Vienna Convention on the Law of Treaties.

[138] See article 61 on impossibility of performance when the object indispensable for the execution of the treaty disappears. This could happen if overlapping areas (regarded as the 'object') no longer overlap: AP, p. 58, para 147.

[139] On judicial delimitation, see Cogliati-Bantz, n 74. Colombia wrote that there are situations where a geographical formation is also recognized in a judgment or arbitral award for the purposes of delimitation of maritime spaces but can no longer be considered as such because of SLR: comment of 2022 to the ILC, available at https://legal.un.org/ilc/sessions/74/pdfs/english/slr_colombia.pdf.

[140] E.g. FIP, pp. 46–55, paras 120–141.

[141] See the discussion in the AP, pp. 55–56; UN Doc A/76/10, n 85, p. 173, para 281.

[142] UN Doc A/76/10, n 85, p. 103, para 211. Singapore cautiously stated that 'maritime boundary delimitation treaties and the decisions of international courts or tribunals should *not be easily* re-opened'. Emphasis added. It also referred to the extent to which the interests of third States and the freedom of navigation are engaged: n 104.

[143] World Meteorological Organization (2023) State of the climate in the South-West Pacific in 2022 (WMO-No.1324), p. 12.

play to the advantage of Pacific SIDS.[144] Their Western, developed supporters, particularly those in the region, are undoubtedly animated by some laudable sentiments; yet, altruism or a sense of post-colonial responsibility is rarely a single motivator of foreign policies. Geopolitical considerations are ever-present. There is strategic anxiety, notably in both the U.S. and Australia, about China's increasing influence in the Pacific, as donor, economic, military and diplomatic partner.[145] This prompted several new national or multilateral strategies; especially the U.S.'s first Indo-Pacific Strategy identifying 'mounting challenges, particularly from the PRC',[146] and the Partners in the Blue Pacific, emphasizing 'growing pressure on the rules-based free and open international order'.[147] These add to or update a plethora of pre-existing programmes of security and development relations within the region.[148] The security element has been recently exemplified by the Aukus security partnership[149] or the Agreement on defense cooperation between the U.S. and Papua New Guinea.[150] Interestingly, the U.S. also recently updated its policy on SLR and maritime zones. In contrast to its previous view that baselines are generally ambulatory,[151] it now 'recognizes new trends', and 'applauds the Pacific Island States' initiative'.[152] The U.S. is evidently in a difficult position, not being a party to the UNCLOS and having long advocated that most of its provisions reflect customary law. It refrains from referring to an interpretation of the UNCLOS that does not require updating; however, it 'will not challenge such baselines and maritime zone limits that are not subsequently

[144] See e.g. Parsons M, Nalau J (2019) Adaptation policy and planning in Pacific Small Island Developing States'. In: E. C. H. Keskitalo E C H, Preston B L (eds), Research handbook on climate change adaptation policy. Edward Elgar, Cheltenham, p. 279.

[145] Sora M (2022) Geopolitical competition among the larger powers in the Pacific. Journal of International Affairs 74:111–125, pp. 111–113. For some journalists' accounts on power-play in the Pacific, see e.g. https://www.news.com.au/finance/work/leaders/the-truth-about-chinas-power-play-in-the-pacific/news-story/fb8e8be28d65fd4df0141d59109a230d (20 June 2018); https://www.brookings.edu/articles/the-risks-of-chinas-ambitions-in-the-south-pacific/ (20 July 2020); https://www.scmp.com/week-asia/politics/article/3244443/us-chinas-tense-pacific-power-play-persist-after-australia-papua-new-guinea-security-pact (9 December 2023).

[146] https://www.whitehouse.gov/wp-content/uploads/2022/02/U.S.-Indo-Pacific-Strategy.pdf (February 2022), p. 5.

[147] https://www.whitehouse.gov/briefing-room/statements-releases/2022/06/24/statement-by-australia-japan-new-zealand-the-united-kingdom-and-the-united-states-on-the-establishment-of-the-partners-in-the-blue-pacific-pbp/ (24 June 2022). The initiative groups the U.S., Australia, Japan, New Zealand, the UK, and Canada, Germany and South Korea are partner nations.

[148] On the top lenders and grantors in the Pacific, see https://pacificaidmap.lowyinstitute.org/. Pledges of aid and cooperation have been made by several countries, including the U.S., UK, Australia, New Zealand, Indonesia, France, Japan: https://www.stuff.co.nz/national/china-and-nz/300504115/pawns-of-the-pacific-region-becoming-increasingly-caught-up-by-uschina-geopolitical-struggle (20 February 2022).

[149] https://www.defense.gov/spotlights/aukus/ (September 2021).

[150] https://www.state.gov/wp-content/uploads/2023/10/63374-Papua-New-Guinea-Defense-08.16.2023.pdf (22 May 2023).

[151] N 71.

[152] https://www.state.gov/marine-environment/#sea-level-rise.

updated despite [SLR] caused by climate change'. The upside of geopolitical competition is that it can provide an opportunity for the receiving States to advocate for positive competition on development cooperation. The downside is that geopolitical competition also has negative impacts, be they destabilizing effects, elite capture or corruption.[153] Further, the interests of great powers are not necessarily aligned with those of the receivers and the game could change at any time.[154] Some Pacific leaders are concerned that major powers are developing strategies with little, if any, consultation with Pacific Island countries.[155] Yet, as the chief security concern of low-lying island nations is climate change, independent choices and options are limited. Decisions not to update baselines and outer limits on charts, in accordance with a seemingly novel interpretation of the UNCLOS, just like the previous calls to 'freeze' maritime spaces (baselines, limits, boundaries) are decisions that cannot dispense with wide-ranging support. Such support appears to be existing; but the international community needs to carefully consider the ways to go about translating such support into agreeable solutions, what motivates such support, and what scope the solutions will have.

Only carefully balanced solutions negotiated in a multilateral setting, following multilateral processes taking account of all interests at stake, and within integrated legal and policy frameworks, should be acceptable. This in no way excludes bilateral or regional agreements; they are encouraged and sometimes required by the UNCLOS.[156] They will, arguably, become necessary to address other issues such as 'climate refugees'.[157] Global problems requiring global solutions mean that processes are as important as substantive rules. The risk of bilateral deals, when varied strategic interests are coupled with varied levels of power, is that they become a substitute for equitable solutions with wide-ranging support. The legitimacy of a particular legal solution to SLR must be anchored in the rule of law, not diluted in transactional bargains. Greening geopolitics is no less ubiquitous than greening coastal creeping jurisdiction. Unsurprisingly, the Pacific Islands Forum Declaration on the continuity of statehood and the protection of persons in the face of climate change-related sea-level rise, calls for the 'international community to support this Declaration and cooperate in achieving its purposes, consistent with…principles of equity and fairness'.[158] On the same day, the Falepili Union Treaty was signed between Australia and Tuvalu; there, provisions on climate cooperation and human mobility are accompanied by Tuvalu's duty to 'mutually agree with Australia any partnership, arrangement or engagement with any other State or entity on security and

153 Sora n 145, pp. 116, 120.

154 See Nath E, Klingebiel S (2023) Geopolitical competition in the Indo-Pacific: managing development cooperation. IDOS Policy brief 8/2023, pp. 6–7.

155 https://pasifika.news/2022/05/pacific-elders-voice-statement-on-climate-security/ (2 May 2022).

156 E.g. articles 51, 74, 83, 123, 125.

157 See the work of the ILC on statehood and the protection of persons affected by SLR, especially the second issues paper by two Co-Chairs, UN Doc A/CN.4/752 (19 April 2022).

158 https://www.forumsec.org/wp-content/uploads/2023/11/Annex-D-2023-PIF-Declaration-on-Statehood-and-Protections-of-Persons.pdf (9 November 2023).

defence-related matters. Such matters include but are not limited to defence, policing, border protection, cyber security and critical infrastructure, including ports, telecommunications and energy infrastructure'.[159] This led a former Tuvalu Prime Minister to claim that this was 'revers[ing] Tuvalu political status to that of 45 years ago'.[160]

Those who cannot see the forest for the trees could be accused of crafting solutions catering to contemporary challenges without due regard for the long-term stability, credibility of, and enduring support for, the UNCLOS. So far, there has been a resounding call for respecting the integrity of the UNCLOS. But clear guardrails must also emphasize the controlled setting in which climate change and SLR, as global challenges, prompt credible legal solutions within the UNCLOS; otherwise, the danger is to set precedents validating, through either interpretation or practice, the primacy of particular interests over self-restraint; this was the hallmark of centuries of the 'old' law of the sea. The signs are here already. Witness the view that the special powers of coastal States over ice-covered regions within the EEZ (article 234 of the UNCLOS) should remain when the ice has reduced.[161] This does not mean that self-restraint, that is, due regard for the rights of others, should lead to self-destruction. The emphasis here is on multilateralism, not sacrifice. The programme of work of the ILA and ILC was springboarded by a few sympathetic individuals. Yet, the choices to be made need not, and should not, be hastened. Firstly, because, as was pointed out in this chapter, certain important aspects need to be fleshed out. Secondly, because there is a variety of options available, be they related to climate change measures of adaptation and resilience, including coastal protection, or other accommodations of coastal States apart from the maintenance of baselines and limits. One also wonders how only maintaining maritime zones assists affected States if the land disappears. The whole array of rights and duties of a coastal State in that situation might not be necessary and would be less practically helpful than, say, additional quotas of, income or usufruct from, resources, especially if the (living) resources previously found in their maritime zones have moved away anyway because of climate change.[162]

---

[159] https://www.dfat.gov.au/geo/tuvalu/australia-tuvalu-falepili-union-treaty, article 4(4).

[160] https://www.rnz.co.nz/international/pacific-news/503354/australia-tuvalu-falepili-union-shameful-former-tuvalu-pm (27 November 2023).

[161] 'The Russian Federation…has indicated that it takes the view that there is no requirement to change legal regime in reaction to the shrinking ice coverage': Dremliuga R (2017) A note on the application of article 234 of the Law of the Sea Convention in light of climate change: views from Russia. Ocean Development and International Law 48:128–135, p. 133; Gavrilov V, Dremliuga R, Nurimbetov R (2019) Article 234 of the 1982 United Nations convention on the law of the sea and reduction of ice cover in the Arctic Ocean. Marine Policy 106:103518, p. 5: 'Clearly, the provisions of Article 234 should be applied in the light of current conditions and independent of existing and near-future changes in Arctic ice coverage'.

[162] On research on the risks and impacts of climate change on fish stocks, see UN Doc. A/72/70, Oceans and the law of the sea: report of the Secretary-General (6 March 2017), p. 15, para 44; Lennan M (2023) Fisheries redistribution under climate change. In: Platjouw F M, Pozdnakova A (eds) The Environmental rule of Law for oceans: designing legal solutions. Cambridge University Press, pp. 163–177.

The maintenance of current baselines and limits is predicated on the idea that permanence, measured from moment *x* as decided by the coastal State (the establishment and notification of baselines and limits), best serves stability. This assumes that this is the objective of stability. At the same time, it is claimed that a flexible interpretation of the UNCLOS is needed to accommodate the changing needs of certain coastal States because ambulation is inequitable. Yet, as quipped by Judge Schwebel, what is equitable can be as variable as the weather in The Hague. While the interests of coastal States and the rest of the international community in the use of the oceans arguably remain the same, the practical opportunities to realize, or frustrate, those interests do change over time. The practical opportunity for vigorous debates over whose interests are at stake and over which impact of climate change, is also very real. Any such debate might bring about unintended side effects, for other coastal or landlocked States that are victims of climate change would, no doubt, also be inclined to seize opportunities. For instance, some could claim that, while some SIDS received disproportionate advantages under the UNCLOS, and would now be assisted to keep those advantages, others like landlocked States have been less fortunate.[163] Some might be keen on openly raising the status of ice and the legal consequences of ice melting.[164]

For a long time, there has been an interest in linking geography to entitlements and continuation of entitlements and this, too, was considered conducive to stability and predictability. On the other hand, most principles have exceptions. Even the sacrosanct principle of territorial integrity suffers exceptions, for instance when the international community has decided that secession, to the detriment of the existing State, is justified in the circumstances. One may argue that the same could be true for the revered principle that the land dominates the sea, and that it could be twisted in favour of reduced or disappeared land, to the advantage of the existing State; or even that that principle could mean that, once the land has dominated the sea, it continues to do so, even without any land anymore. But this, too, is for the international community to decide. It is sometimes professed that the UNCLOS is inadequate because the circumstances of its adoption are different from today's. But the real question is whether the UNCLOS is equipped to deal with changing circumstances. There are many reasons to think that it is, both at substantive and institutional levels, including by authentic or authoritative interpretation, incorporation of compatible norms and principles, or the adoption of multilateral compatible complementary agreements.

[163] Climate change also destabilizes environments remote from the sea: for glaciers receding in Bhutan and risk for Glacial Lakes Outburst Floods, see https://www.adaptation-undp.org/explore/bhutan.

[164] The melting of ice raises many issues, including increased possibilities of transport and access to resources. But ice also raises the possibility of using the edge of shelves as the inner limit of the territorial sea. So far as limits are concerned, their maintenance in case of melting of sheets and shelves has not attracted the same attention as SLR, arguably because claims by those concerned have been either unclear, or fluctuating, or not significant. The international community might feel less sympathetic towards powerful Arctic nations and Antarctic claimants. There have been proposals for geographically fixed lines which would prevail regardless of the current location of the margin of the shelf: see Auburn F M (1982) Antarctic Law and Politics. Indiana University Press, Bloomington, p. 37.

The risk of a rhetoric trumpeting shortcomings or silence of the UNCLOS is matched by the risk of fast-tracking solutions which in the long run might do more harm than good.

'Le mieux est le mortel ennemi du bien', Charles de Montesquieu

Chapter 7
Marine Scientific Research in the Protection of the Marine Environment Under the International Legal Framework: A Sustainable Development Goals Perspective

Minerva Batool and Yen-Chiang Chang

Abstract Marine Scientific Research (MSR) under Sustainable Development Goal—14 (SDG 14) has envisioned a new dimension of cooperation for marine environmental protection. This chapter has taken the approach of MSR as provided in SDG 14 to provide a cooperative approach for MSR to protect the marine environment. This chapter analyzes the international law provisions dealing with MSR envisioning cooperation for the protection of the marine environment. The chapter has taken three perspectives of the marine environment: (i) climate change, (ii) fisheries preservation, and (iii) marine protected areas, along with scientific approaches required for marine pollution prevention. The conclusion of this chapter follows the challenges and opportunities for MSR cooperation, which could be a future course of research on the subject matter.

Keywords Marine scientific research · Marine environmental protection · UNCLOS · Sustainable development goal—14

1 Introduction

The marine environment (or ocean/marine ecosystem) is a vast and intricate ecosystem that plays a pivotal role in sustaining life on Earth. This ecosystem provides habitat for many species, regulates climate, and provides livelihoods for several communities. However, this fragile ecosystem faces unprecedented challenges due to human activities, climate change, and pollution. In this context, Marine Scientific Research (MSR) emerges as a crucial tool for understanding, preserving, and

M. Batool · Y.-C. Chang (✉)
School of Law, Dalian Maritime University, Dalian, China
e-mail: ycchang@dlmu.edu.cn

L. A. T. Nguyen and H. D. Vu (eds.), *Viability of UNCLOS amid Emerging Global Maritime Challenges*, https://doi.org/10.1007/978-981-97-5838-8_8

protecting the delicate balance of the marine environment.[1] MSR can serve as the foundation for comprehending the complexities of marine ecosystems.

The 1956 report of the International Law Commission on 'Law of the Sea' stated that "scientific research in oceans is among other freedoms provided under international law."[2] Under such provisions, the United Nations Convention on Law of the Sea (UNCLOS) provides a specific part on the conduct and governance of MSR.[3] The coastal States regulate the MSR under UNCLOS in their Exclusive Economic Zones (EEZs) or Continental Shelf (if determined). Furthermore, the coastal States cannot unreasonably deny permission for the conduct of MSR in normal circumstances.[4]

Scientists explore the oceans to study the diverse array of marine species, their habitats, and their interactions.[5] Through advanced technologies such as unmanned marine vehicles (UMVs) and marine sensors, scientists delve into the depths of the ocean, unlocking mysteries and gaining insights into the intricate web of life beneath the surface.[6] In this scenario, the trajectory of MSR is subject to ongoing developments in the international legal system. Therefore, the evolving nature of the international legal system has greatly impacted the purposes and meaning of MSR.

Since the emergence of Sustainable Development Goals or Agenda—2030 (SDGs), the landscape of MSR has undergone a profound transformation, encompassing a broad spectrum of physical and biological changes in the marine environment under Goal 14 or SDG 14 (life below water).[7] Such a transformative shift is significantly influenced by extensions of coastal state jurisdiction beyond the territorial sea and EEZ, which inclined the international community to develop the Agreement under the United Nations Convention on the Law of the Sea on the Conservation and Sustainable Use of Marine Biological Diversity of Areas beyond National Jurisdiction (BBNJ Agreement).[8]

---

[1] Luciana Fernandes Coelho, 'Marine Scientific Research and Small Island Developing States in the Twenty-First Century: Appraising the United Nations Convention on the Law of the Sea' (2022) 37 The International Journal of Marine and Coastal Law 493.

[2] Articles concerning the Law of the Sea with commentaries 1956 (The report, which also contains commentaries on the draft articles, appears in Yearbook of the International Law Commission, 1956, vol II).

[3] Article 246, United Nations Convention on Law of the Sea 1982 (came into force on 16 November 1994, (1833 UNTS 397)).

[4] Articles 238–257 of the UNCLOS. See also, PK Mukherjee, 'The Consent Regime of Oceanic Research in the New Law of the Sea' (1981) 5 Marine Policy 98.

[5] Alfred Soons, 'The Legal Regime of Marine Scientific Research: Current Issues', *Law, Science & Ocean Management* (Brill Nijhoff 2007). p. 76.

[6] Shijun Zhang and M Jahanzeb Butt, 'Marine Scientific Research, New Marine Technologies and the Law of the Sea, Edited by Keyuan Zou and Anastasia Telesetsky' (2023) 1 The International Journal of Marine and Coastal Law 1.

[7] 'Final List of Proposed Sustainable Development Goal Indicators' of Sustainable Development Goals (SDGs) (2016) (E/CN.3/2016/2/Rev.1), Annex IV <https://sustainabledevelopment.un.org/content/documents/11803Official-List-of-Proposed-SDG-Indicators.pdf> .

[8] Agreement under the United Nations Convention on the Law of the Sea on the Conservation and Sustainable Use of Marine Biological Diversity of Areas beyond National Jurisdiction, A/RES/78/272 UNTS 2023.

The two critical developments in ocean governance have transformed the landscape of MSR and urged coastal states to make substantial progress in legislative mechanisms for marine environmental protection.[9] A significant factor of SDG 14 that can contribute to protecting and preserving the marine environment is multilateral cooperation in MSR to develop capacities for developing and least-developed (small island developing) coastal states.[10] This position of SDG 14 supplements that MSR shall be conducted in a manner providing mechanisms for equitable exploitation and sustainable utilization of marine resources that shall not impact the needs of future generations and not harm the marine ecosystems (including fisheries, resources, and environment).

It is apparent that a universally applicable regulatory process for MSR is critical for maintaining and promoting a protected and peaceful marine environment while enabling international cooperation in the advancement of MSR and sharing its results.[11] In this scenario, other targets and goals provided in the SDGs indicators become relevant because of their impacts on the vast and intricate marine environment. Therefore, MSR cooperation has been strengthened with SDG 14, envisioning certain mechanisms from the dynamic interplay of legal and scientific systems.[12]

MSR cooperation would serve to supplement existing MSR programs, which, it appears, can spatially expand to areas falling under EEZs and the high seas. This ambitious endeavor seeks to address a gap between MSR and marine environmental protection framework by adopting a legislative framework, aiming to discern prevailing trends in the evolution of scientific research and its interconnected policy issues.[13] The inherent advantage of this approach lies in ability of the MSR to focus on the scale of the scientific phenomena of interest—the intricate marine ecosystem—while simultaneously addressing international issues within the context suggested by the UNCLOS.[14] Notably, UNCLOS frequently emphasizes the need for regional solutions, providing a contextual backdrop for our analysis.

---

[9] Fran Humphries and others, 'A Tiered Approach to the Marine Genetic Resource Governance Framework under the Proposed UNCLOS Agreement for Biodiversity beyond National Jurisdiction (BBNJ)' (2020) 03 Marine Policy 910.

[10] Catherine Colard-Fabregoule, 'Chapter 7—Maritime Spatial Planning: A Means of Organizing Maritime Activities Measured Iin Terms of Sustainable Development Goals' in MohananBhaskaran Pillai and Geetha Ganapathy Dore (eds), *Global Commons: Issues, Concerns and Strategies* (1st edn, SAGE Publishing India 2020) 14.

[11] Yen-Chiang Chang, Sirong Xin and Xu Zhang, 'A Proposal for Joint Marine Scientific Research Activities in the Disputed Maritime Areas of the South China Sea' (2022) 50 Coastal Management 215.

[12] Atsuko Kanehara, 'Marine Scientific Research Conducted in Disputed Sea Areas Including Seabed Where Delimitation Is Not Agreed: An Analysis from General and Particular Perspectives of the East China Sea', *Marine Scientific Research, New Marine Technologies and the Law of the Sea* (Brill Nijhoff 2021).

[13] Yoshifumi Tanaka, 'Obligation to Co-Operate in Marine Scientific Research and the Conservation of Marine Living Resources' (2005) 65 The Heidelberg Journal of International Law 937.

[14] Harriet Harden Davies, 'The Regulation of Marine Scientific Research:: Addressing Challenges, Advancing Knowledge', In R. M. Warner and S. B. Kaye (Eds.) (pp. 212–230). Abingdon: Routledge. *Routledge Handbook of Maritime Regulation and Enforcement* (Routledge 2015).

While many research articles, policy papers and books have inquired meticulously about MSR and analyzed the evolution of the global legal regime on the subject matter, there remains a notable dearth of a comprehensive examination of the latest developments on MSR under SDG 14 with marine environmental protection perspectives. This chapter has conducted a thorough analysis of diverse prospects of MSR under international law (particularly UNCLOS) that envisions legally binding obligations on the States to conduct MSR for marine environmental protection. SDG 14 has been utilized as a catalyst to provide a 'theoretical and legal basis' for the research. Following the 'theoretical and legal basis of MSR', the sections below offer suggestions based on an analysis of how MSR governance frameworks can be developed under SDG 14 for marine environmental protection.

2 MSR-Cooperation for Marine Environmental Protection: Theoretical and Legal Basis

The threat to the marine environment posed by MSR is relatively less than industrial exploration, fishing, or other similar activities.[15] However, unregulated MSR conducted to explore ocean resources (oil, minerals, and deep-sea fishing) may adversely impact the marine environment.[16] While MSR is essential, it must be conducted responsibly to avoid negative impacts on the marine environment. UNCLOS emphasizes the need for States to take measures to prevent marine pollution and minimize the potential environmental consequences of research activities.[17] International organizations and state authorities must adhere to environmental standards, employ sustainable practices, and consider the long-term consequences of their MSR to ensure the protection of marine ecosystems.

MSR is coupled with the complex nature of scientific problems, which underscores the advisability of fostering international cooperation as a strategic imperative.[18] This can also help develop a more stringent regulation of MSR as it is one of the primary contributions to identifying and assessing threats to the marine environment. MSR under UNCLOS is generally categorized into three broad distinctions in terms of its objectives: 'pure', 'resource-oriented', and 'military'. Pure MSR is simply conducted for scientific knowledge, which includes 'physical, biological, chemical,

[15] Rogelio Cabrera Camaya, 'The Consent Regime for Marine Scientific Research in the Philippines Feature Papers' (2000) 4 Ocean Law and Policy Series 17.

[16] Shijun Zhang, M Jahanzeb Butt and Khadija Zulfiqar, 'Interconnected Principles of Ocean Governance through Science-Policy Integration under the Judgements of the International Dispute Settlement Bodies' (2023) 106 Science Progress 4.

[17] Part XIII of the United Nations Convention on Law of the Sea.

[18] Zou Keyuan, 'Marine Scientific Research and Foreign Cooperation', in Keyuan Zou (Ed) *China's Marine Legal System and the Law of the Sea* (Brill Nijhoff 2005). p. 64.

geological and hydrographical characteristics of the marine environment'.[19] The resource-oriented MSR is conducted for industrial purposes, and the military MSR is conducted for strategic and defense purposes.[20] The 'resource-oriented' and 'military' MSR are mainly based on 'pure research.' Pure and resource-oriented MSR allows the investigation of the impact of human activities on marine ecosystems, such as overfishing, coastal development, and pollution. Studying these threats can provide valuable information to develop effective conservation strategies and assist governing authorities in sustainably managing the marine environment.[21]

In the context of this chapter, MSR is the research that must be conducted for the 'benefit of mankind' under the UNCLOS.[22] This implicitly recognizes the existence of MSR, which is fundamental and represents a revival in SDG 14.[23] The structure outlined by SDG 14 for MSR cooperation also distinguishes between pure resource-oriented research and military research.[24] Given that, military research does not fall within the scope of SDG 14 unless it serves peaceful purposes, as 'peace and justice' are key agendas of the SDGs. Such objectives align with MSR, as outlined by UNCLOS, which mandates that "all States and competent organizations shall conduct research to promote international cooperation and for peaceful purposes."[25] In this context, MSR under the UNCLOS is designed to promote international cooperation. The framework of MSR also mandates that all relevant information about such activities be made publicly available.

The present chapter focuses on 'marine environmental protection'; therefore, this section delves into MSR from the perspective of pure and resource-oriented research. Scientific cooperation under the SDGs is a relatively new concept, encompassing a broad spectrum of diverse interests in the oceans beyond trade and shipping lanes, notably the preservation of ocean ecosystems and their resources.[26] For

---

[19] Roland Cormier and Michael Elliott, 'SMART Marine Goals, Targets and Management—Is SDG 14 Operational or Aspirational, Is "Life Below Water" Sinking or Swimming?' (2017) 123 Marine Pollution Bulletin 28.

[20] Khadija Zulfiqar and M Jahanzeb Butt, 'Preserving Community's Environmental Interests in a Meta-Ocean Governance Framework towards Sustainable Development Goal 14: A Mechanism of Promoting Coordination between Institutions Responsible for Curbing Marine Pollution' (2021) 13 Sustainability 9983.

[21] Article 240 of the United Nations Convention on Law of the Sea.

[22] Jai Acharya, 'Marine Pollution and SDG 14 Implementation Degree of Challenges and Combat Strategies' (2023) 7 IIRE Journal of Maritime Research and Development 14.

[23] Dhruv Gautam, 'Trans-Boundary Marine Oil Pollution and Its International Legal Aspects' (2011) 4 International Journal of Liability and Scientific Enquiry 151.

[24] Edgardo D Gomez, 'Marine Scientific Research in the South China Sea and Environmental Security' (2010) 32 Ocean Development & International Law 2.

[25] Shijun Zhang and others, 'China's Belt and Road Initiative (BRI) under the Vision of'maritime Community with a Shared Future'and Its Impacts on Global Fisheries Governance' [2023] 9 Heliyon 4.

[26] Agreement for the Implementation of the Provisions of the United Nations Convention on the Law of the Sea of 10 December 1982 relating to the Conservation and Management of Straddling Fish Stocks and Highly Migratory Fish Stocks 1995 (UNTS 37,924).

such purposes, scientific cooperation can serve as a catalyst for the further development of multilateral agreements aimed at addressing challenges faced by oceans through MSR. Cooperation in MSR, although still in its infancy concerning SDGs, has nonetheless reached the threshold of rapid advancement in the near future. In this way, the implications for existing UNCLOS and IEL are of growing significance.

The developed States advocate that unrestricted MSR is vital for enhancing scientific knowledge of marine ecosystems. The developing States disagreed with the idea of unrestricted MSR due to concerns about the motives of developed nations. However, it's recognized that no single State possesses all the technology, resources, and expertise needed for comprehensive MSR, which is essential for addressing the multifaceted challenges facing marine ecosystems. Cooperation in MSR facilitates the sharing of knowledge, technology, and resources among States. MSR can enable States to leverage each other's strengths, whether in advanced research facilities, cutting-edge technologies, or specialized expertise. This sharing of resources accelerates the pace of scientific discovery and enhances the capacity of States to collectively address environmental threats.

MSR cooperation under SDG 14 lays the groundwork for crafting treaties and conventions, ensuring that the latest scientific knowledge informs policies. SDG 14 aims to conserve and sustainably use the oceans, seas, and marine resources, with the overarching goal of ecosystem protection and preservation. The three main targets of SDG-14 in terms of MSR are: (i) mitigating ocean acidification (including through enhanced scientific cooperation at all levels), (ii) effectively regulating fishing by eliminating overfishing and illegal, unreported, and unregulated (IUU) fishing (through the implementation of science-based management plans), and (iii) conserving at least 10 percent of coastal and marine areas (in accordance with national and international law and based on the best available scientific information).

The scientific approach required to achieve ocean goals through MSR is further established in Target 14.a of SDG 14, which emphasizes the sharing of scientific knowledge, research capacity, and the transfer of marine technology to improve ocean health and enhance the contribution of marine biodiversity. SDG 14 also emphasizes that the effective implementation of such objectives relies on MSR as provided under the UNCLOS, which underscores the importance of scientific cooperation for marine environmental protection. Besides UNCLOS, the Agreement for the Implementation of the Provisions of the UNCLOS Relating to the Conservation and Management of Straddling Fish Stocks And Highly Migratory Fish Stocks (UNFSA), Convention on the Conservation of Migratory Species of Wild Animals (CMS),[27] Convention on International Trade in Endangered Species of Wild Fauna and Flora (CITES),[28] the Convention on Biological Diversity (CBD)[29] and United Nations

[27] Convention on the Conservation of Migratory Species of Wild Animals, 1983, (Enforced 1991), UNTS 1651.

[28] Convention on International Trade in Endangered Species of Wild Fauna and Flora, 1973 (Enforced 1975) (993 UNTS 243).

[29] Convention on Biological Diversity 1992 (came into force on 29 December 1993, (1760 UNTS 79)).

Framework Convention on Climate Change (UNFCCC)[30] supports the provisions related to cooperation in scientific research which mutatis mutandis applies on the MSR (as established by SDG-14).

The UNFCCC, the Kyoto Protocol, and the Paris Agreement are integral for analyzing climate change mitigation in the context of marine environmental protection.[31] Similarly, the preservation of fisheries and the sustainable exploitation of marine habitats rely on the effective implementation of UNFSA, CMS, and CITES, which should be complemented by the Agreement to Promote Compliance with International Conservation and Management Measures by Fishing Vessels on the High Seas (the Compliance Agreement) and the Code of Conduct for Responsible Fisheries (CCRF).[32] Further emphasis on MSR is provided by, and can be governed under, existing Multilateral Environmental Agreements (MEAs) and agreements governing Regional Fisheries Management Organizations (RFMOs).[33]

The following section discusses the three targets of SDG-14, which aim for comprehensive MSR to achieve marine environmental protection, including addressing ocean acidification, fisheries preservation, and the conservation of marine areas. It argues that MSR cooperation is instrumental in establishing comprehensive monitoring systems for marine environmental protection. Furthermore, it suggests that by integrating data from diverse sources, such as satellite observations, underwater sensors, and research expeditions, states can develop a data-sharing mechanism to track changes in ocean temperature, salinity, biodiversity, and pollution levels. Shared data provides a foundation for evidence-based decision-making, enabling policymakers to formulate effective marine conservation and sustainable management strategies.

[30] United Nations Framework Convention on Climate Change 1992 (came into force 21 March 1994, (1771 UNTS 107)).

[31] Kyoto Protocol to the United Nations Framework Convention on Climate Change 1997 (came into force on 16 February 2005, (UN Doc FCCC/CP/1997/7/Add1, Dec 10, 1997)); Paris Agreement (adopted 12 December 2015, entered into force 4 November 2016 (CN632016TREATIESXXVII7.d)).

[32] Agreement to Promote Compliance with International Conservation and Management Measures by Fishing Vessels on the High Seas, 1993. (Enforced: 2003); Code of Conduct for Responsible Fisheries, 1995. (FAO(092.1)/C669/ENG). Available Online: https://digitallibrary.un.org/record/195400?ln=en.

[33] Chen-Ju Chen, 'The Ecosystem Approach to International Marine Management under International Law: A Case Study of the East China Sea' in Keyuan Zou (ed), *Sustainable Development and the Law of the Sea*, vol 2 (Brill Nijhoff 2017).

3 SDG-14 Under International Law for MSR-Cooperation

As already discussed, MSR is integral to achieving the marine environmental targets of SDG 14 by providing the necessary knowledge to inform policies, enhance conservation efforts, and address threats to ecosystems.[34] MSR focuses on ocean acidification, biodiversity, and the impact of human activities on marine environments, contributing to evidence-based decision-making for achieving SDGs.[35] The research framework discussed in the previous section is designed to be applicable not only to coastal States but also to States engaged in marine research beyond their regional confines.

As States are reciprocally obligated to actively promote the flow of information, scientific data, and knowledge resulting from MSR, international cooperation is paramount in addressing the challenges posed by marine environmental issues.[36] Developing States, often lacking the resources and infrastructure for extensive research, benefit from collaborative efforts that promote knowledge exchange and capacity building. According to UNCLOS, developed States are encouraged to assist developing states in enhancing their scientific and technical capabilities to conduct MSR.[37] Furthermore, joint MSR initiatives, facilitated by international organizations and partnerships, foster a collective approach to marine environmental protection.[38] Sharing data, technology, and expertise contributes to a more comprehensive understanding of global ocean systems and promotes sustainable practices.

The *Aegean Sea Continental Shelf Case* is a landmark example in the realm of international law that underscores the importance of MSR for effective marine environmental protection. The case involves a dispute between Greece and Turkey over the delimitation of their respective continental shelves in the Aegean Sea, highlighting the intricate connection between MSR and the protection of the marine environment in a geopolitically significant region. The International Court of Justice (ICJ) redefined MSR in the context of marine environmental protection, stating that "MSR plays a pivotal role in resolving disputes related to the delimitation of continental shelves and the protection of marine ecosystems." The *Aegean Sea case* exemplifies the application of MSR in safeguarding the marine environment while navigating complex geopolitical issues.

[34] Kenneth RN Anthony, 'Coral Reefs Under Climate Change and Ocean Acidification: Challenges and Opportunities for Management and Policy' (2016) 41 Annual Review of Environment and Resources 59.

[35] Montserrat Gorina-Ysern, 'Legal Framework for International Marine Scientific Research Cooperation', In Montserrat Gorina-Ysern (ed) *An International Regime for Marine Scientific Research* (Brill Nijhoff 2004) p. 527.

[36] Montserrat Gorina-Ysern, 'The New Frontier: A Bottomless Pot of Gold at the End of the Biotechnology Rainbow-Proprietary and Non-Proprietary Marine Scientific Research', in Montserrat Gorina-Ysern (ed), (Brill Nijhoff 2004) p. 353

[37] *Aegean Sea Continental Shelf (Greece v Turkey), Judgment, International Court of Justice Reports, 495, 1978.*

[38] AvukatFeridunKoymen, 'The Aegean Sea Continental Shelf Problem-Presentation of the Turkish Case' (1978) 6 International Business Lawyer 495.

The interim ruling of the Special Chambers of the International Tribunal for the Law of the Sea (ITLOS) in the Ghana v Cote d'Ivoire case, also known as the Delimitation of the Maritime Boundary in the Atlantic Ocean, fostered collaboration among the disputing parties in areas of mutual interest.[39] This cooperation was encouraged in line with their respective obligations for mutual benefit. The decision clarified that provisions within the UNCLOS do not impose specific restrictions on MSR.[40] However, it emphasized the necessity of a cooperative spirit in disputed regions, where states should strive to understand and cooperate with each other.[41] States were explicitly required to exert maximum effort to avoid jeopardizing or obstructing the final agreement. This ruling outlined distinctions between obligations, interim measures criteria under UNCLOS, and violations of international law. Nevertheless, it remains evident that there is a notable degree of similarity across all three aspects.

In the *Aegean Sea Continental Shelf Case and* the *Ghana v Cote d'Ivoire cases*, the interpretation of MSR provided the scientific foundation for understanding the geological and geomorphological characteristics of the oceans, which assisted international courts in delimitation.[42] The oceans are ecologically diverse, housing unique marine ecosystems and sensitive habitats. MSR has facilitated an in-depth assessment of these areas' ecological significance and vulnerability. Through studies of marine biodiversity, habitats, and the potential environmental impacts of resource exploitation, MSR has contributed to the development of measures to preserve the ocean's environmental integrity.

4 MSR for Protection of Marine Environment from Climate Vulnerability

In recent decades, coastal regions have faced unprecedented challenges due to climate-change-induced phenomena.[43] The marine environment is significantly influenced by climate change, with rising sea temperatures, coastal flooding, ocean

---

[39] *Dispute Concerning Delimitation of the Maritime Boundary between Ghana and Côte d'Ivoire in the Atlantic Ocean (Ghana/Côte d'Ivoire)* International Tribunal for the Law of the Sea ITLOS/PV.17 (Case no 23, 2017).

[40] Raymond BaguloBening, 'The Ghana-La Côte D'Ivoire Maritime Boundary Dispute' (2014) 6 Ghana Journal of geography 81.

[41] Millicent McCreath and Zoe Scanlon, 'Prospects for the Future Use of ITLOS Ad Hoc Special Chambers after the Ghana/Côte d'Ivoire Case' (2018) 17 The Law & Practice of International Courts and Tribunals 309.

[42] Yoshifumi Tanaka, 'Unilateral Exploration and Exploitation of Natural Resources in Disputed Areas: A Note on the Ghana/Côte d'Ivoire Order of 25 April 2015 before the Special Chamber of ITLOS' (2015) 46 Ocean Development & International Law 315.

[43] Rakhyun E Kim, 'Is a New Multilateral Environmental Agreement on Ocean Acidification Necessary?' (2012) 21 Review of European Community & International Environmental Law 243.

acidification, and changing weather patterns posing severe challenges.[44] Addressing these issues requires a comprehensive understanding of marine systems, and MSR cooperation has emerged as a powerful tool for developing effective mitigation strategies.[45] This part explores the pivotal role of MSR cooperation in mitigating coastal flooding, rising sea levels, and ocean acidification, emphasizing the importance of interdisciplinary collaboration and sustainable management practices.

Target 14.3 of SDG 14 specifically calls for minimizing and addressing the impacts of ocean acidification, acknowledging the need for MSR to inform mitigation measures.[46] The global community should invest in MSR initiatives that enhance our understanding of ocean acidification's environmental consequences and identify sustainable management practices to protect marine ecosystems.[47] For such purposes, SDG-13, also known as 'Climate Action', connects with Target 14.3 of SDG 14 under the UNFCCC, recognizing the close linkages between climate and the oceans.

Furthermore, the Kyoto Protocol and the Paris Agreement of the UNFCCC represent commitments by states to reduce greenhouse gas (GHG) emissions. Achieving the goals of SDG 14 (Life Below Water) requires aligning SDG 13 (Climate Action) with the preservation of marine ecosystems.[48] Therefore, MSR becomes essential in understanding the intricate connections between climate change, ocean acidification, and sea-level rise.[49] Sea-level rise is intricately linked to the broader issue of climate change, and understanding the complex interactions between oceanic and atmospheric systems is crucial for effective mitigation.

4.1 MSR-Cooperation for Monitoring and Assessment of Ocean Acidification, Sea-Level Rise and Coastal Flooding

The oceans act as a carbon sink, absorbing a substantial portion of the greenhouse gases (mainly carbon) emitted into the atmosphere. However, this absorption has consequences, leading to ocean acidification, which negatively impacts marine life,

---

[44] Alexander Bisaro and others, 'Multilevel Governance of Coastal Flood Risk Reduction: A Public Finance Perspective' (2020) 112 Environmental Science & Policy 203.

[45] Charlotte Salpin and others, 'Marine Scientific Research in Pacific Small Island Developing States' (2018) 95 Marine Policy 363.

[46] Ellycia R Harrould-Kolieb, 'Implications of the Paris Agreement for Action on Ocean Acidification within the UNFCCC', *Research Handbook on Ocean Acidification Law and Policy* In David L. VanderZwaag, Nilüfer Oral, and Tim Stephens (Eds) p 24 (Edward Elgar Publishing 2021).

[47] Thomas Wernberg, Dan A Smale and Mads S Thomsen, 'A Decade of Climate Change Experiments on Marine Organisms: Procedures, Patterns and Problems' (2012) 18 Global Change Biology 1491.

[48] Thomas A Okey and others, 'Effects of Climate Change on Canada's Pacific Marine Ecosystems: A Summary of Scientific Knowledge' (2014) 24 Reviews in Fish Biology and Fisheries 519.

[49] Mark R Payne and others, 'Uncertainties in Projecting Climate-Change Impacts in Marine Ecosystems' (2016) 73 ICES Journal of Marine Science 1272.

particularly fisheries and shell-forming organisms. MSR cooperation can play a crucial role in monitoring and understanding climatic changes. By collecting and analyzing ocean temperature, salinity, and current data, scientists can assess climate change's impact on marine ecosystems and contribute to developing strategies to mitigate its effects.[50]

MSR enables monitoring and predicting sea level changes, providing valuable data for developing adaptive strategies and infrastructure planning. Additionally, research helps identify vulnerable regions, allowing for targeted efforts to protect communities through the construction of resilient anti-flooding systems in coastal areas and sustainable land-use planning.[51] Through MSR cooperation, cutting-edge technologies such as satellite observations, oceanographic modelling, and data analysis can be employed jointly to accurately monitor sea-level changes.[52] This information is invaluable for policymakers at regional levels and urban planners at national levels in developing strategies to adapt to rising sea levels, ranging from the construction of elevated infrastructure to the implementation of green infrastructure solutions, such as mangrove restoration and coastal wetland preservation.

MSR cooperation is indispensable for studying the effects of ocean acidification on marine ecosystems and species. By identifying vulnerable species and ecosystems, scientists can inform conservation and management efforts, facilitating the development of strategies to mitigate the impacts of acidification, such as reducing greenhouse gas emissions and promoting the restoration of critical marine habitats.[53] Concerning the Kyoto Protocol and the Paris Agreement, mitigating ocean acidification and rising sea levels necessitates a multidimensional approach that integrates scientific research, international collaboration, and policy coherence.[54] By aligning efforts under SDG 14, UNCLOS, and UNFCCC, the global community can harness the collective expertise and resources needed to safeguard the health of our oceans. Through sustained investment in MSR, states can develop effective strategies to mitigate the impacts of these threats, ensuring the long-term resilience and sustainability of marine ecosystems and the communities that depend on them.[55]

---

[50] Yen-Chiang Chang and others, 'Legal Practices and Challenges in Addressing Climate Change and Its Impact on the Oceans—A Chinese Perspective' (2020) 111 Marine Policy 103,355.

[51] Ellycia R Harrould-Kolieb, '(Re)Framing Ocean Acidification in the Context of the United Nations Framework Convention on Climate Change (UNFCCC) and Paris Agreement' (2019) 19 Climate Policy 1225.

[52] Rachel Baird, Meredith Simons and Tim Stephens, 'Ocean Acidification: A Litmus Test for International Law' (2009) 3 Carbon & Climate Law Review 459.

[53] Manuel Bellanger and others, 'Addressing Marine and Coastal Governance Conflicts at the Interface of Multiple Sectors and Jurisdictions' (2020) 7 Frontiers in Marine Science 1.

[54] Loraine McFadden, Edmund Penning-Rowsell and Sue Tapsell, 'Strategic Coastal Flood-Risk Management in Practice: Actors' Perspectives on the Integration of Flood Risk Management in London and the Thames Estuary' (2009) 52 Ocean & Coastal Management 636.

[55] Xianli Zhu, Matthew M Linham and Robert J Nicholls, 'Technologies for Climate Change Adaptation. Coastal Erosion and Flooding', UNEP Risoe Centre on Energy, Climate and Sustainable Development (ISBN: 978-87-550-3855-4) <https://www.osti.gov/etdeweb/biblio/1010716> accessed 4 February 2024.

4.2 *MSR-Cooperation for Knowledge, Expertise, and Marine Technology*

Coastal regions are interconnected, and the impacts of climate change respect no borders. Therefore, effective solutions require cooperation on a global scale. Such cooperation in MSR can facilitate data-sharing, expertise allocation, and the sharing of resources among States. This collaboration allows scientists to collect comprehensive datasets, conduct comparative analyses, and develop holistic strategies for mitigating the impacts of coastal flooding, rising sea levels, and ocean acidification.[56] Cooperation in MSR can enhance the accessibility of critical resources and technologies. Participating States can pool their resources to fund large-scale research initiatives, deploy advanced monitoring systems, and share research vessels and equipment.[57] This collaborative effort can not only accelerate the pace of scientific discovery but also ensure that states with varying levels of technological and financial capabilities can contribute meaningfully to the global understanding of the impacts of climate change on marine environments.[58]

MSR cooperation is grounded in the UNFCCC, UNCLOS, and Paris Agreement, which promote knowledge exchange and capacity building, empowering states to develop their scientific expertise and infrastructure.[59] By establishing joint research projects and educational programs, states can strengthen their ability to monitor and respond to climate-induced challenges. This capacity building is particularly crucial for developing States, as suggested by the UNFCCC, which may be disproportionately affected by the impacts of coastal flooding, rising sea levels, and ocean acidification.[60] Scientific research forms the foundation for evidence-based policymaking. International collaboration enables the development of comprehensive policy frameworks that address climate change's root causes and consequences on coastal regions.[61] By sharing best practices and lessons learned, states can collectively formulate and implement adaptive strategies, ranging from resilient infrastructure development to sustainable land-use planning.

---

[56] Julia GuifangXue, 'Climate Change and the Law of the Sea: Challenges of the Sea Level Rise and the Protection of the Affected States' in Keyuan Zou (ed), *Sustainable Development and the Law of the Sea*, vol 2 (Brill Nijhoff 2017) p. 241.

[57] Ellycia R Harrould-Kolieb and Ove Hoegh-Guldberg, 'A Governing Framework for International Ocean Acidification Policy' (2019) 102 Marine Policy 10.

[58] Davor Vidas, David Freestone and Jane McAdam, 'International Law and Sea Level Rise: Report of the International Law Association Committee on International Law and Sea Level Rise' (2019) 2 Brill Research Perspectives in the Law of the Sea 1.

[59] Tony George Puthucherril, 'Climate Change, Sea Level Rise and Protecting Displaced Coastal Communities: Possible Solutions' (2012) 1 Global Journal of Comparative Law 225.

[60] David Freestone and Millicent McCreath, 'Climate Change, the Anthropocene and Ocean Law: Mapping the Issues', *Research Handbook on Climate Change, Oceans and Coasts* (Edward Elgar Publishing 2020) p. 54.

[61] Tim Stephens, 'Adapting to Climate Change in Marine and Coastal Areas: The International Legal Perspective' J Verschuuren (ed), *Research Handbook on Climate Adaptation Law* (Edward Elgar 2013), Edward Elgar: UK p.76.

4.3 Regional-Cooperation in MSR for Climate Action

Addressing the multifaceted challenges of coastal flooding, rising sea levels, and ocean acidification requires collaboration among various states. States can collaborate under existing MEAs to develop holistic solutions.[62] Regional cooperation is pivotal for MSR in tackling complex marine challenges, given the interconnectedness of oceanic systems and shared vulnerabilities.[63] Collaborative efforts enable the pooling of resources, expertise, and data, fostering a more comprehensive understanding of regional variations in ocean acidification and sea-level rise. Such an approach facilitates the development of context-specific mitigation and adaptation strategies, recognizing the unique characteristics of different oceanic regions.

SDG 14 is a catalyst for regional mechanisms for MSR, underscoring the importance of regional collaboration in addressing marine issues. Target 14.a explicitly calls for the enhancement of scientific knowledge on the impacts of ocean acidification, aligning regional priorities with global sustainability goals. Regional cooperation under SDG 14 can lead to the establishment of joint research programs, data-sharing mechanisms, and capacity-building initiatives, strengthening the scientific foundation for informed decision-making at both regional and global levels.[64]

MSR under the UNCLOS emphasizes the significance of regional cooperation.[65] States are encouraged to coordinate and facilitate joint research initiatives, recognizing the mutual benefits of shared knowledge. Regional bodies established under UNCLOS, such as the regional seas programs of the United Nations Environmental Programme (UNEP), offer platforms for collaborative research and the formulation of regional action plans, promoting sustainable ocean management practices.[66] Furthermore, the UNFCCC's emphasis on climate change mitigation aligns with regional efforts to address rising sea levels due to global warming. By integrating regional climate action plans, States can work collectively to reduce greenhouse gas emissions and implement adaptive measures. Regional cooperation under the UNFCCC fosters shared responsibility, encouraging states to collaborate on research initiatives that bridge climate science with marine impacts.

---

[62] Article 242 of the United Nations Convention on Law of the Sea.

[63] Clive Schofield, 'Rising Waters, Shrinking States: The Potential Impacts of Sea Level Rise on Claims to Maritime Jurisdiction' (2010) 53 German Yearbook of International Law 189.

[64] M Jahanzeb Butt and others, 'Maritime Dispute Settlement Law towards Sustainable Fishery Governance: The Politics over Marine Spaces vs. Audacity of Applicable International Law' (2022) 7 Fishes 81.

[65] Catherine Blanchard, 'Fragmentation in High Seas Fisheries: Preliminary Reflections on a Global Oceans Governance Approach' (2017) 84 Marine Policy 327.

[66] 'Code of Conduct for Responsible Fisheries, International Plan of Action to Prevent, Deter and Eliminate Illegal, Unreported and Unregulated Fishing' in David Joseph Attard, Malgosia Fitzmaurice, Alexandros XM Ntovas (Eds) The IMLI Treatise On Global Ocean Governance: Volume II: UN Specialized Agencies and Global Ocean Governance(*Oxford Public International Law*, 2018) p. 17.

Examples of successful regional cooperation, such as the Baltic Sea and Caribbean Sea initiatives, demonstrate the efficacy of collaborative approaches.[67] These regional efforts leverage joint research programs, policy coordination, and the sharing of best practices to address common challenges related to ocean acidification and rising sea levels. Regional cooperation for MSR emerges as a critical component in the collective pursuit of mitigating ocean acidification and rising sea levels. By aligning regional strategies with the principles outlined in SDG 14, UNCLOS, and UNFCCC, states can harness the power of shared knowledge, resources, and expertise to develop region-specific solutions. The collaborative spirit embedded in regional partnerships advances scientific understanding and strengthens the resilience of coastal communities and ecosystems, ultimately contributing to the sustainable management of our oceans in the face of evolving environmental challenges.

5 MSR-Cooperation for Integrated Management of Fisheries

Fisheries, by their nature, extend across national borders, making them inherently international resources. Shared fish stocks migrate through vast oceanic expanses, and their management requires coordinated efforts among states. Unilateral actions by one state can have cascading effects on the sustainability of fisheries, necessitating collaborative approaches grounded in scientific research and international cooperation.[68] It is also recognized that overfishing is a pressing issue that threatens marine ecosystems and the livelihoods of millions who depend on fisheries.[69] Existing scientific cooperation mechanisms, such as MSR cooperation, play a pivotal role in the integrated management of fisheries, allowing states to share data on fish stocks, migratory patterns, and the impacts of fishing practices.[70]

The importance of MSR for fisheries management is highlighted in the UNFSA, CMS, CITES, and the International Plan of Action on Illegal, Unreported, and Unregulated Fishing (IPOA-IUU). All these treaties, conventions, and agreements encourage states to cooperate in sharing information and conducting joint MSR to combat IUU fishing. The approach forwarded by SDG 14 for MSR cooperation can help establish sustainable fishing quotas, implement effective conservation measures, and combat IUU fishing activities that undermine global efforts to preserve marine

---

[67] Maria Hammer and Alf HåkonHoel, 'The Development of Scientific Cooperation under the Norway–Russia Fisheries Regime in the Barents Sea' (2012) 3 Arctic Review on Law and Politics 244.

[68] Gilles Hosch, Gianluca Ferraro and Pierre Failler, 'The 1995 FAO Code of Conduct for Responsible Fisheries: Adopting, Implementing or Scoring Results?' (2011) 35 Marine Policy 189.

[69] Warwick Gullett, 'Incorporating Fisheries Interests in National Oceans Policymaking' (2012) 40 Coastal Management 222.

[70] Keyuan Zou and Sen Wang, 'Introducing the Seasonal Closure into the CCAMLR Fishery Management Framework: Problems, Methods, and Prospects' (2021) 13 Sustainability 9770.

biodiversity. As SDG 14 recognizes that the sustainable management of fisheries is a pressing global concern, it connects with SDG 2 and 15 owing to its critical role in supporting biodiversity, food security, and livelihoods. While recognizing the transboundary nature of fisheries resources, states worldwide are increasingly acknowledging the importance of cooperation in MSR to inform integrated management approaches.

5.1 MSR-Cooperation for Monitoring and Assessment of Fish Stocks

The UNCLOS serves as the foundational legal framework for the management of fisheries on a global scale, mandating cooperation among states for the conservation and sustainable use of shared fish stocks beyond national jurisdiction. Under UNCLOS, coastal states are responsible for managing their fisheries sustainably, but cooperation is required to address the broader challenges posed by highly migratory and straddling fish stocks. In this context, UNFSA, CMS, CITES, and the IPOA-IUU become relevant for the sustainable management and preservation of fisheries.[71]

Besides UNCLOS, UNFSA, and other related agreements, the Compliance Agreement and the CCRF emphasize the importance of MSR for the sustainable development of fisheries.[72] MEAs and agreements dealing with RFMOs are established to manage and conserve fishery resources in specific regions. These organizations often promote cooperative MSR programs to assess the status of fish stocks and establish conservation measures, as seen in examples like the Northwest Atlantic Fisheries Organization (NAFO) and the Commission for the Conservation of Antarctic Marine Living Resources (CCAMLR). Collaboration often involves the exchange of scientific data, methodologies, and technologies for monitoring and assessment. This facilitates a more comprehensive understanding of fish stocks and promotes sustainable management practices.

As SDG 14 provides a new means of ocean and fisheries governance, it urges the facilitation of sharing scientific data and information related to fish stock assessments among states. Align national policies with the objectives of UNCLOS, UNFSA, and other relevant agreements (including MEAs) to ensure a comprehensive and coordinated approach to fisheries governance. As part of these objectives, MSR cooperation supports capacity-building initiatives to enhance the scientific and technical capabilities of states, particularly developing ones, to actively participate in monitoring and assessment efforts.

[71] Alicia Said and Ratana Chuenpagdee, 'Aligning the Sustainable Development Goals to the Small-Scale Fisheries Guidelines: A Case for EU Fisheries Governance' (2019) 107 Marine Policy 103,599.

[72] Code of Conduct for Responsible Fisheries, 1995. (FAO(092.1)/C669/ENG). Available Online: https://digitallibrary.un.org/record/195400?ln=en

5.2 *Sharing of Knowledge, Expertise, and Marine Technology in Fisheries Governance through MSR*

Sharing knowledge, expertise, and the transfer of marine technology in fisheries governance through MSR is vital for achieving the SDGs, as outlined in SDG-14. The provisions dealing with MSR in the UNCLOS encourage states to promote and facilitate international cooperation in capacity building and the transfer of marine technology for the conservation and sustainable use of marine resources, including fisheries. Furthermore, the CCRF also calls for international cooperation in the exchange of scientific data, information, and technology related to fisheries management.[73]

Another important instrument is the Food and Agriculture Organization's (FAO) International Plan of Action on Capacity Management, which encourages states to share knowledge and expertise to enhance the effectiveness of fisheries management.[74] Under this instrument, states can engage in joint research programs to share expertise and technology for assessing and managing fish stocks. This includes collaborative surveys, data collection, and analysis. Developed states often assist developing ones in building their capacity for fisheries research and management, including the transfer of technology and expertise.[75]

At regional levels, RFMOs often serve as platforms for member states to share knowledge, best practices, and technology for effective fisheries governance. Collaborative research initiatives are common within these regional frameworks, involving sharing fisheries data, scientific findings, and research methodologies. Open access to information contributes to a more comprehensive understanding of the status of fish stocks. Developed states may assist developing ones in acquiring and implementing advanced marine technologies for fisheries monitoring, control, and surveillance, including vessel monitoring systems, satellite technology, and data analysis tools.

5.3 *Regional Cooperation in MSR for Fisheries Preservation*

Regional cooperation for MSR is essential for transferring advanced capabilities, often achieved by providing access to research vessels and infrastructure for

[73] Anastasia Telesetsky, 'UN Food and Agriculture Organization: Exercising Legal Personality to Implement the UN Convention on the Law of the Sea' in Marta Chantal Ribeiro, Fernando Loureiro Bastos and Tore Henriksen (eds), *Global Challenges and the Law of the Sea* (Springer International Publishing 2020).

[74] M Jahanzeb Butt and Khadija Zulfiqar, 'Chapter 6. The Role of China in Global Ocean Governance: A Marine Environmental Perspective' in Proshanto K Mukherjee, Jingjing Xu and Maximo Q Mejia Jr. (eds), *Maritime Law Perspectives Old and New*, vol II (Nova Science Publishers 2023) p. 101.

[75] Giuseppe Bonanno, '7—Marine-Protected Areas and Plastic Pollution' in Giuseppe Bonanno and Martina Orlando-Bonaca (eds), *Plastic Pollution and Marine Conservation* (Academic Press 2022). p. 83.

joint projects. This facilitates comprehensive studies of fish stocks and ecosystems. Additionally, UNEP and FAO engage in capacity development programs to train fisheries scientists and managers from developing states, fostering a pool of skilled professionals.[76] Collaboration between states, research institutions, and private enterprises can lead to developing and applying cutting-edge technologies for sustainable fisheries management. Developed states transfer marine technologies such as satellite monitoring, artificial intelligence, and underwater robotics, significantly contributing to effective fisheries governance by enhancing surveillance and enforcement capabilities.

6 Biodiversity Conservation—BBNJ Agreement and MSR

Target 14.5 of SDG-14 emphasizes conserving at least 10 percent of coastal and marine areas in accordance with national and international law and based on the best available scientific information.[77] MSR cooperation is instrumental in establishing and managing Marine Protected Areas (MPAs), which serve as sanctuaries for marine life.[78] Collaborative research aids in identifying areas of high biodiversity, migratory pathways, and critical habitats. Through shared knowledge and coordinated efforts, states can create and manage MPAs that transcend borders, offering refuge to endangered species and contributing to the overall health of the marine environment.[79]

The marine environment is susceptible to natural disasters such as oil spills, tsunamis, and hurricanes, which can have catastrophic consequences. MSR cooperation is essential for developing effective disaster preparedness and response strategies. Collaborative research enhances understanding of the potential impacts of disasters, facilitates the sharing of technologies for rapid response, and promotes joint efforts in mitigating and recovering from environmental crises.[80] MSR cooperation fosters capacity building and education, particularly in developing states that may lack resources for advanced research and technology. Collaborative initiatives promote the exchange of scientific knowledge, training programs, and capacity-building exercises, empowering states to actively participate in global efforts for

[76] Charles N Ehler, 'Integrating Management of Marine Protected Areas with Coastal and Ocean Governance: Principles and Practices' (2005) 48 Ocean & Coastal Management 843.

[77] M Jahanzeb Butt, Khadija Zulfiqar and Yen-Chiang Chang, 'The Role of the International Law in Shaping the Governance for Sustainable Development Goals' (2021) 28 Journal of Law and Political Sciences 87.

[78] Mariano Koen-Alonso and others, 'The Northwest Atlantic Fisheries Organization Roadmap for the Development and Implementation of an Ecosystem Approach to Fisheries: Structure, State of Development, and Challenges' (2019) 100 Marine Policy 342.

[79] Julian Roberts, 'Designating Particularly Sensitive Sea Areas in Areas Beyond National Jurisdiction' (2024) 55 Ocean Development & International Law 1-2.

[80] Deyi Ma and Jietao Zhou, 'The Binding Force of the BBNJ Agreement on Third Parties' (2021) 212 Ocean & Coastal Management 105818.

marine environmental protection.[81] This inclusivity is vital for creating a collective consciousness and commitment to preserving our oceans for future generations.

The interpretation of international courts in the Aegean Sea Continental Shelf Case and Ghana v Cote d'Ivoire cases highlighted the application of UNCLOS principles, particularly those related to the exclusive rights of coastal states over their continental shelves and the obligation to cooperate in the conservation and management of shared resources.[82] MSR, conducted in accordance with UNCLOS, served as a tool for ensuring that decisions made by international courts were based on a thorough understanding of the marine environment, promoting fair and equitable resolutions. International courts underscored the need for international collaboration in MSR. States engaged in MSR activities presented their findings to the ICJ, emphasizing the role of shared knowledge and transparency in resolving disputes.[83]

The BBNJ Agreement emerged as a response to the challenges posed by human activities in the high seas and the international seabed area, where governance gaps have left marine biodiversity vulnerable.[84] The agreement not only underscores the importance of sustainable use and conservation but also recognizes the pivotal role of MSR in enhancing our understanding of these complex ecosystems. One of the critical pillars of the BBNJ Agreement is the promotion of MSR as a means to advance scientific knowledge about marine biodiversity.[85] By emphasizing international cooperation and the exchange of scientific information, the agreement seeks to bridge existing knowledge gaps and facilitate a more comprehensive understanding of the diverse ecosystems in areas beyond national jurisdiction.

The BBNJ Agreement encourages collaborative efforts among states, fostering a spirit of shared responsibility for the conservation of marine biodiversity. States are urged to engage in cooperative MSR initiatives, ensuring the free exchange of data and information.[86] This cooperation enhances the scientific community's collective ability to assess and address the challenges faced by these ecologically significant regions. Recognizing the disparities in scientific capabilities among states, the BBNJ

---

[81] Elisa Morgera, 'The Relevance of the Human Right to Science for the Conservation and Sustainable Use of Marine Biodiversity of Areas beyond National Jurisdiction: A New Legally Binding Instrument to Support Co-Production of Ocean Knowledge across Scales', in Vito De Lucia, Lan Nguyen and Alex G. Oude Elferink (eds) *International Law and Marine Areas beyond National Jurisdiction* (Brill Nijhoff 2021) p. 128.

[82] Sarah M Watson, 'Conservation Target for Marine Biodiversity in Areas Beyond National Jurisdiction' in Walter Leal Filho and others (eds), *Life Below Water* (Springer International Publishing 2021). p. 37.

[83] M Jahanzeb Butt and Yen-Chiang Chang, 'Regulation of Autonomous Maritime Weapon Systems under the Governance Framework of International Law', Marine Scientific Research, New Marine Technologies and the Law of the Sea, vol 11 (1st edn, Brill Nijhoff 2021) p. 105 accessed 29 September 2021.

[84] Marta Coll and others, 'Sustainability Implications of Honouring the Code of Conduct for Responsible Fisheries' (2013) 23 Global Environmental Change 157.

[85] Article 240 of the United Nations Convention on Law of the Sea.

[86] International Convention for the Prevention of Pollution from Ship (MARPOL 73/78) 1973 (came into force on 26 November 1983, (1340 UNTS 184)).a.

Agreement strongly emphasizes capacity building and technology transfer. Developing states are provided support to enhance their scientific capacities, enabling them to actively participate in MSR activities. This inclusivity ensures that the benefits of scientific knowledge are shared globally.

SDG 14, with its focus on the conservation and sustainable use of oceans, seas, and marine resources, complements the objectives of the BBNJ Agreement.[87] Both frameworks aim to safeguard marine biodiversity for present and future generations. The BBNJ Agreement serves as a practical and legal instrument through which states can actively contribute to achieving the ambitious targets set forth in SDG 14. The BBNJ Agreement incorporates the necessity of conducting Environmental Impact Assessments (EIAs) for MSR activities. This requirement ensures that potential adverse effects on marine biodiversity are thoroughly evaluated and measures are put in place to minimize these impacts. The agreement thus promotes responsible and sustainable MSR practices.

6.1 Cooperation in Research Initiatives for Biodiversity Conservation

MSR plays a crucial role in providing the data and knowledge necessary for the sustainable management of fisheries. It enables the assessment of fish stocks, their migration patterns, and the impact of environmental factors on their abundance. Through advanced technologies such as satellite monitoring, acoustic surveys, and genetic analysis, scientists can gain insights into the complex dynamics of marine ecosystems, informing evidence-based management strategies. International collaboration in MSR is paramount for comprehensively understanding fish stocks and ecosystems. States must come together to conduct joint research initiatives that span geographic boundaries and involve sharing expertise, data, and resources. Collaborative research projects contribute to a more accurate assessment of fish stocks, enabling the formulation of effective management plans that consider the diverse interests and needs of participating States.

6.2 MSR Cooperation in Ecosystem-Based Management for Marine Environmental Protection

Integrated and ecosystem-based approaches to ocean governance recognize the interconnectedness of marine ecosystems and the need to address the broader ecological context. Cooperation in MSR under SDG 14 can facilitate the development of holistic management strategies that consider not only individual issues but also

[87] Mark H Carr, 'Marine Protected Areas: Challenges and Opportunities for Understanding and Conserving Coastal Marine Ecosystems' (2000) 27 Environmental conservation 106.

the health of entire ecosystems. This approach helps prevent overfishing, minimizes bycatch, and protects marine habitats and environments, contributing to the long-term sustainability of fisheries.

Various international and regional institutions and agreements have been established to facilitate cooperation in ecosystem-based ocean governance. RFMOs and MEAs under the UNEP are crucial platforms, where states collaborate to develop and implement conservation and management measures. These organizations rely on the best available scientific information to establish and implement measures aimed at preventing threats to marine ecosystems. With the assistance of such institutions, climatologists, ecologists, engineers, policymakers, and local communities can conduct interdisciplinary MSR to enhance understanding of the interconnectedness of marine systems and foster innovative and sustainable approaches to mitigation and adaptation.

7 Pollution Prevention and Remediation

Marine pollution, whether from oil spills, plastic debris, or chemical contaminants, poses a significant threat to the marine environment. MSR can help understand the sources, pathways, and impacts of pollution. This knowledge is crucial for the development of effective pollution prevention and remediation strategies. Researchers are working on innovative solutions, such as bioremediation techniques and sustainable waste management practices, to address the challenges posed by marine pollution. Scientific evidence from MSR informs the development and revision of policies and regulations related to marine pollution prevention. It provides a basis for setting standards, guidelines, and best practices at both national and international levels.

MSR for marine pollution prevention also intersects with SDG 6 (Clean Water and Sanitation). Understanding the interconnectedness of these goals is essential for developing holistic strategies to address the complex challenges of marine pollution. As suggested by SDG 14, MSR can play a vital role in supporting the objectives of UNCLOS by providing scientific evidence and data to inform regulatory measures and policies aimed at preventing and mitigating marine pollution. Beyond UNCLOS, various MEAs emphasize the need for cooperation in addressing marine pollution. For example, the International Maritime Organization's (IMO) MARPOL (International Convention for the Prevention of Pollution from Ships) sets standards for discharging pollutants from ships, and MSR contributes to the development and assessment of these standards.

MSR can also assist in identifying the sources of marine pollution, whether from industrial discharges, shipping activities, or land-based runoff. This information is crucial for implementing targeted prevention measures. Furthermore, MSR enables the assessment of marine pollution's ecological and human impacts. Understanding these impacts is essential for devising effective pollution prevention and remediation strategies. Additionally, MSR can contribute to the development of new technologies for monitoring and preventing marine pollution. Innovations in sensing, data collection, and clean-up technologies enhance the effectiveness of pollution prevention measures.

8 Challenges and Opportunities

Although indispensable, MSR cooperation faces challenges, including political differences, economic disparities, and competing national interests that can impede collaborative efforts. Successful cooperation hinges on equitable benefit-sharing, transparent data exchange mechanisms, and diplomatic dialogue, presenting opportunities for technology transfer and capacity-building initiatives. Challenges encompass issues of data transparency, equitable benefit-sharing, and the need for capacity building, requiring diverse monitoring techniques such as stock assessments, tagging programs, acoustic surveys, and ecosystem modeling. International cooperation in MSR is essential for addressing transboundary challenges and ensuring the sustainable use of marine resources in line with international law.

Aligned with SDG 14, MSR holds the key to addressing complex challenges. The global community can advance our understanding of marine ecosystems and work towards sustainable development through collaboration, capacity building, and responsible practices. Achieving a harmonious balance between human activities and ocean health requires prioritizing MSR for a resilient and thriving marine environment. The role of MSR cooperation in marine environmental protection is crucial. Oceans demand collective and united efforts to address challenges. Collaborative research deepens understanding, develops effective conservation strategies, and reinforces global interconnectedness in safeguarding our oceans' future. By fostering global harmony through scientific cooperation, the States initiating such cooperation can leave a legacy of a healthy, resilient marine environment.

9 Conclusion

Integrating MSR into the governance structure of various RFMOs and MEAs offers a crucial opportunity to promote the conservation of marine environments in line with the objectives of the SDGs. The international legal framework, particularly UNCLOS, UNFSA, UNFCCC, and CBD, provides a comprehensive basis for tackling the complex issues confronting marine ecosystems. UNCLOS, as a fundamental framework, defines the rights and obligations of States in maritime areas and emphasizes the importance of MSR to ensure the sustainable utilization of marine resources, as outlined in its provisions, with particular emphasis on collaboration and knowledge exchange. Furthermore, UNFCCC supports worldwide endeavors to address climate change, acknowledging the crucial connection between the health of the oceans and their ability to withstand climate impacts. Integrating MSR enhances decision-making and promotes a shared dedication to protecting the seas for current and future generations. By operating within the governance framework of international law, states can advance marine conservation initiatives beyond geographical limits while safeguarding the planet's and its inhabitants' well-being.

Part III
UNCLOS and Cooperation in the South China Sea

Chapter 8
Ocean Science Collaborations: Towards a Complex Interdependence in the South China Sea

Suzette V. Suarez

1 Introduction

The need for claimant States and other stakeholders to cooperate in the South China Sea (SCS) in the conflict area has been a refrain oft reiterated. A semi-enclosed sea, the SCS is one of Asia's 13 Large Marine Ecosystems (LME) with an estimated area of 3,10 million sq. km. Located at the western border of the world's most diverse coral reefs, the Coral Triangle, the SCS though less studied, is also known to possess comparably high biodiversity which supports marine biological processes including spawning, nurseries or feeding areas critical to the marine ecologies of all littoral states.[1] It has "one of the world's most diverse marine ecosystems, hosting 76 percent of the world's coral species".[2] It is therefore not a surprise that the SCS ranks very high globally in terms of fish diversity and fish production.[3] The populations of all littoral States rely on the SCS for their food security and livelihood.[4]

Unfortunately, the SCS region also ranks high as one of the most over-exploited fisheries in the world not only on account of illegal, unregulated and unreported fishing but also due to the excessive government support and subsidies provided to

[1] Huang, D. (2015). Extraordinary diversity of reef corals in the South China Sea. *Mar Biodiv, 2015*(45), 157–168.

[2] Trajano, J. C., Gong, L., Sembiring, M., & Astuti, R. (2017). Marine environmental prottecion in the South Chia Sea: Challenges and prospects part 1.

[3] Coulter, D. Y. (1996). South China sea fisheries countdown to calamity. *Contemporary Southeast Asia,* 371–388.

[4] Coulter, D. Y. (1996). South China sea fisheries countdown to calamity. *Contemporary Southeast Asia,* 371–388.

S. V. Suarez (✉)
Center of Maritime Studies, Hochschule Bremen City University of Applied Sciences,
Flughafendamm 40, 28199 Bremen, Germany
e-mail: Suzette.Suarez@hs-bremen.de

L. A. T. Nguyen and H. D. Vu (eds.), *Viability of UNCLOS amid Emerging Global Maritime Challenges*, https://doi.org/10.1007/978-981-97-5838-8_9

legal fishing.[5] Dire warnings of the catastrophic state of the marine living resources and the habitats in the SCS have been given by scientists in the last thirty years.[6,7]

Despite such admonitions of calamity, claimant States to the SCS have not been able to overcome their differences and undertake cooperative activities in the disputed areas. Indeed, the history of cooperation among and between SCS claimant States conducted in areas and on resources where claims overlap has been sparse. The Joint Oceanographic and Marine Scientific Research Expedition in the South China Sea (JOMSRE-SCS) from 1994 to 2007 between the Philippines and Vietnam was one of the very few scientific collaborative efforts specific to the SCS conflict that took place.[8] There has been no follow-up to this collaboration so far, although in 2021 the Philippines and Vietnam announced the resumption of its joint research cooperation in 2022.[9]

Another notable cooperative arrangement involving more SCS littoral States in the past that may be mentioned here was the UNEP/GEF project "Reversing Environmental Degradation Trends in the South China Sea and Gulf of Thailand." It must be underscored, however, that the UNEP/GEF project focussed on the coastal sea coastlines of the littoral States and not within the conflict areas in the Spratlys.[10]

In order to address the deteriorating ecological situation in the SCS several proposals have been forwarded. In addition to bilateral ocean research between disputing States, trilateral as well as regional mechanisms have also been proposed including: (i) introducing a multinational scientific expedition so that regional states could contribute different equipment and specializations; (ii) developing a regional regime to consult, collaborate and promote MSR; and (iii) establishing a Spratly Islands Marine Peace Park.[11] None of these proposals have so far materialized. Whether at a bilateral, trilateral or regional level makes the most sense, the current geopolitical situation in the SCS region has remained a major stumbling block for any kind of cooperation involving only SCS claimant States.

---

[5] Coulter, D. Y. (1996). South China sea fisheries countdown to calamity. *Contemporary Southeast Asia,* 371–388.

[6] Coulter, D. Y. (1996). South China sea fisheries countdown to calamity. *Contemporary Southeast Asia,* 371–388.

[7] Sumaila, U. R., Cheung, W. W., Teh, L. S., Bang, A. H., Cashion, T., Zeng, Z., & Sadovy de Mitcheson, Y. (2021). Sink or swim the future of fisheries in the East and South China Seas. ADM Capital Foundation.

[8] McManus, J. W., Shao, K. T., & Lin, S. Y. (2010). Towards establishing a Spratly Islands International Marine Peace Park ecological importance and supportive collaborative activitis with an emphais on the role of Taiwan. *Ocean Development and International Law,* 270–280.

[9] Mangosing, F. (2021). *Inquirer.net.* Retrieved November 1, 2022, from https://globalnation.inquirer.net/2003382/ph-vietnam-resume-joint-research-work-in-south-china-sea#ixzz71JEdCyiZ

[10] Pernetta, J. C., & Jiang, Y. (2013). Managing multi-lateral, intergovernmental projects and programmes: The case of the UNEP/GEF South China Sea project. *Ocean & Coastal Management,* 141–152.

[11] McManus, J. W., Shao, K. T., & Lin, S. Y. (2010). Towards establishing a Spratly Islands International Marine Peace Park ecological importance and supportive collaborative activitis with an emphais on the role of Taiwan. *Ocean Development and International Law,* 270–280.

Section 2 of this contribution argues that any proposal to address common ecological problems in the SCS should be in the context of and towards the goal of claimant States achieving complex interdependence with each other. As proven by the example of the cooperation in the Arctic, international relations among States are more resilient in times of crises when they have achieved a state of complex interdependence with one another. Applying the concept of complex interdependence to the SCS conflict and since direct bilateral and regional cooperation remains filled with political obstacles, Sect. 3 proposes that claimant States cooperate in ocean science research in existing international institutions with mandates in ocean science. The history of inter-state conflicts in maritime areas shows that ocean science research plays a critical role in motivating conflicting States to jointly address and overcome challenges relating to cross-border issues despite their conflicts.

2 International Cooperation in a State of Conflict and the Arctic Model of Complex Interdependence

Inter-state cooperation in the Arctic is a good example to consider because, similar to the SCS setting, the conflict also involves several States. Eight States have various overlapping territorial claims and resource claims in the Arctic: the United States, Canada, Sweden, Norway, Denmark, Russia, Iceland and Finland. Despite their conflicts, these 8 States were able to establish the Arctic Council, a university and three binding agreements including the 2017 Agreement on Enhancing International Arctic Scientific Cooperation among the 8 Arctic States.[12] In addition, other agreements among some of the Arctic States such as the bilateral and trilateral fisheries agreements and agreements which include non-Arctic States, may also be mentioned here to underscore the usefulness of the Arctic experience as a model for SCS States on how to go forward.

The success of the Arctic model of inter-state relations came to renewed scholarly attention among international relations experts in 2014 when Russia's occupation of Crimea tested its relations with its fellow Arctic States.[13] One study explains the cooperative mechanisms in the Arctic according to the concept of complex interdependence. The concept of complex interdependence was developed by international relations scholars Keohane and Nye to explain and analyse international relations and inters-state conflicts which could not be done according to traditional realist frameworks.[14] The realist school of thought explains and analyses international relations under the lens of "security" as its "the dominant goal" whereby "states are the only

[12] Berkman, P. A., Kullerud, L., Pope, A., Vylegzhanin, A. N., & Young, O. R. (2017). The arctic science agreement propels science diplomacy. *Science*, 596–598.

[13] Byers, M. (2017). Crisis and international cooperation: An Arctic case study. *International Relations*, 375–402.

[14] Keohane, R. & Nye, J. (2012). *Power and interdependence*. 4th edn. Longman Pearson.

significant actors; and force is the dominant instrument."[15] Unlike the realist school of thought, complex interdependence sees a more complicated and entangled world with interests and issues beyond the traditional security matters which are considered not necessarily as triggers of discord but as opportunities to jointly solve and manage common problems.[16,17] Complex interdependence continues to acknowledge inequalities and asymmetries in power that exist between powerful States and their weaker counterparts and the dominance that the former could continue to exert over the latter. However, since there are multiple issues that connect the States at different levels, the significance of the military power of the stronger States is thereby reduced.[18]

Keohane and Nye underscore that complex interdependence does not mean that international relations from a realist perspective do not exist. Rather, according to them, complex interdependence and realism are ideals on the extreme sides of the same line and most of the time, international relations "fall somewhere between the two extremes."[19]

To better understand international relations between and among States in a complex interdependence, Keohane and Nye identified three political processes that "translate power resources into power as control over outcomes: (1) linkage strategies, (2) agenda setting and (3) international institutions."[20]

In realist settings, powerful States normally will attempt to link issues as a strategy in order to influence and control the outcome in their favour. In the Arctic setting, however, relations between States developed in a way where they had opportunities to interact on issues separately, avoiding a breakdown in their relations when there is conflict in one issue. In the area of ocean politics, for example, Arctic States have had opportunities to engage and cooperate separately in fisheries during the Cold War period. The trigger for cooperation was the overfishing fishery crises that pushed three Arctic States—Norway, Russia and later Iceland—to engage with each other and eventually to agree on binding rules and procedures by way of fishery agreements. Norway and the former Soviet Union established the Russian-Norwegian Fisheries Commission in the Barents Sea and began fishery management based on science-based quotas. This bilateral cooperation later became trilateral with the inclusion of Iceland.[21] Fisheries in the Arctic are therefore managed and resolved separately from other issues involving the Arctic States.

[15] Keohane, R. & Nye, J. (2012). *Power and interdependence.* 4th edn. Longman Pearson.

[16] Ibid.

[17] Keohane, R. & Nye, J. (2012). *Power and interdependence.* 4th edn. Longman Pearson.

[18] Keohane, R. & Nye, J. (1987). Power and interdependence revisited. *International Organization,* 725–753.

[19] Keohane, R. & Nye, J. (2012). *Power and interdependence.* 4th edn. Longman Pearson.

[20] Byers, M. (2017). Crisis and international cooperation: An Arctic case study. *International Relations,* 375–402.

[21] Byers, M. (2017). Crisis and international cooperation: An Arctic case study. *International Relations,* 375–402.

Continental shelves under national jurisdiction and control is an issue that developed under the UNCLOS regime. Arctic States engaged with each other via the Third United Nations Conference on the Law of the Sea which eventually adopted the treaty which contains provisions on the continental shelf regime, the 1982 UN Convention on the Law of the Sea (UNCLOS). All Arctic States took part in the negotiations of the UNCLOS which took place for about ten years during the Cold War period from 1972 to 1982. The long history of negotiations on the continental shelf provided the States and their scientists, a stable, regular avenue of communications between and among diplomats, scientists and academics.[22] Under the UNCLOS, rules and procedure for establishing the limits of the continental shelf were put in place which ensure that States do not resort to war in order to establish their continental shelf claims and the claims to the resources therein To date, the following Arctic States that have extended areas of the continental shelf in the Arctic Ocean have submitted their information on the extended limits of the continental shelf in the Arctic Ocean to the Commission on the Limits of the Continental Shelf: Canada, Norway, Denmark and Russia.[23] Though not a member of UNCLOS, the United States considers Art. 76 of UNCLOS as customary law and it thus makes its continental shelf claims in accordance with UNCLOS. The US is of the view that it can submit information concerning its extended continental shelf in accordance with Art. 76 to the Commission on the Limits of the Continental Shelf.[24] Though the submissions made by the Arctic States reveal overlapping claims and have induced some tensions at least in the media, the practice of the Arctic States shows that they cooperate with each other and make their claims within the bounds allowed under Art. 76. The tensions relating to their continental shelf claims have therefore been contained from other issues generating conflict among the Artic claimants. Despite the fact that two Arctic States are military powers, military force became for the most part "largely irrelevant" or not linked to other issues in the Arctic setting, enabling the States and non-States to undertake cooperative efforts. This confirms what Keohane and Nye posited that in complex interdependence, military force becomes "largely irrelevant" amidst the multiplicity of "state policies (that) are not arranged in stable hierarchies (and)multiple channels of contact exist among societies,.."[25]

Agenda in complex interdependence is not driven by one powerful State; depending on the issues, agenda may be set even by a coalition of weaker States or by consensus by all relevant stakeholders.[26] Following the post-Cold War period,

---

[22] Suarez, S. (2008). *The outer limits of the continental shelf: Legal aspects to their establishment*. Springer.

[23] United Nations Division for Ocean Affairs and the Law of the Sea. (2023). *Submissions, through the secretary-general of the United Nations, to the commission on the limits of the continental shelf, pursuant to article 76, paragraph 8, of the United Nations convention on the Law of the Sea of 10 December 1982*. United Nations.

[24] United States Department of State. (2023). *The outer limits of the extended continental shelf of the United States executive summary*. U.S. Department of State.

[25] Byers, M. (2017). Crisis and international cooperation: An Arctic case study. *International Relations*, 375–402.

[26] Keohane, R. & Nye, J. (2012). *Power and interdependence*. 4th edn. Longman Pearson.

"the politics of agenda setting are more subtle, affected 'by changes in the distribution of resources within issue areas."[27] In the Arctic experience, the agenda for cooperation on environmental and ocean research matters was driven by non-State actors, notably the scientific agencies of the various Arctic States. These agencies were instrumental in establishing the International Arctic Science Council (IASC) in 1990 after the end of the Cold War. The IASC was instrumental in pushing for the first Arctic Environmental Protection Strategy and also led to the formation of the Arctic Council.

Finally, political processes in international institutions are also relevant in explaining why cooperation in the Arctic has endured notwithstanding the advent of political crises. The foremost institution that plays a critical role in the relations among States and non-State actors in the Arctic is the Arctic Council, which was established in 1996. The Arctic Council is extraordinary in its complexity in that it consists not only of States representatives but also representatives of indigenous communities and organizations as well as with the active participation of six technical and science-based working groups. Collaboration within the Arctic Council has borne many fruits. It led to the establishment of the Arctic University in 1998 and three binding agreements. The first agreement was on search and rescue operations in 2011.[28] The second agreement was on the prevention of oil pollution and coordination of emergency and clean-up operations in case of oil pollution.[29] The third agreement is on scientific cooperation adopted in 2017.[30]

In addition to and operating separately and independently from the Arctic Council are other institutional mechanisms where Arctic States have international relations with each other. On ocean issues, the Arctic States deal with each other via mechanisms established under the UNCLOS, such as the CLCS on extended continental shelf issues, as mentioned above. The existence of several institutional mechanisms where the Arctic States can meet and communicate and deal with issues affecting them enhances the complex interdependence that developed among them.

The history of the Arctic model of cooperation shows that it evolved into a multiplicity of linkages on common and non-military interests and concerns among State and non-State actors. The cooperation between and among Arctic stakeholders is not just within the confines of the Arctic Council but also within other regimes including the law of the sea regime in general, the continental shelf regime in particular and fishery regimes.

When Keohane and Nye developed the concept of complex interdependence, they did not consider the impact of crises on the international relations between and among States that have achieved a level of complex interdependence. Russia's annexation of Crimea in 2014 and its consequences on the Arctic cooperation proved

[27] Byers, M. (2017). Crisis and international cooperation: An Arctic case study. *International Relations,* 375–402.

[28] Agreement on Cooperation on Aeronautical and Maritime Search and Rescue in the Arctic, 2011.

[29] Agreement on Cooperation on Marine Oil Pollution Preparedness and Response in the Arctic, 2013.

[30] Agreement on Enhancing International Arctic Scientific Cooperation, 2017.

a good laboratory that showed the resilience of international relations of States in complex interdependence. Developments in the Arctic following the Crimea annexation showed that notwithstanding the sanctions imposed on Russia, cooperation among Arctic States with Russia continued. Byers argues that cooperation among them continued notwithstanding the political crisis brought about by the Crimea annexation because of complex interdependence among the Arctic States.[31]

However, the situation is much different today with the Russian invasion of Ukraine in 2022. When the war started in February 2022, Arctic States boycotted the activities in the Arctic Council because it was under Russian leadership. Arctic States only resumed to participate in the activities of the Arctic Council when the term of Russia as Chair ended and was handed to Norway in May 2023. Currently, the Arctic Council continues to undertake its programmes without the participation of Russia. The relations between Arctic States vis-à-vis Russia are further impacted by the joining of Finland and Sweden in the North Atlantic Treaty Organization. The Western States line of defense or offense (as Putin sees it) is now directly in its front yard so Russia sees the new memberships as provocative. Putin has vowed "to take appropriate military-technical measures."[32]

The resilience shown by the Arctic cooperation in 2014 clearly appears to be on the decline and there is a real threat that the war in Ukraine might spread to Europe. Does this mean that, at least in Europe, one will witness a return to a realist setting, with military and security issues at the top of the hierarchy of issues? Despite the pendulum swinging closer to a more realistic setting, cooperation on other issues, especially those not within the mandate of the Arctic Council would survive. For instance, the establishment and delimitation of any overlapping areas of the continental shelf is governed by another legal process under Art. 76 UNCLOS will not be affected by the consequences of the Russian invasion of Ukraine. Search and rescue efforts in the Arctic involving the Russians and other Arctic States also have continued despite the worsening political situation caused by the Russia-Ukraine war.[33] The fact that some cooperative efforts in the Arctic remain to be undertaken despite the military and security crisis demonstrates that international relations in a state of complex interdependence is a goal worth pursuing by States in conflict.

Interestingly, in a recent survey among SCS experts and analysts, citing the geopolitical and geographical differences between the two regions, many have expressed doubts that the Arctic cooperation could serve as a model for the SCS claimant States.[34] The author does not have any access to the question posed in the survey nor the context in which the question concerning the appropriateness of the Arctic type

[31] Byers, M. (2017). Crisis and international cooperation: An Arctic case study. *International Relations,* 375–402.

[32] Chatterjee, P. (2023). *BBC News*. Retrieved March 7, 2024 from https://www.bbc.com/news/world-europe-61397478

[33] Rosen, Y. (2022). *Arctic Business Journal*. Retrieved March 8, 2024, from https://www.arctictoday.com/despite-ukraine-war-us-and-russia-continue-emergency-cooperation-in-the-bering-strait/

[34] RANE Stratfor Center for Applied Geopolitics. (2023). *South China Sea Maritime Survey,* s.l.: RAE Stratfor Center for Applied Geopolitics.

of interstate cooperation was formulated. However, the author posits that there is probably a misunderstanding on the part of respondents as to how the Arctic model could be useful in the SCS conflict. As argued above, the Arctic type of cooperation provides useful insights when viewed in the context of complex interdependence. The Arctic type of cooperation is mentioned here not for the purpose of proposing that SCS claimant States copy what the Arctic States have undertaken together. It is to highlight that relations between and among Arctic stakeholders that have achieved complex interdependence prove resilient even in critical situations, enabling them to continue undertaking cooperative efforts.

3 Cooperation in Ocean Science Research Through International Organizations

In the same survey mentioned above, there was general agreement among respondents that science diplomacy could be helpful in alleviating the problems of environmental degradation as well as addressing the looming food security issues brought about by overfishing and illegal fishing in the South China Sea.[35] Respondents to the survey, however, were also not confident that scientific cooperation would be enough to resolve the dispute. The author agrees with the respondents that "a shared scientific understanding around resources and the broader South China Sea environment" must be pursued and this can only be done by way of scientific cooperation.[36] However, the current geopolitical tensions between SCS claimant States are hindering any form of direct scientific cooperation among them.

Applying the concept of complex interdependence, this author proposes that in addition to efforts to directly cooperate in ocean science research, ocean scientists from SCS claimant States should engage and collaborate via international organizations with mandates on ocean science. Keohane and Nye posited that political processes that transpire in international institutions are significant for States in complex interdependence with one another.[37] International institutions "provide decision-making environments for enhancing communication and information flows reducing uncertainty and arenas for agenda setting, coalition formation, bargaining, and influence peddling.[38]

Existing intergovernmental institutions with ocean science research mandates could contribute towards a culture of scientific collaboration among claimant States

[35] RANE Stratfor Center for Applied Geopolitics. (2023). *South China Sea Maritime Survey,* s.l.: RAE Stratfor Center for Applied Geopolitics.

[36] RANE Stratfor Center for Applied Geopolitics. (2023). *South China Sea Maritime Survey,* s.l.: RAE Stratfor Center for Applied Geopolitics.

[37] Keohane, R. & Nye, J. (1987). Power and interdependence revisited. *International Organization,* 725–753.

[38] Coate, R., Griffin, J., & Elliott-Gower, S. (2015). *Interdependence in international organization and global.* Oxford Research Encyclopedia of International Studies.

in the SCS. Three intergovernmental organizations (IGOs) of which all claimant and littoral States to the SCS are members may be mentioned here: the International Hydrographic Organization (IHO), the International Seabed Authority (ISA) and the Intergovernmental Ocean Commission (IOC). All three are competent organizations under the various provisions relating to marine science research (MSR), surveying and/or marine scientific activities outside the purview of the MSR regime in the UNCLOS.

The IHO was established in Monaco in 1921 to promote surveying and chartering of the oceans, seas and all navigable waters for purposes of maritime safety. It acts as a coordinating body of hydrographic offices of its Member-States and establishes standards and best practices in hydrographic surveying, as well as provides and or supports capacity-building of States. Under UNCLOS, the IHO is the competent international organization on hydrographic surveying.

The ISA is the youngest among the three organizations. Established under the 1982 UNCLOS, it commenced operations in 1994 when the UNCLOS entered into force. All claimant States in the SCS are members of the ISA. The ISA is the regulatory body mandated to organize and control all development deep-sea activities of mineral resources in the international seabed and subsoil beyond the national jurisdiction and control.[39] The ISA mandate includes marine scientific research activities related to minerals in the international area. While much seabed and subsoil of the SCS is part of continental shelves under the national jurisdiction and control of coastal States, there is an area in the SCS that is part of the international area under the regulatory authority of the ISA. Hence, claimant States could harness the existing institutional structure and MSR programme of action of the ISA to collaborate in scientific research activities in the international seabed area in the SCS.

Among the three, the IOC has the most comprehensive mandate on ocean science. It also has the most "comprehensive network comprising a large number of expert bodies, which facilitates the exchange of information and experience, project co-ordination and shared utilisation of resources."[40] It is tasked to promote cooperation in ocean science not only "to learn more about the nature and resources of the ocean and coastal areas" but also in order to "to apply that knowledge for the improvement of management, sustainable development, the protection of the marine environment, and the decision-making processes of its Member States." (Art. 2.1) (*Statutes of The Intergovernmental Oceanographic Commission* 1960). Claimant States to the SCS could consider harnessing the IOC's ongoing programmes such as the Global Ocean Observing System (GOOS), the International Oceanographic Data and Information Exchange (IODE), the Ocean Biogeographic Information System (OBIS), the Tsunami Intergovernmental Coordination Groups (ICGs), and the World Climate Research Programme (WCRP) and establish a sub-group that focuses on the SCS.

---

[39] Anon. (1982). United Nations Convention on the Law of the Sea. s.l.:s.n.

[40] Ehlers, P. (2000). The intergovernmental oceanographic commission: An international organisation for the promotion of marine research. *The International Journal of Marine and Coastal Law,* 533–544.

These three institutions take into consideration the interests and circumstances of developing States, an element which is important for the littoral States in the SCS. The IOC, the ISA and the IHO have training, capacity building as well as marine technology transfer components in their ocean science programmes.[41]

Maximising scientific cooperation through these international organizations is opportune because 2021–2030 has been declared as the UN Decade of the Ocean Science for Sustainable Development. All three international organizations with the IOC being designated as the overall coordinator are taking an active part in the UN Decade of the Ocean Science for Sustainable Development. Both the IHO and the ISA are in partnership with the IOC and other organizations for the purpose of pushing forward ocean science as a tool to sustainably manage and develop marine habitats and resources.

The Decade of Ocean Science has identified four scientific objectives that the SCS claimant States could adopt in their collaborative efforts in the SCS. These are:

(a) Increase capacity to generate, understand, manage and use ocean knowledge;
(b) Identify and generate required ocean data, information and knowledge;
(c) Build a comprehensive understanding of the ocean and ocean governance systems; and;
(d) Increase the use of ocean knowledge.[42]

In summary, the claimant States to the SCS as well as their scientists should review their participation in these IGOs and consider how they could bring forward the goals of building confidence and achieving sustainable development in the SCS within these international institutions. These existing institutions are ideal as they provide a ready-made infrastructure for the littoral States and their scientists as well as non-claimant States and their scientists who are interested in undertaking ocean science in the SCS to collaborate and integrate their research agenda, results and expertise.[43] The established procedures in these institutions could contribute to creating and/or increasing an atmosphere of trust between and among SCS littoral States and their scientists and experts. The IHO has an East Asia Sub-commission whereby all claimant States are represented either as Members or Observers.[44] The IOC also has a regional structure in place; it has among others a Western Pacific Subcommission (WestPac) established in 1989 with offices in Thailand.

[41] Kay, D. (1974). International transfer of marine technology: The transfer process and international organizations. *Ocean Development & International Law,* 351–377.

[42] ISA, S. G. (2020). *Action plan of the international seabed authority in support of the united nations decade of ocean science for sustainable development.* International Seabed Authority.

[43] Markus T., Hillebrand H., Hornidge A-K., Krause G., & Schlüter A. (2018) Disciplinary diversity in marine sciences: The urgent case for an integration of research, *ICES Journal of Marine Science,* 502–509.

[44] IHO. (2022). *International Hydrographic Organization.* Retrieved November 17, 2022, https://iho.int/en/east-asia-hc

4 Concluding Remarks

The marine environment and marine living resources in the SCS are in a dire state. There are many obstacles that have hindered littoral States from directly cooperating in ocean science research in areas of conflict in the SCS. Cooperation among and between States that are in conflict with each other while difficult to undertake is not impossible as proven by the 8 Arctic States. The Arctic type of inter-State cooperation which demonstrates the characteristics of complex interdependence, i.e., multiplicity of channels or linkages between and among States as well as non-States, the absence of a hierarchy of issues among them, and finally, a reduced role of military force, proved to be resilient in the face of geopolitical issues affecting their relations. Engagements between and among SCS claimant States and the relevant non-State stakeholders on different issues in different venues should therefore be encouraged and indeed pursued with the goal of achieving a state of complex interdependence among them.

Based on the example of the Arctic States, ocean science cooperation has been a game changer and has been fundamental to their decisions and actions concerning the marine environment and marine resources. However, establishing a specific ocean science cooperative regime similar to what the Arctic States established is currently out of reach for claimant States in the SCS. However, State and non-State stakeholders in the SCS conflict should, with the goal of achieving a state of complex interdependence among them, should consider other venues where their scientists can engage and collaborate. International institutions with mandates in ocean science research are ideal vehicles by which cooperation in ocean science may take place despite the ongoing geopolitical conflict. These organizations do not only provide for the scientific expertise but their standing infrastructure and procedures will facilitate cooperation between and among the disputant States and their scientists. It will be a pity if the Decade of Ocean Science ends without any improvement in the shared scientific understanding of the marine habitats and resources in the SCS.

Chapter 9
BBNJ in the Context of the South China Sea: With a Focus on Area-Based Management Practice

Nong Hong

1 Introduction

The Biodiversity Beyond National Jurisdiction (BBNJ) Agreement, now commonly referred to as the High Seas Treaty, represents the culmination of discussions initiated in 2004 under the United Nations Convention on the Law of the Sea (UNCLOS). The primary aim is to enhance the conservation and sustainable use of biological diversity in the oceans beyond the exclusive economic zones (EEZ) and continental shelves of states. In March 2023, international negotiations concluded successfully, and on 19 June 2023, the Agreement was unanimously adopted at the 5th BBNJ Intergovernmental Conference in New York. Officially opened for signing and ratification at the UN General Assembly on 20 September 2023, this innovative instrument is set to provide protection to nearly two-thirds of the ocean beyond national jurisdiction. Furthermore, it aims to address existing inequalities in the equitable sharing of benefits derived from the organisms in these areas.

Area-based management is a pivotal component of the BBNJ negotiations. Ocean and coastal area-based management, which involves the integrated and sustainable management of a comprehensive range of human activities within large, spatially defined areas, represents the practical application of ecosystem-based management. This approach considers biophysical, socioeconomic, and jurisdictional factors to ensure comprehensive and effective management strategies.[1] Protected areas, while valuable and beneficial, are not adequate on their own to comprehensively tackle

[1] "Area-based Management," *Conservation Gateway*, https://www.conservationgateway.org/ConservationPractices/Marine/Area-basedManagement/Pages/area-based-management.aspx (accessed December 8, 2018).

N. Hong (✉)
Institute for China-America Studies, Washington DC, United States
e-mail: hongnong@chinaus-icas.org

Beijing Club for International Dialogue, Beijing, China

L. A. T. Nguyen and H. D. Vu (eds.), *Viability of UNCLOS amid Emerging Global Maritime Challenges*, https://doi.org/10.1007/978-981-97-5838-8_10

issues arising from human activities in ocean and coastal areas. Realizing the long-term sustainable use of the seas demands a comprehensive approach, where thoughtfully designed and efficiently managed protected areas operate synergistically within the broader context of sustaining the health of adjacent waters and landscapes.[2] This need is effectively addressed through Ocean and Coastal Area-Based Management (ABM). Utilizing area-based management as a vital tool is paramount for achieving long-term conservation and sustainable use of biodiversity. Specifically, Area-Based Management Tools (ABMTs) play a crucial role in mitigating the impacts of ongoing human activities and global climate change, along with their associated cumulative and synergistic effects.

Among the various strategic challenges confronting the South China Sea (SCS), such as territorial and maritime disputes and geological competition, none is as underestimated as the degradation of the marine ecosystem.[3] The SCS, as a critical waterway, is one of the world's most diverse global marine bio-systems, hosting 76 percent of the world's coral species and 37 percent of reef-fish species.[4] Over the past two decades, there have been documented instances of fishermen in the SCS indulging in large-scale illegal capture of fish using cyanide, dynamite, and detonating cords. A broad spectrum of marine life has been targeted, encompassing endangered sea turtles, giant clams, giant oysters, sharks, eels, and sizable fragments of intricately ornamental coral.[5] The SCS is one of the most biologically diverse marine ecosystems in the world. Marine scientists, however, have warned that pollution caused by busy shipping lanes has threatened the SCS environment and its future food supplies.[6] The SCS is an integral ecosystem, and as such it needs to be treated in a comprehensive manner by all the states surrounding it.[7] Given the complexity and inter-connectedness of the marine environment, the littoral countries need to take collective actions to reverse the environmental degradation trends, and thereby prevent adverse impacts on economic and security issues.[8] However, there has been minimal concern about the imperatives for maintaining the environmental integrity of the territories in question.[9]

This paper initiates the discussion by exploring conceptual models of Area-Based Management (ABM) and examining existing efforts dedicated to ABM. Two distinct

---

[2] Ibid.

[3] Abhijit Singh, "Why the South China Sea is on the Verge of an Environmental Disaster", *The National Interest*, August 13, 2016, https://nationalinterest.org/blog/the-buzz/why-the-south-china-sea-the-verge-environmental-disaster-17348 (accessed December 8, 2018).

[4] Abhijit Singh, "A Looming Environmental Crisis in the South China Sea", *CSIS*, August 12, 2016, https://amti.csis.org/looming-environmental-crisis-south-china-sea/ (assessed December 8, 2018).

[5] Ibid.

[6] http://lateline.muzi.net/news/ll/english/10066636.shtml?cc=18140&ccr = .

[7] Karin Dokken, Environment, "Security and regionalism in the Asia–Pacific: is environmental security a useful concept"? *The Pacific Review,* Vol. 14 No. 4 2001: 509–530, p. 514.

[8] Sulan Chen, *Instrumental And Induced Cooperation: Environmental Politics In The South China Sea*, PhD dissertation, pp. 135–140.

[9] Francisco A. Magno, "Environmental Security in the South China Sea", *Security Dialogue*, Vol. 28, No. 1, 97–112 (1997), p. 98.

approaches—namely, the cross-sectoral approach (e.g., marine protected areas) and the sectoral approach (e.g., marine environmental protection)—will be employed to delve into the regional and state practices of ABM in the SCS. The paper accentuates challenges associated with ABM in areas both beyond national jurisdiction and within national jurisdiction within the South China Sea context. Additionally, it delves into the future prospects of ABMs in this region, considering the global trend, regional governance framework, and political will.

2 Conceptual Area-Based Management

Area-based management encompasses the integrated, sustainable management of the full suite of human activities occurring in spatially defined areas ranging from discrete patches to larger ecosystem-scale areas.[10] Applied in the context of an ecosystem approach, area-based management provides tools to respond to cumulative impacts. Area-based management tools (ABMTs) include marine spatial planning (MSP), as well as marine protected areas (MPAs) and ecological networks, and "other effective area-based conservation measures" including indigenous, community and privately managed areas.[11] Area-based management can also include sectoral tools, such as the closure of certain vulnerable areas to fishing, shipping or mining. While no universally accepted definition exists, area-based management is generally expected to result in higher protection than exists in the surrounding area due to more stringent regulation of one or more human activities.[12]

The preservation and sustainable utilization of the oceans and their biodiversity rely on the effective planning and management of human activities, both within and beyond national jurisdiction. ABMTs, including marine protected areas, pollution control zones, and fisheries closures, are acknowledged as essential mechanisms for safeguarding vulnerable biodiversity. They play a crucial role in restoring and stabilizing the values derived by humans from marine and coastal ecosystems.

While lacking a universally accepted definition, ABM can integrate various models. For instance, it can encompass marine spatial planning, a collaborative process involving multiple ocean users—such as energy, industry, government, conservation, and recreation—to make informed and coordinated decisions regarding

---

[10] Marjo Vierros et al., "Space for Conservation and Sustainable Use: Area-based Management in Areas beyond National Jurisdiction," *Nereus Program*, https://nereusprogram.org/wp-content/uploads/2016/08/BBNJ-Policy-brief-area-based-management.pdf (accessed December 8, 2018).

[11] "Measures such as Area-based Management Tools, including Marine Protected Areas," *UN*, http://www.un.org/depts/los/biodiversity/prepcom_files/area_based_management_tools.pdf (accessed December 9, 2018).

[12] David Johnson, Maria Adelaide Ferreira, and Ellen Kenchington, "Climate Change is Likely to Severely Limit the Effectiveness of Deep-sea AMBTs in the North Atlantic", *Marine Policy* 87, January (2018): 111–122. *ScienceDirect*, https://www.sciencedirect.com/science/article/pii/S0308597X17304268 (accessed December 9, 2018).

the sustainable use of marine resources. Additionally, ABM may involve the establishment of marine protected areas to safeguard critical zones, protect habitats of migratory species, promote species replenishment, ensure precautionary measures, and enhance resilience. It may also employ sectoral approaches to mitigate the impacts of specific sectors, along with utilizing environmental impact assessment (EIA) and strategic environmental assessment (SEA) to assess cumulative impacts resulting from new activities.

Various efforts are underway to pinpoint priority ocean areas for protection or management. These include the identification of Ecologically or Biologically Significant Areas (EBSAs) requiring protection according to the Convention on Biological Diversity (CBD), the recognition of Vulnerable Marine Ecosystems (VMEs) under the Food and Agriculture Organization of the United Nations (FAO), the designation of Particularly Sensitive Sea Areas (PSSAs) by the International Maritime Organization (IMO), the establishment of Preservation Reference Areas (PRAs) by the International Seabed Authority (ISA), and the creation of Marine Protection Areas under Regional Sea Conventions and Action Plans.

3 State Practice of Cross-Sectoral Approach: A Case Study of MPAs

Numerous definitions of protected areas and marine protected areas are already in existence, with notable ones provided by the Convention on Biological Diversity (CBD) and the International Union for Conservation of Nature (IUCN). Many national and regional entities also have their own established definitions. According to IUCN, a protected area is a distinctly defined geographical space, officially recognized, dedicated, and managed through legal or other effective means. The primary objective is to achieve the long-term conservation of nature, encompassing associated ecosystem services and cultural values.[13]

There are a variety of objectives for MPAs that offer differing degrees of protection, from strictly protected areas to areas that allow multiple sustainable uses with limited formal protections.[14] "They can provide comprehensive protection for ecologically or biologically significant areas, sustain spatially-dispersed habitats of migratory species, contribute to sustainable use by replenishing species and offering reference zones to inform management, be precautionary tools to protect characteristic habitats and species on a biogeographic basis, and provide insurance for the future by building resilience and giving ecosystems time to adapt."[15] Research findings suggest that areas with stronger and more stringent protection measures

[13] "Protected Areas", *IUCN*, https://www.iucn.org/theme/protected-areas/about (assessed December 9, 2018).

[14] Vierros, "Space for Conservation and Sustainable Use: Area-based Management in Areas beyond National Jurisdiction,".

[15] Ibid.

experience substantial biodiversity benefits compared to less strictly protected areas.[16]

Nearly all SCS states have implemented a national system of marine protected areas. China, as the world's largest producer and exporter of wild-caught and farmed fish, bears significant environmental costs due to this distinction. Since the 1990s, China has established marine nature reserves and fisheries conservation zones, aiming in part to counteract the ongoing degradation of the marine environment. In the early 2000s, China introduced two additional types of marine zones—special marine protected areas and marine parks, encompassing fully protected areas and multiple-use zones. As of 2012, approximately 1.65 percent of China's waters were covered by these protective designations. According to China's 2008 National Ocean Development Plan, there is an expectation that by 2020, 5 percent of its waters will be officially designated as marine protected areas, indicating a rapid expansion in MPA establishment over the next decade.[17]

Indonesia has embraced the CBD Strategic Plan for Biodiversity 2011–2020. Within the priority landscapes of the Sustainable Landscape Partnership (SLP), there exist diverse conservation areas, encompassing Nature Reserves (Cagar Alam), Nature Tourism Parks (Taman Wisata), Wildlife Reserves (Suaka Margasatwa), and National Parks (Taman Nasional). The fundamental objective of these protected area types is the conservation of biodiversity.[18]

In its 4th Country Report on Vietnam's Implementation of the Biodiversity Convention, it recommends 14 priority activities, including the sustainable development of Vietnam's protected areas system by integrating the objectives of protection and conservation. Vietnam has achieved certain results during the period of implementing the CBD through the pursuit of national objectives. The report highlights objectives such as biodiversity conservation and sustainable use, as well as the equal sharing of benefits from biodiversity, acknowledging these as controversial issues that require special consideration in the next steps. The notable achievements, such as increased forest coverage, an improved terrestrial protected area system, a planned inland water protected area system, and a proposed marine protected area system, reflect Vietnam's successes in nature conservation in recent years.[19]

Malaysia was urged to establish a dedicated law facilitating the exploration of marine biodiversity resources and overseeing marine resources beyond its national jurisdiction. During a forum on Malaysia's interests and role in the sustainable use

[16] Ibid.

[17] "An Analysis of Marine Protected Areas in China", *LENFEST OCEAN PROJECT*, April 27, 2017, https://www.lenfestocean.org/en/research-projects/an-analysis-of-marine-protected-areas-in-china (assessed December 10. 2018).

[18] Zaki Mubarok Busro and Genevieve Quirk, "Indonesia Must Seize Role in Drafting Rules for High Seas: The Jakarta Post columnists," *The Strait Times*, April 19, 2016, https://www.straitstimes.com/asia/se-asia/indonesia-must-seize-role-in-drafting-rules-for-high-seas-the-jakarta-post-columnists (assessed December 10, 2018).

[19] "4th Country Report Vietnam's Implementation of the Biodiversity Convention," *Convention on Biodiversity*, 2008, https://www.cbd.int/doc/world/vn/vn-nr-04-en.pdf (assessed December 10, 2018).

and conservation of biodiversity beyond national jurisdiction (BBNJ) held at Wisma Putra, Putrajaya, on 13 March 2011, participants reached a consensus for a team comprising marine science and legal experts to convene at the national level. Their objective was to provide valuable input to the government for the formulation of an effective ocean governance and management policy framework.[20] Indicators have been identified to assess marine protected areas based on the marine waters controlled by each state in Malaysia. The target ranking aims for 10% of the State Territorial Water for Peninsular Malaysia, controlled by each state. This is defined as the area within three nautical miles from the shore of each state, calculated based on the 3-nautical-mile limit from the low-water mark shoreline, as specified in the National Land Code (Act 56 of 1965). "Marine Protected Areas serve to protect and restore the ecosystems in our seas and around our coasts. It ensures that the species and habitats within the protected area are protected from physical disturbance, pollution and climate change. It serves the general public by providing recreational and research opportunities."[21]

A significant milestone has been achieved as a whopping 1,013,340 hectares, encompassing both coastal and offshore waters of Cagayancillo, along with an additional 80,000 hectares in Aborlan, within the Philippine province of Palawan, have been officially declared as MPAs.[22] This marks the initiation of a two-country initiative led by the World Wide Fund for Nature (WWF) and Fondation Segré, aimed at replenishing fish stocks in the Coral Triangle. The approach involves a paradigm shift in perceiving protected areas, with a strong emphasis on engaging local fishermen and communities in the management of marine resources. This is achieved by assisting them in acquiring exclusive rights to fisheries within or near MPAs and collaborating with them to enhance the health and productivity of their fisheries.[23] An example would be *Seven Lines*, a coral reef system in Aborlan. "Seven Lines supplies fish to smaller coral reefs in the region. This means fisherfolk don't need to travel far for fishing," says Aborlan Municipal Agriculture Officer Cacatian. This guarantees that even if certain areas are off-limits to fishers, the spillover effects of protection will seed large areas with life.[24]

Thailand has established 28 MPAs with a robust legislative framework. The country boasts 5 Ramsar sites, 3 ASEAN Heritage Parks, and is currently considering a World Heritage proposal for the marine parks in the Andaman Sea. These parks have a mean size of 178.3 km^2, with an average marine component of 160.5 km^2. The surveyed area encompasses a total of 2674.5 km^2. On average, these parks

[20] "Status and Options for Malaysia on Biodiversity Conservation beyond National Jurisdiction," *MIMA*, April 6, 2018, http://www.mima.gov.my/news-list/265-status-and-options-for-malaysia-on-biodiversity-conservation-beyond-national-jurisdiction (assessed December 10, 2018).

[21] "Status and Options for Malaysia on Biodiversity Conservation beyond National Jurisdiction."

[22] "Large MPAs set in Palawan to rebuild fish stocks," *BusinessMirror*, https://businessmirror.com.ph/large-mpas-set-in-palawan-to-rebuild-fish-stocks/ (assessed December 10, 2018).

[23] Alan T. White, Porfirio M. Aliño, and Anna Blesilda T. Meneses, "Creating and Managing Marine Protected Areas in the Philippines," *Oneocean*, 2006, http://www.oneocean.org/download/db_files/creating_and_managing_mpas.pdf.

[24] Ibid.

welcome 44,930 Thai visitors and 22,691 international visitors, totaling 1,081,946 visitors annually to the selected parks. The median of 9,485 neighbors provides a more accurate indication of true visitor numbers. Additionally, seven of the parks house residents within their boundaries, with an average of 1,397 people (ranging from 79 to 3,000) living within each park.[25]

4 Regional Practice of Sectoral Approach: A Case Study of Marine Environment Protection

In the pursuit of a cleaner environment and regional marine environmental cooperation within the intricate dynamics of the SCS, various programs, including the United Nations Environment Programme (UNEP), have played a pivotal role. The subsequent sections assess the progress of marine environmental cooperation within the framework of these programs. They explore how these initiatives identify issues for collaboration and cultivate a sense of community by engaging with the countries bordering the SCS. This interaction aims to promote multilateral environmental cooperation in the region.

SCS Large Marine Ecosystem

SCS Large Marine Ecosystem (LME) is characterized by its tropical climate. Different sub-systems within the ecosystem have been identified.[26] Intensive fishing stands as the primary driving force behind the SCS LME, with climate serving as the secondary force. The Global Environment Facility (GEF) is actively backing the SCS LME project to tackle crucial threats to the coastal and marine environment. The project aims to foster ecosystem-based management of coastal and marine resources, addressing challenges and promoting sustainable practices in the region.

Eight parties (Cambodia, China, Taiwan, Indonesia, Malaysia, Philippines, Thailand, and Vietnam) are involved in the governance of the SCS LME, sharing concerns about the marine environment and an awareness of the importance of the Sea as a source of protein for the growing coastal populations.[27] The entire region is undergoing rapid economic development and population growth, despite political tensions and competing claims in the SCS. Notably, seven countries have taken a collaborative stance in protecting the marine environment. In 2001, they signed a joint agreement endorsing a regional plan sponsored by the UNEP. This plan is designed to address the degradation of the SCS by initiating nine pilot projects for sustainable

[25] Petch Manopawitr, "Thailand's Marine and Coastal Protected Area Management Effectiveness Evaluation, July, 2012,"https://www.icriforum.org/sites/default/files/ICRIGM27-MEworkshop-Thailand.pdf (assessed December 11, 2018).

[26] See Pauly, D. and V. Christensen, " Stratified models of large marine ecosystems: a general approach, and an application to the South China Sea", in Kenneth Sherman, Lewis M. Alexander, Barry D. Gold (eds.) *Large marine ecosystems: stress, mitigation, and sustainability* (Washington: AAAs Publication, 1993).

[27] Ibid.

development at priority trans-boundary sites in the region. The GEF is providing $16 million in support for this plan, aiming to enhance human and institutional capacity. Concurrently, environmental laws and regulations are being formulated. The seven countries are adopting an ecosystem-based approach to management, marked by the creation of a Trans-boundary Diagnostic Analysis (TDA). This science-based analysis of trans-boundary concerns and their root causes will guide the setting of priorities for action in a Strategic Action Programme (SAP).[28]

The UNEP/GEF Project

Following the Informal Working Group[29] activities, the UNEP took the lead in launching the UNEP/GEF SCS Project in 1996. This marked the inception of the first intergovernmental project involving all major littoral countries bordering the SCS. The UNEP/GEF Project, titled "Reversing Environmental Degradation Trends in the SCS and Gulf of Thailand," is funded by the GEF and executed by UNEP in collaboration with seven riparian states along the SCS—Cambodia, China, Indonesia, Malaysia, Philippines, Thailand, and Vietnam..[30] Leveraging the trust and confidence fostered by the Informal SCS Working Group, the UNEP/GEF SCS Project has achieved groundbreaking advancements in formalizing regional marine environmental cooperation in the SCS. The project has actively undertaken substantive cooperative activities aimed at addressing marine environmental problems in the region.[31] The project became fully operational in February 2002.[32]

The project document outlines the overall goals of the project as follows: "to create an environment at the regional level, in which collaboration and partnership in addressing environmental problems of the SCS, between all stakeholders, and at all levels is fostered and encouraged; and to enhance the capacity of the participating governments to integrate environmental considerations into national development planning."[33] In the medium term, the project aims to "elaborate and agree at an intergovernmental level, the Strategic Action Programme (SAP) encompassing specific targeted and cost actions for the longer-term, to address the priority issues

[28] Ibid.

[29] Since 1990, a series of workshops on "Managing Potential Conflicts in the SCS" have been held in Indonesia under the auspices of the Research and Development Agency within the Department of Foreign Affairs. These non-governmental gatherings, attended by government and military officials in their private capacities as well as by academics from the region and Canada, have been convened to explore ways to engender cooperation among the nations bordering on the SCS. The alternative is a jurisdictional void and the threat of armed conflict, since maritime boundary delimitation is an unlikely scenario at least in the short term.

[30] http://www.unepscs.org/project_background.html

[31] Chen Sulan, p. 225.

[32] http://pemsea.org/knowledge-center/links-to-coastal-and-marine-topics/habitat-protection-restoration-and-management/reversing-environmental-degradation-trends-in-the-south-china-sea-and-gulf-of-thailand/

[33] http://www.unepscs.org/project_background.html

and concerns. More specifically the proposed activities are designed to assist countries in meeting the environmental targets specified in the framework SAP that was developed over the period 1996–1998."[34]

Miguel D. Fortes claims that the UNEP/GEP SCS project is the first attempt to develop regionally coordinated programmes of actions designed to reverse environmental degradation in the SCS.[35] The outcomes achieved thus far provide a clearer understanding of the strategic significance of the SCS within the current regional coastal and marine environmental landscape. The project is actively constructing a framework for regional cooperation aimed at effectively addressing the environmental challenges prevalent in the SCS.

UNEP/Action Plan

UNEP has played a pivotal role as the primary source of financial support for the East Asian Seas Action Plan.[36] Its contributions to the development and implementation of the Action Plan have been crucial, spanning intellectual and technical inputs, financial assistance, and institutional support. These multifaceted roles have positioned UNEP as a facilitator for collective action and a catalyst for other regional initiatives. Particularly noteworthy is UNEP's significant intellectual input and coordinating role, which proved decisive during the preparatory phase of the action plan.[37] UNEP assumed overall responsibility for managing the logistics and administrative arrangements throughout the entire process of preparing, consulting, drafting, and revising the text of the East Asian Seas Action Plan.

Throughout the process, UNEP enlisted the services of regional experts or consultants to draft the East Asian Seas Action Plan and associated policy documents. Additionally, UNEP organized several expert meetings to facilitate the review of these documents. UNEP wielded influence over the meeting outcomes, not only through direct participation and the articulation of technical opinions (which were often well-received by other participants) but also by selecting experts to attend the meetings and shaping the meeting agenda.

UNEP's symbolic power as an authoritative international organization plays a crucial role in attracting countries to engage in multilateral cooperation. Participation in UNEP-sponsored activities allows countries to present themselves as responsible states actively addressing regional environmental challenges. UNEP's influence has had a dual impact on the development and implementation of the Action Plan. On the positive side, UNEP has been effective in garnering government support and participation, leveraging its authority as a program approved by the Governing

---

[34] The mid-term evaluation of the SCS Project was conducted in 2004 at http://www.unepscs.org/scsdocuments/Mid-Term-Evaluation.pdf

[35] See Miguel D. Fortes at "The SCS: Towards a Cooperative Management Regime." Conference report, May 16–17, 2007, Singapore, p. 6.

[36] East Asian Seas Action Plan is steered by the Coordinating Body on the Seas of East Asia (COBSEA) that is consisting of the ten member countries.

[37] Sulan Chen, p. 199.

Council of UNEP. However, on the negative side, the Action Plan's focus on environmental issues was influenced or determined by factors external to the region. The plan mirrored the global trend in addressing marine pollution, primarily driven by major oil spill accidents in the temperate northern hemisphere during the 1970s, which garnered extensive global attention due to their severe impacts on the marine environment. The issue of oil spills was not a top priority in the East Asian Seas region, except in the Straits of Malacca, when compared to the rapid loss and degradation of coastal habitats in the region.[38] With the exception of projects specifically addressing the control of pollution from accidental oil spills, many other program activities predominantly focused on environmental assessment, including research and monitoring. However, these activities often did not translate into substantial impacts on the management of environmental problems in the region.[39] The failure to identify regional priorities and shared marine environmental problems in the region likely constituted the primary factor contributing to the lack of strong governmental financial support for the Action Plan.

5 Challenges to Area-Based Management Approach

The existing challenges encompass both legal and conceptual dimensions. A universal legal framework for area-based management is currently absent. The governance of the ocean and its resources operates within a fragmented structure of national, regional, and international institutions (e.g., the IMO for shipping, the ISA for seabed-mining, the FAO and RFMOs for fisheries, and the Regional Seas Conventions for conservation and sustainable use of the marine environment). Furthermore, questions persist about who should define, review, and update criteria for identifying areas that may necessitate area-based management tools, including marine protected areas, based on the best available science. The determination of the authority responsible for deciding on the identification of such areas remains unresolved. These challenges extend to areas both beyond national jurisdiction and within national jurisdiction.

In Areas Beyond National Jurisdiction

The implementation of area-based management in Areas Beyond National Jurisdiction (ABNJ) encounters several challenges, encompassing both technical and governance aspects. On the technical front, the distinctive characteristics of the ABNJ environment, such as its remoteness, depth, and dynamic nature, have led to a scarcity of scientific information and restricted observing programs.[40] The lack of

---

38 Ibid. p. 201.

39 UNEP/GEF/SCS/RTF-L.1/13. 2002. *Review of Obligations of Signatory States under Global. Environmental Conventions with Regard to Regional Cooperation*. www.unepscs.org.

40 Vierros, "Space for Conservation and Sustainable Use: Area-based Management in Areas beyond National Jurisdiction,".

funding mechanisms for data collection further exacerbates this situation, hindering the availability of essential information to inform management in ABNJ. These challenges raise questions about the feasibility of effectively monitoring and enforcing Area-Based Management Tools (ABMTs) in ABNJ.

Looking at it from a governance standpoint, the development and implementation of ABMTs in ABNJ face a minimum of four significant hurdles. The lack of overarching governance principles for ABNJ leads to varying interpretations among different actors about the utilization of ABNJ, fostering pronounced differences of opinion regarding the methods and timing of ABMT usage. Additionally, the fragmented institutional framework for resource management in ABNJ constrains the capacity and potential effectiveness of ABMTs.[41] As an illustration, certain regions in ABNJ have been designated as VMEs by fisheries, while simultaneously being allocated for exploration in deep-sea mining. These concurrent uses are incompatible, and the absence of coherence in management measures underscores a significant lack of coordination among management authorities. Furthermore, the absence of a comprehensive mechanism to implement ABMTs in ABNJ confines the potential measures' objectives to those determined by sectoral management organizations.

Geographic and thematic gaps in sectoral governance or competence pose challenges to the effective implementation of ABMTs in ABNJ. For Regional Fisheries Management Organizations (RFMOs), this translates to their utility being confined to the species, stocks, and regions they actively manage. Similarly, for Regional Sea Organizations (RSOs), the limitations involve restricting the consideration of ABMTs for biodiversity conservation to the four RSOs whose competence extends into ABNJ.[42]

An additional objective that is currently absent is that of enhancing the resilience of specific ecosystems to the impacts of climate change. ABM goes beyond addressing various local human impacts; it can also contribute to increasing biodiversity resilience against the effects of climate change, encompassing acidification, warming, and deoxygenation. Although reducing CO_2 emissions remains a pivotal action for mitigating climate-change impacts, ABM can serve as a means to alleviate the pressure from other stressors, thereby providing time for marine ecosystems to adapt. Moreover, some researchers argue that the identification and protection of sites resilient to the impacts of climate change, including acidification, could be a crucial adaptation strategy. These sites may potentially serve as vital refuges for important biodiversity in the future.

Other commonly encountered challenges of ABM include the absence of a supportive legal and political framework, an ineffective system for compliance and enforcement, insufficient involvement of all relevant stakeholders, the absence of a sustainable financing mechanism for maintaining the MPA network, the lack of a social network of MPAs, failure to utilize the best available knowledge, potential strong resistance from existing users of the seas, and the diversity among SCS states, which differ significantly in various aspects.

[41] Ibid.

[42] Ibid.

The South China Sea in Context

The status of the high seas or ABNJ in the SCS remains an unresolved question. According to the 1953 report of the International Hydrographic Organization (IHO), the southern boundary of the SCS extends to the "Eastern and Southern limits of Singapore and Malacca Straits as far West as Tanjong Kedebu (1006'N, 102,058'E) down the East coast of Sumatra to Lucipara Point (3014'N, 106,005'E) thence to Tanjong Nanka…"[43] If this definition is accepted, it suggests the presence of the high seas or ABNJ outside the U-shaped Line in the SCS. However, within the confines of the U-shaped Line, the status of the high seas remains unclear.

As per the SCS arbitration award in July 2016, it appears that there is a substantial expanse of high seas within the U-shaped Line in the South China Sea.[44] It's important to note that China rejects the awards. Furthermore, the award did not adjudicate every aspect of historic rights, and its brief examination of offshore archipelagos was a side matter. Consequently, other states should exercise caution in shaping state practices based solely on certain aspects of the Award.

In the SCS, political considerations and a lack of mutual trust impact maritime cooperation, even in less sensitive areas. While some cooperative activities are confined to workshops and mutual visits, there is a need to advance concrete cooperative projects and joint cruises. Overall, environmental interdependence presents both a source of conflict and an opportunity for international cooperation. When political actors view significant environmental issues as matters of security, they are more likely to prioritize them and address them satisfactorily, fostering cooperation and acceptable solutions for all parties involved. The direction of development, whether leading to conflict or cooperation, largely hinges on how decision-makers perceive the situation.

In general, the marine environmental problem is not a top priority for most SCS countries. Many researchers studying the environmental situation in the SCS region emphasize the necessity of regional cooperation to address the growing problem. However, regionalism has not made significant progress in tackling international environmental issues so far. ASEAN, being the most prominent institution in this regard, has collaborated on environmental matters for many years. However, it seems that environmental issues are not given the highest priority on its agenda. To elevate their importance, ASEAN would likely need to perceive these serious environmental problems as security matters, prompting them to be placed higher on the agenda.

In addition to political obstacles, there are also technical challenges in the respective state practices. For instance, the management status of MPAs in the Philippines

---

[43] International Hydrographic Organization (IHO), "Limits of Oceans and Seas (Special Publication NO. 23)", 3rd Edition 1953, available at <https://epic.awi.de/29772/1/IHO1953a.pdf> , p. 30.

[44] Awards include: 1. none of the maritime features in the SCS can claim EEZ and CS; 2. China's claims to historic rights within the "nine-dash line" are groundless[contrary to UNCLOS, and UNCLOS superseded any historic rights claimed by China]; and 3. the Tribunal maintained that continental States' offshore archipelagos (/outlying archipelagos) should not be enclosed within a system of archipelagic or straight baseline pursuant to the Convention, and denied China's Nansha Qundao as a unit any maritime entitlement.].

is documented through a shared database established by several collaborating institutions.[45] However, documentation exists for only about 350 of all MPAs in the Philippines.[46] This lack of monitoring and documentation is one of the main reasons why so many MPAs in the Philippines are not managed properly.[47] Consistent monitoring and evaluation of all MPAs could enhance their effectiveness by addressing challenges such as determining how to form effective networks among existing MPAs to address larger ecosystem conservation needs, scaling up efforts to cover strategically selected larger areas, and providing monetary and moral support to both new and existing MPAs.

6 Way Forward

In the SCS, there has been some progress in implementing ABMTs despite encountering political and operational challenges. The future of ABM in the SCS is influenced by various factors, encompassing the geopolitical, environmental, and diplomatic landscape of the region.

The success of area-based management relies significantly on collaborative efforts among nations bordering the SCS. However, the geopolitical tensions in the SCS, driven by overlapping territorial claims among neighboring countries, pose challenges. The resolution of these disputes and the establishment of cooperation mechanisms will profoundly impact the effectiveness of area-based management.

In this context, diplomatic dialogues and initiatives aimed at finding common ground on environmental protection and sustainable resource management are deemed essential. The growing recognition of the significance of marine biodiversity conservation may stimulate increased efforts toward area-based management. Preserving the rich marine biodiversity in the SCS not only holds vital importance for the region but also aligns with global conservation goals. Despite the seemingly local nature of the physical and ecological degradation of coastal and nearshore areas, along with the depletion of their resources, the impacts of these problems extend far beyond their origin. The evidence of these issues is now widespread, reaching sites far away, emphasizing the need for globally applied strategies to achieve long-term solutions.

Several areas warrant further attention in the realm of area-based management. Technological advancements, particularly in satellite monitoring and remote

[45] Karin Post, "Increasing the Resilience of Marine Ecosystem: Creating and Managing Marine Protected Areas in the Philippines," *Marine Conservation Philippines*, February, 2018, https://marineconservationphilippines.org/wp-content/uploads/2018/02/marine-protected-areas-in-the-philippines.pdf (assessed December 11, 2018).

[46] White et al., 2006, "Creating and Managing Marine Protected Areas in the Philippines.".

[47] Karin Post, "Increasing the Resilience of Marine Ecosystem: Creating and Managing Marine Protected Areas in the Philippines," *Marine Conservation Philippines*, February, 2018, https://marineconservationphilippines.org/wp-content/uploads/2018/02/marine-protected-areas-in-the-philippines.pdf (assessed December 11, 2018).

sensing, present opportunities to augment the monitoring and enforcement of area-based management measures. These technologies can significantly enhance surveillance capabilities, enabling better tracking of activities that may impact the marine environment.

Moreover, the involvement of local communities and stakeholders in decision-making processes related to area-based management is crucial. Sustainable management practices are more likely to succeed when they take into account the needs and perspectives of those directly affected by the measures. Inclusivity in decision-making ensures that the implemented strategies align with the local context and garner support from the communities involved.

The future of area-based management in the SCS may be influenced by global initiatives focused on biodiversity conservation and sustainable development. International support and funding for regional conservation projects have the potential to enhance effective management practices. Worldwide endeavors for biodiversity and ecosystem protection encompass a blend of international agreements, conservation initiatives, and sustainable development practices. Goal 14 of the Sustainable Development Goals (SDGs), "Life Below Water," specifically addresses the conservation and sustainable use of marine resources.

Initiatives like the GEF play a crucial role by providing financial support for projects dedicated to biodiversity conservation, sustainable development, and ecosystem protection. These projects often entail collaborative efforts between governments, non-governmental organizations (NGOs), and the private sector. Businesses and industries are increasingly acknowledging the significance of incorporating biodiversity and ecosystem considerations into their operations. This involves adopting sustainable sourcing practices, minimizing environmental impacts, and actively supporting conservation efforts.

Global research initiatives and monitoring programs play a crucial role in assessing the status of biodiversity and ecosystems. The data collected through these efforts are invaluable for decision-making, policy development, and targeted conservation actions. The interconnectedness between addressing climate change and protecting biodiversity and ecosystems is evident. Given the increasing impacts of climate change on marine ecosystems, future area-based management strategies may need to incorporate measures to enhance resilience and mitigate the effects of climate-related stressors. Actions to reduce greenhouse gas emissions, promote sustainable land use, and enhance resilience to climate change collectively contribute to the overall health of ecosystems.

To further enhance cooperation and address environmental issues in the SCS, strengthening or establishing regional governance mechanisms could be beneficial. This may involve creating joint management areas, initiating collaborative research projects, and sharing best practices among nations in the region. Such efforts would contribute to more effective environmental management and sustainable use of marine resources in the SCS.

Dr. Hong Nong is the Executive Director and Senior Fellow of Institute for China–America Studies. She is concurrently a senior fellow with National Institute for South China Sea Studies and Beijing Club for International Dialogue. She holds a PhD of interdisciplinary study of international law and international relations from the University of Alberta, Canada and held a Postdoctoral Fellowship in the University's China Institute. She was ITLOS-Nippon Fellow for International Dispute Settlement and Visiting Fellow at Australian National Centre for Ocean Resources and Security, the Center of Oceans Law and Policy, University of Virginia, and at the Max Planck Institute for Comparative Public Law and International Law. Her selected publications include US and China Global Maritime Relations (Routledge, 2024), China's Role in the Arctic: Observing and Being Observed (Routeldge, 2020), UNCLOS and Ocean Dispute Settlement: Law and Politics in the South China Sea (Routledge, 2012).

Chapter 10
Challenges to Navigation Rights and High Seas Freedoms in the Indo-Pacific

Robert Beckman

This paper analyses the current challenges to navigation rights and high seas freedoms in the Indo-Pacific, with a particular focus on the South China Sea. First, it sets out the possible actions the Indo-Pacific States could take to challenge what they believe are China's excessive maritime claims that pose a threat to the rules-based legal order set out in the 1982 United Nations Convention on the Law of the Sea ("UNCLOS").[1] Second, it recommends that the Indo-Pacific States engage in discussions with China to attempt to reach a consensus on how certain provisions in UNCLOS could be interpreted and applied so as to reduce tensions and possible conflict concerning navigation rights and high seas freedoms in the Indo-Pacific.

1 Legal Challenges to Excessive Maritime Claims

1.1 Excessive Maritime Claims of China in the South China Sea

Many States in the Indo-Pacific believe that China has made excessive maritime claims from disputed offshore features in the South China Sea, and that such claims infringe the rights and freedoms of other States.

[1] United Nations, *United Nations Convention on the Law of the Sea*; <https://www.un.org/depts/los/convention_agreements/texts/unclos/closindx.htm> (accessed September 30, 2021).

R. Beckman (✉)
Centre for International Law, National University of Singapore, 469A Bukit Timah Road, Tower Block, #09-01, Singapore 259770, Singapore
e-mail: cilbeckman@nus.edu.sg

L. A. T. Nguyen and H. D. Vu (eds.), *Viability of UNCLOS amid Emerging Global Maritime Challenges*, https://doi.org/10.1007/978-981-97-5838-8_11

The main issues concern China's maritime claims from the disputed features it occupies in the Spratly Islands, but there are also issues arising from its maritime claims from the Paracel Islands. China occupies the Paracel Islands, but both Vietnam and China claim sovereignty over them. The main issue under UNCLOS with regard to the Paracel Islands is that China has drawn straight baselines enclosing the islands in the mid-ocean archipelago.[2] It claims the waters inside the baselines as internal waters, where the passage of foreign ships is subject to its consent. It also claims a territorial sea and an EEZ measured from the straight baselines.

China, Brunei, Malaysia, the Philippines and Vietnam claim sovereignty over and occupy one or more of the islands or geographic features in the Spratly Islands. Brunei, Malaysia, the Philippines and Vietnam have not asserted a right to claim an EEZ or continental shelf from any of the disputed Spratly Islands. They have made their EEZ and continental shelf claims from the baselines along their coast or from their archipelagic baselines. On the other hand, China has asserted that it enjoys "sovereign rights and jurisdiction" within the waters inside the "nine-dash line map" it attached to a diplomatic note sent to the UN Secretary-General.[3] China has also asserted that it is entitled to claim an EEZ and a continental shelf from several of the individual islands and from the group of islands as a whole.[4]

In the 2016 Award of the Arbitral Tribunal in the South China Sea case,[5] the tribunal ruled that none of the features in the Spratly Islands was an "island" entitled to an EEZ or continental shelf as defined in Article 121 of UNCLOS. Rather, they were all either low-tide elevations entitled to no maritime zones of their own, or "rocks which cannot sustain human habitation or economic life of their own" entitled only to a 12 nm territorial sea. The Tribunal also ruled that even if China did possess "historic rights" to explore and exploit the natural resources in areas that are now within the EEZ of the other States bordering the South China Sea, it gave up such rights when it ratified UNCLOS. Further, it ruled that China could not claim maritime zones from the island groups over which it claims sovereignty in the South China Sea because only archipelagic States have the right to draw straight baselines connecting the outermost points of their islands and drying reefs.

China refused to participate in the arbitration but the case proceeded in its absence as provided in UNCLOS.[6] Although the Award of the Arbitral Tribunal is legally

---

[2] UNDOALOS, Law of the Sea Bulletin No. 32, pages 39–40; < https://www.un.org/Depts/los/doalos_publications/LOSBulletins/bulletinpdf/bulletinE32.pdf> (accessed September 30, 2021).

[3] United Nations, The Communication of China of 7 May 2009 to the CLCS in response to that submission, with the "nine-dash line" map attached; < https://www.un.org/depts/los/clcs_new/submissions_files/mysvnm33_09/chn_2009re_mys_vnm_e.pdf> (accessed September 30, 2021).

[4] Ministry of Foreign Affairs of the People's Republic of China, *Statement of the Government of the People's Republic of China on China's Territorial Sovereignty and Maritime Rights and Interests in the South China Sea*, 12 July 2016; < https://www.fmprc.gov.cn/mfa_eng/zxxx_662805/t1379493.shtml> (accessed September 30, 2021).

[5] Permanent Court of Arbitration, *The South China Sea Arbitration (The Republic of Philippines v. The People's Republic of China), Award of Arbitral Tribunal of 12 July 2016*; < https://pca-cpa.org/en/cases/7/> (accessed September 30, 2021).

[6] Ministry of Foreign Affairs of the People's Republic of China, *Position Paper of the Government of the People's Republic of China on the Matter of Jurisdiction in the South China Sea Arbitration*

binding on both the Philippines and China, China has declared that it considers it null and void.[7] China has continued to maintain that it is entitled to claim an EEZ and a continental shelf from the individual islands in the Spratly Islands and from the four islands groups it claims in the South China Sea, including the Spratly Islands.[8]

2 Actions by Indo-Pacific States to Challenge China's Excessive Maritime Claims

The United States has issued studies setting out its position on the extent to which China's maritime claims are inconsistent with UNCLOS.[9] The United States has also continued to challenge China's excessive maritime claims through naval operations under its Freedom of Navigation Programme.[10]

Some other States in the Indo-Pacific have continued to exercise high seas freedoms or passage rights in the waters near the Chinese-occupied disputed features in the South China Sea in order to demonstrate support for the rules-based order in UNCLOS. They have justified their actions by stating that their navies sail where international law allows. However, as a general rule, they seem to prefer actions that are less confrontational than the US Freedom of Navigation Programme exercises.

In addition, several States interested in maintaining a rules-based legal order in the Indo-Pacific have publicly and officially challenged China's position on the 2016 Award of the Arbitral Tribunal in the *South China Sea Case* by sending Diplomatic Notes to the UN Secretary-General. The impetus for these notes was a note sent by Malaysia in December 2019 advising the Commission on the Limits of the Continental Shelf that it intended to make a separate submission for an extended continental shelf in the South China Sea. China sent a diplomatic note to the UN

Initiated by the Republic of the Philippines, 7 December 2014; <https://www.fmprc.gov.cn/mfa_eng/zxxx_662805/t1217147.shtml> (accessed September 30, 2021).

7 Ministry of Foreign Affairs of the People's Republic of China, *Statement of the Ministry of Foreign Affairs of the People's Republic of China on the Award of 12 July 2016 of the Arbitral Tribunal in the South China Sea Arbitration Established at the Request of the Republic of the Philippines, 12 July 2016*; <https://www.fmprc.gov.cn/mfa_eng/zxxx_662805/t1379492.shtml> (accessed September 30, 2021).

8 Ministry of Foreign Affairs of the People's Republic of China, *Statement of the Government of the People's Republic of China on China's Territorial Sovereignty and Maritime Rights and Interests in the South China Sea, 12 July 2016*; <https://www.fmprc.gov.cn/mfa_eng/zxxx_662805/t1379493.shtml> (accessed September 30, 2021).

9 US State Department, *Limits in the Seas No. 143 China: Maritime Claims in the South China Sea, 5 December 2014*; < https://www.state.gov/wp-content/uploads/2019/10/LIS-143.pdf> (accessed September 30, 2021); US State Department, *Limits in the Seas No. 117, Straight Baseline Claims: China, 9 July 1996*; < https://www.state.gov/wp-content/uploads/2020/01/LIS-117.pdf> (accessed September 30, 2021).

10 US Department of Defense, *Report to Congress, Annual Freedom of Navigation Report, Fiscal Year 2020*; <https://s3.documentcloud.org/documents/20509421/fy20-dod-fon-report-final.pdf> (accessed September 30, 2021).

Secretary-General objecting to Malaysia's submission. China's diplomatic note triggered a series of diplomatic notes from States interested in upholding the rules-based legal order set out in UNCLOS.[11]

2.1 Action by ASEAN States on Maritime Claims in the South China Sea

The ASEAN member States bordering the South China Sea have one important issue in common. China is claiming sovereign rights and jurisdiction in waters which the ASEAN States believe are either their exclusive economic zone, their extended continental shelf or high seas. If the ASEAN States bordering the South China Sea were to resolve their own overlapping maritime boundary claims, it would be easier for them to cooperate to challenge what they believe are China's excessive maritime claims that challenge navigation rights and high seas freedoms.

In 2019 Indonesia and the Philippines entered into an agreement resolving their EEZ boundary in the South China Sea, and in 2023 Indonesia and Vietnam resolved their EEZ boundary. These agreements will help minimize incidents in which the authorities of one ASEAN State arrest fishing vessels from another ASEAN State. It may be more difficult for Malaysia and the Philippines to resolve their EEZ boundary because of the Philippines' historic claim to Sabah, but it would be in the common interest of Malaysia and the Philippines to work out a "provisional arrangement" regarding fishing activities in the disputed area.

Another step that could be taken would be for the Philippines to make a submission for an extended continental shelf in the South China Sea that does not overlap with the claims of Indonesia and Malaysia. This would enable the three States to cooperate in promoting the existence of an area of high seas in the South China Sea. In addition, it would enable them to argue that the South China Sea is a semi-enclosed sea and that States bordering the South China Sea, including China, have an obligation to cooperate as provided in Article 123 of UNCLOS. If the ASEAN States were able to clarify their maritime claims and boundaries in the South China Sea, it would also be easier for them to cooperate to challenge threats to navigation rights and high seas freedoms. It would also enable them to cooperate to challenge excessive claims to the natural resources in the South China Sea.

---

[11] United Nations, Communications to the CLCS responding to the points in China's Notes and further responses; <https://www.un.org/depts/los/clcs_new/submissions_files/submission_mys_12_12_2019.html> (accessed September 30, 2021).

2.2 *Invocation of Dispute Settlement Provisions in UNCLOS*

A more controversial option would be for one or more Indo-Pacific States that are party to UNCLOS to bring a case against China by challenging the legality of China's restrictions on passage rights and/or high seas freedoms. Under Article 286 of UNCLOS, a State can invoke the dispute settlement procedures in Part XV of UNCLOS if a dispute arises on the interpretation or application of UNCLOS that cannot be resolved through negotiation.[12] States who believe that China's laws restricting passage rights or high seas freedoms are contrary to UNCLOS could consider this option.

For example, a State could send one of its ships through the Paracel Islands, and if China objected because the ship failed to obtain its permission to enter its territorial sea or internal waters, a dispute would arise on the legality of China's use of straight baselines around the Paracel Islands and its declaration that the waters inside the baselines are internal waters. States that are interested in how UNCLOS provisions on baselines apply to mid-ocean archipelagoes could share the costs of bringing this case. The Award of a court or tribunal in this case would likely have an impact on whether and how China attempts to draw straight baselines around the Spratly Islands as well as the Paracel Islands.

However, it should be noted that China has made an optional clause declaration under Article 298 excluding all disputes concerning military activities.[13] Therefore, although the United States and some of its Allies believe that naval operations such as naval exercises involving live firing of weapons are "other lawful uses of sea relating to the freedom of navigation" under Article 58 of UNCLOS, it may not be possible to challenge China's actions of attempting to restrict such naval operations. Although the term "military activities" is not defined in UNCLOS, it is likely to include naval exercises.

The more important issue, however, is whether invoking the dispute settlement provisions in UNCLOS against China is a wise move politically. It would likely make it impossible to engage in discussions with China to attempt to reach a consensus on how UNLCOS should be applied. It is also highly unlikely that China would either participate in the case or abide by the decision rendered by a court or tribunal.

2.3 *Domestic Legislation on Restrictions for Innocent Passage of Warships*

China's Territorial Sea Law requires foreign warships to either provide notice or request authorization to exercise the right of innocent passage in the territorial

[12] Supra n 1.

[13] Supra n 1.

sea. The United States challenges such legislation under its Freedom of Navigation Program.

Most coastal States in the region have no restrictions on the passage of warships in their territorial sea, and they do not send their warships through the territorial sea of China. However, they may fear that if tensions arise with China, China may signal its displeasure by sending its warships through their territorial sea. Such coastal States could address this issue by enacting domestic legislation to provide that any warship flying the flag of a State that requires notice and/or authorization for the exercise of innocent passage of warships through its territorial sea is subject to the same requirements for the exercise of innocent passage through the territorial sea of that coastal State. The legislation should state that this requirement is based on the principle of reciprocity and is not intended to create a new rule of customary law. In addition, the legislation could state that these requirements do not apply to warships from States that do not impose such restrictions on the passage of foreign warships through their territorial sea.

2.4 Consultations Concerning Incidents at Sea and Chinese Legislation

Another way to address issues concerning navigation rights and high seas freedoms is to organize consultations between China and major States with interests in navigational rights and high seas freedoms in the Indo-Pacific Region. During these consultations, States can discuss how to address incidents at sea that may arise because of Chinese laws and regulations.

It is also important to explore avenues of discussion and communication with Chinese government officials so that they understand why some of their laws and regulations are a matter of concern to other States. Such discussions might explore the prospect of finding practical solutions that address China's concerns without undermining the rules-based legal order set out in UNCLOS.

These discussions could also include issues concerning the Chinese Coast Guard and China's reported use of fishing vessels as part of its "maritime militia" in protecting China's maritime interests. These vessels are arguably not warships or auxiliary vessels and are therefore not entitled to sovereignty immunity, and their acts would not be imputable to China. However, China may be internationally responsible for such vessels' conduct if they engage in illegal activity and it can be shown that they were acting under the direction and control of an organ of the Chinese Government.

3 Consultations on How to Interpret and Apply 1982 UNCLOS

Another option that might be considered is for the Indo-Pacific States to invite China to engage in discussions on the provisions in UNCLOS, which give rise to differing interpretations and which may raise tensions. The purpose of the exercise would be to try to reach a consensus on how those provisions should be interpreted in the Indo-Pacific so that it would reduce tensions and the risk of armed conflict.

4 Restrictions on Naval Exercises in the EEZ

The first issue is the extent to which a coastal State can restrict foreign warships from engaging in naval operations in its EEZ. China has not challenged the right of foreign merchant ships to exercise freedom of navigation in its EEZ. However, it has challenged the right of foreign warships to engage in naval operations in its EEZ that it believes pose a threat to its security. This includes naval exercises involving the live firing of weapons, reconnaissance activities, survey activities and marine data collection by US research vessels.

China is not the only State in the Indo-Pacific that has expressed concern about the conduct of naval exercises in their EEZ. Several States in Southeast Asia and South Asia have also made formal declarations to the United Nations stating that it is their understanding that UNCLOS provisions do not authorize other States to carry out military exercises or maneuvers in the EEZ and on the continental shelf without the consent of the coastal State. This is especially so for exercises involving the use of weapons or explosives. Such declarations were made by Bangladesh (2009), India (1995), Pakistan (1997) and Malaysia (2019). When it ratified UNCLOS in 2011, Thailand made an even broader declaration with regard to military activities in its EEZ.[14]

The United States has challenged the legality of such unilateral declarations through diplomatic notes and Freedom of Navigation Operations. The issue is whether it is possible to find a mutually agreeable position that addresses the major concerns of States involved in sensitive areas such as the South China Sea. A possible solution is for interested States to adopt a memorandum of understanding ("MOU") on military exercises in the South China Sea.

The MOU could provide that they agree to interpret the "due regard" obligation in Article 58(3) of UNCLOS as a duty to informally consult the coastal State in good faith with regard to the timing, location and nature of the planned naval exercises involving the live firing of weapons. This would prevent military exercises from interfering with a coastal State's planned activities while avoiding a coastal State's requirement that such exercises require its express consent. Such an MOU could

[14] Supra n 1.

provide that such informal consultations are without prejudice to the legal positions of the parties on the interpretation or application and application of the provisions in UNCLOS.

5 Restrictions on Survey Activities in the EEZ of Other States

There is no provision in UNCLOS restricting States from engaging in survey activities such as hydrographic surveys in the EEZ of coastal States. The United States maintains that States can engage in such activities in the EEZ of other States because they are "other internationally lawful uses of the sea" relating to the freedom of navigation that is set out in Article 58(1) of UNCLOS. It would enhance trust and confidence if an agreement could be reached by the Indo-Pacific States, including the United States and China, on what activities are "internationally law uses of the sea" related to the freedom of navigation and on what types of survey activities can be conducted in the EEZ of other States without their consent.

6 Marine Scientific Research Activities in the EEZ and on the Continental Shelf

Another issue concerns research activities in the EEZ and on the continental shelf. Under UNCLOS coastal States have the exclusive right to regulate, authorize and conduct marine scientific research (MSR) in their territorial sea and in their archipelagic waters. Coastal States also have the right to regulate, authorize and conduct marine scientific research in their EEZ and on their continental shelf. MSR in the EEZ and on the continental shelf may only be conducted with the consent of the coastal State. The provisions of UNCLOS provide that in normal circumstances, coastal States should grant their consent for MSR in their EEZ and on their continental shelf. In addition, coastal States have an obligation to establish rules and procedures to ensure that their consent will not be delayed or denied unreasonably.

The major problem is that there is no definition of MSR in UNCLOS and no consensus on what are other lawful activities relating to the freedom of navigation in Article 58. Consequently, the position of the United States is that it can engage in "marine data collection" for naval warfare purposes in the EEZ of other States because it is not MSR. States may also undertake surveys or other activities that may prejudice the economic interests of the coastal State.

Consequently, it would greatly increase trust and confidence between coastal States and the major powers in the Indo-Pacific if agreement could be reached on what types of activities come within the definition of MSR.

7 Restrictions on the Right of Innocent Passage

Another issue is the extent to which coastal States can regulate or restrict the right of innocent passage of foreign ships in general and foreign warships in particular through its territorial sea. China's 1992 Law on the Territorial Sea[15] states that foreign military ships must obtain permission to enter its territorial sea. The Law on the Territorial Sea further states that foreign nuclear-powered ships and other ships carrying nuclear, toxic or other dangerous substances must carry certain documents and observe special precautionary measures when they pass through the territorial sea. In 2021, China amended its Maritime Traffic Safety Law[16] to require mandatory reporting to the coastal authorities by foreign ships entering the territorial sea that may pose a threat to the marine environment, including ships carrying nuclear, toxic or other dangerous substances.

States in the Indo-Pacific should engage in discussions with China in order to try to reach a consensus on how China's legislation should be interpreted in practice. Such discussions should include an analysis by legal experts of the relevant provisions in UNCLOS as well as the conventions and regulations adopted by the International Maritime Organization (IMO) and the International Atomic Energy Agency (IAEA) on the carriage of nuclear, toxic and other dangerous substances.

8 Unmanned Vehicles and the Rules-Based Legal Order for the Oceans

The major maritime powers, including the United States and China, are developing and deploying unmanned surface vehicles (USVs) and unmanned underwater vehicles (UUVs) for use by their navies. The navies employing USVs and UUVs are likely to assert that they are "warships" entitled to the same passage rights and high seas freedoms as other warships. On the other hand, some coastal States are likely to fear that USVs and UUVs pose a special threat to their economic and security interests, and their passage should be subject to either the notice or consent of the coastal State.

These developments raise important issues concerning the development of the rules-based legal order governing the oceans. UNCLOS was negotiated over nine years with the participation of almost all States. The issue is who gets to decide how the provisions in UNCLOS are to be interpreted in light of developments in

[15] United Nations, *Law on the Territorial Sea and Contiguous Zone of the Peoples' Republic of China of 25 February 1992*; <https://www.un.org/Depts/los/LEGISLATIONANDTREATIES/PDFFILES/CHN_1992_Law.pdf> (accessed September 30, 2021).

[16] China Maritime Safety Administration, *Maritime Traffic Safety Law*; < https://www.egcsa.com/wp-content/uploads/China-MSA-implementation-regulation-on-IMO-2020-Google-English-translation.pdf> (accessed September 30, 2021).

technology? Should the technologically advanced States decide, or should less technologically advanced States have a voice in how the rules-based legal order set out in UNCLOS is to be interpreted?

One issue concerns the employment of USVs and UUVs in waters subject to the sovereignty of coastal States. The territorial sea and archipelagic waters are subject to the sovereignty of coastal States, but such sovereignty must be exercised subject to the provisions in UNCLOS. "Ships" have a right of innocent passage through the territorial sea and archipelagic waters, the right of transit passage through straits used for international navigation, and the rights of innocent passage and archipelagic sea lanes passage through archipelagic waters. However, there is no definition of "ship" in UNCLOS. Are all USVs and UUVs "ships" entitled to such passage rights?

Article 20 of UNCLOS provides that, in the territorial sea, "submarines and other underwater vehicles" are entitled to the right of innocent passage, but they are required to navigate on the surface and to show their flag. Are UUVs "other underwater vehicles" that must surface and fly their flag?

Under Parts III and IV of UNCLOS ships may exercise transit passage through straits used for international navigation and archipelagic sea lanes passage through archipelagic waters in their "normal mode", that is, while submerged. Is a UUV a ship entitled to exercise such passage rights while submerged?

Ships exercising passage rights in the territorial sea and archipelagic waters are prohibited from carrying out any research or survey activities. However, the main function of some USVs and UUVs is to engage in research and survey activities for military purposes. How does a coastal State ensure that a USV exercising transit passage or archipelagic sea lanes passage while submerged is not engaging in research or survey activities?

In addition, under UNCLOS a "warship" has immunity from the jurisdiction of the coastal State. A warship is defined in Article 29 of UNCLOS as a ship under the command of an officer and manned by a crew under regular armed forces discipline. Is a USV or UUV that is either completely autonomous or controlled by a remote-control operator on shore or on another ship a "warship" entitled to immunity from arrest by the coastal State if it is engaging in activities that are prohibited under UNCLOS? If a naval power classifies a UUV as a warship, are coastal States obligated to accept that classification?

Coastal States have a right to prevent the passage of a USV or UUV that they believe is not innocent. If the USV or UUV in question is not entitled to immunity, the coastal State can arrest it. If the USV or UUV purports to be a warship or government ship entitled to immunity, and it fails to comply with the laws and regulations of the coastal State, the coastal State can require it to leave its territorial sea immediately.

In practice, the authorities in the coastal State would contact the warship in question and inform it of the reasons it questions the innocence of the passage, and give the warship a reasonable opportunity to clarify its intentions or correct its conduct in a reasonably short period of time. These procedures assume that the authorities of the coastal State are able to communicate with whoever is in charge of the warship; whether it is the master on board, a remote-control operator on shore, or an on board computer. The issue that arises is how the authorities in the coastal State can exercise jurisdiction if they are not able to communicate with a USV or UUV that purports to have sovereign immunity?

On these issues, the position of the ASEAN member States bordering the South China Sea may not be entirely in conformity with the positions of the superpowers and developed states that are developing and employing USVs and UUVs. Therefore, the fundamental question raised by these developments is who will decide how the provisions in UNCLOS are to be interpreted in light of developments in technology. In other words, who will determine the content of the "rules-based legal order"? If a dialogue between China and the Indo-Pacific States is undertaken to try to reach a consensus on how UNCLOS should be interpreted in the Indo-Pacific to address the issues raised by USVs and UUVs, it could reduce tensions.

9 Conclusion

The UNCLOS rules-based legal order is under threat in the Indo-Pacific and in the South China Sea. This paper has attempted to set out some actions that Indo-Pacific States with an interest in the rules-based order for the oceans can take to challenge China's excessive maritime claims. Some of the actions can be taken by any of the interested Indo-Pacific States while others can only be taken by the ASEAN States bordering South China. Finally, it suggests some actions that the Indo-Pacific States can take to lessen tensions in the South China Sea by engaging in discussions with China on how to interpret the provisions in UNCLOS to reduce tensions and preserve the rules-based legal order set out in the convention.

Robert Beckman is an Emeritus Professor at the Faculty of Law, National University of Singapore (NUS) and is Co-Head of the Ocean Law and Policy Programme at the NUS Centre for International Law (CIL).

Chapter 11
The Battle of *Notes Verbales* and the Future of the South China Sea: An Indonesia's Perspective

Damos Dumoli Agusman

Abstract The international community has recently witnessed a "battle of *notes verbales*" between some claimant States and other States having interests in the South China Sea (SCS). The battle was triggered by Malaysia's partial submission of its extended continental shelf to the Commission on the Limits of the Continental Shelf (CLCS) on 12 December 2019. The subject matter of the battle has extended beyond the Malaysian submission itself as it has already shifted away from the original points of the submission and entered into the core issues of SCS. The article makes some brief observations on how much weight this battle carries in terms of legal lawfare and a political solution to solve the dispute in the SCS. It concludes that while the battle will not end with any solution to the conflict, it will provide some clarification to the conundrum of the SCS dispute. The notes verbales provide valuable insights into the legal positions of the countries concerned and are a useful source in sorting out the positions of certain claimant States. Some legal clarifications might be derived from the exchanged notes concerning maritime status of the disputed features, maritime entitlements, and the positions of the third parties not involved in the dispute.

1 Introduction

The international community has recently witnessed a "battle of *notes verbales*" between some claimant States and other States having interests in the South China Sea (SCS). The battle was triggered by Malaysia's partial submission of its extended continental shelf to the Commission on the Limits of the Continental Shelf (CLCS)

Lecturer at University of Padjadjaran Bandung, Indonesia and formerly Director General for International Law and Treaties, Ministry of Foreign Affairs of Indonesia. This article reflects purely his academic view and was partly presented at the 12th South China Sea International Conference "Maintaining peace and cooperation through time of turbulence", Hanoi, 16–17 November 2020.

D. D. Agusman (✉)
Janur Elok VIII, Kelapa Gading, Jakarta 14240, Indonesia
e-mail: damos@unpad.ac.id

L. A. T. Nguyen and H. D. Vu (eds.), *Viability of UNCLOS amid Emerging Global Maritime Challenges*, https://doi.org/10.1007/978-981-97-5838-8_12

on 12 December 2019.[1] The submission led to a response from China, which subsequently generated more statements from various countries addressing China's position. The reactions to China's response are not only from States bordering the SCS, such as the Philippines, Vietnam and Indonesia, but also countries from other continents, such as Germany, France, Australia, Canada, the United Kingdom and New Zealand. Interestingly, the "battle" turns out to address the core dispute of the SCS instead of Malaysia's submission.

Such correspondences are normal in diplomatic practice and serve as an avenue by which States duly record their position in legal terms. It is neither the first such battle nor is it taking place only under the UN CLCS. The same legal notes battle on the SCS also took place in 2009/2011, triggered by the Joint Submission by Malaysia and Vietnam to the UN CLCS on 6 May 2009. The battle may also be seen elsewhere, such as in other UN bodies like the UN Division for Ocean Affairs and the Law of the Sea.[2] The diplomatic battle has taken place even more frequently in a bilateral context. Indonesia, for example, has been waging a battle with China since 1995, having indicated that China has an ambiguous and unclarified claim over the Natuna waters.[3]

> The exchange of statements submitted to the UN CLCS in 2019/2020 should thus not be considered complete and may not reflect the exhaustive positions of the States submitting the notes.

This article focuses on the "battle of *notes verbales*" at play in the bilateral context, with special reference to Indonesia-China interactions, followed by the discussion raised by the *notes verbales* submitted in 2009/2010 and 2019/2020. The article will then make some brief observations on how much weight this battle carries in terms of *legal law fare* and a political solution to solve the dispute in the SCS.

2 Diplomatic Lawfare on the South China Sea

Diplomatic correspondence has long been considered one of the tools for identifying the rule of international law. Recently, in its recommendation submitted to the UN General Assembly, the International Law Commission listed diplomatic correspondence as one of the items that may be considered in identifying general practices

---

[1] *Malaysia*'s *Note Verbale* No. HA 59/19 dated 12/12/2019. The *Note Verbale* and the responses submitted by States could be accessed at https://www.un.org/depts/los/clcs_new/commission_submissions.htm.

[2] Legal arguments and their counter arguments also appear following the publication of charts or list of geographical coordinates submitted by States as prescribed by UNCLOS. https://www.un.org/Depts/los/LEGISLATIONANDTREATIES/depositpublicity.htm.

[3] Damos Dumoli Agusman 'Natuna Waters: Explaining a Flashpoint between Indonesia and China' (2023) *Indonesian Journal of International Law*: Vol. 20: No. 4, Article 4. https://scholarhub.ui.ac.id/ijil/vol20/iss4/4.

regarded as part of customary international law.[4] This indicates that diplomatic correspondence (in the form of a *note verbale*) has a particular importance in providing a picture of the prevailing rule of international law.

The legal nature of the *note verbale* is very significant. The note shall be considered under international law as not only an official position of the issuing State in a formal manner but also as an expression of the legal foundation underlining its maritime claim over the SCS, which will be binding after that.

2.1 Bilateral Diplomatic Lawfare Indonesia-China

As briefly mentioned above, the diplomatic battle has taken place more frequently in a bilateral context. On the SCS conflict, the bilateral diplomatic quarrel has hardly been made public due to the Asian culture, which prefers to manage issues in a discrete manner and, if not solved, to sweep them under the carpet. Diplomatic law fare between Indonesia and China is the best example to explain this phenomenon.

On the SCS issue, Indonesia and China had enjoyed a "no-conflict" relation until 1994. The relations between the two remained calm even when the conflict emerged on the public stage, particularly during the inception of the standoff between China and Vietnam over the Paracel Islands in 1974. In this context, Indonesia was convinced about its status as a real third party in the conflict. Therefore, in response to the standoff, Indonesia advised both parties to use the ICJ to achieve peaceful settlements.[5]

The belief that Indonesia was not a party in the SCS conflict was the core principle of its foreign policy toward the Southern part of the SCS, i.e. the Natuna Waters, which is located within Indonesia's continental shelf/EEZ and concurrently within the so-called "nine-dash line" (9DL). For instance, China was not bothered when Indonesia and Malaysia concluded their Agreement on the continental shelf within the SCS in 1969,[6] covering the areas apparently categorized within the 9DL. This Agreement was registered to the UN Secretary-General and publicly announced to China without objection.

During the UNCLOS 1982 negotiations, where China's delegation played an active role, there was no indication of any possible overlapping claim between the two countries over the various maritime zones being discussed and established at that time, nor was any historic claim raised to these waters. In the meantime, when the archipelagic regime was discussed, several neighbouring States, but not China, had raised their interests in retaining their existing rights in the area should it be converted

[4] Report of the International Law Commission, 70th Session, A/73/10/2018, p. 119.

[5] Kompas, 05/02/1974.

[6] The agreed line is within the 9DL. See the Agreement between the Government of Malaysia and the Government of Indonesia on the Delimitation of the Continental Shelves between the Two Countries, 27/10/1969.

https://www.un.org/depts/los/LEGISLATIONANDTREATIES/PDFFILES/TREATIES/MYS IDN1969CS.PDF. Accessed 27/06/ 2023.

into Indonesia's archipelagic waters. The issues raised had been the subject of *quid pro quo* negotiations during the Law of the Sea Conference and led to mutually agreed provisions in the Convention. Thailand, Malaysia and Singapore, among others, requested guarantees from Indonesia respecting their existing rights within certain areas falling within Indonesia's archipelagic waters, as reflected in Articles 47 (6) and 51 of UNCLOS 1982.[7] If the 9DL had already been a substantive claim, the Chinese delegation should have raised it accordingly during the conference.

With this honest-broker status, Indonesia, through a prominent diplomat, Hasjim Djalal, initiated a long series of workshops on "Managing Potential Conflicts in the South China Sea" since 1990, engaging all claimant states in informal round-table discussions with Indonesia acting as a non-claimant in an honest broker role.[8]

The Foreign Affairs Ministry of Indonesia, however, became curious when the 9DL appeared for the first time and became known to Indonesia in the 1993 Workshop on SCS, where China's delegation distributed a map depicting the lines.[9] Diplomatic lawfare started from this point. Through informal diplomatic interaction, Indonesia started asking what the 9DL was supposed to mean but failed to receive an answer. Indonesia then pursued a high-level approach to make sure that the 9DL did not constitute any claim that may encroach on Indonesia's Natuna EEZ. Indonesia sent for the first time a written diplomatic note in 1994 questioning again the meaning of the line and, surprisingly, no answer was forthcoming. The ultimate inquiry was finally made by Indonesian Foreign Minister Ali Alatas in 1995, when he met with Chinese Foreign Minister Qian Qichen in Beijing. Ali Alatas received assurance from Qian Qichen in very general terms, i.e. that "China has no dispute in Spratly and no overlapping claim with Indonesia."[10] This assurance comforted Indonesia and since then Indonesia continued to play its non-claimant role without any doubts.

It is clear that China preferred to shelve the 9DL claim and offer cooperation rather than confrontation and was successfully "silent" and vague on its claim. China, through Foreign Minister Qian Qichen, was successful in making a disguised reply to Indonesia's long-standing inquiry on the meaning of the 9DL, by simply convincing Indonesia that there was no overlapping dispute over islands between the two countries. It was a disguised explanation because the statement induced Indonesia to believe that there was no legal constraint for Indonesia extending its EEZ 200 Nm from Natuna Island based on UNCLOS 1982. The answer led Minister Alatas to

---

[7] Thailand, Malaysia and Singapore, among others, requested guarantees from Indonesia respecting their existing rights within certain areas falling within Indonesia's archipelagic waters, as reflected in Article 47 (6) and 51 of UNCLOS 1982, see Hasyim Djalal, *Perjuangan Indonesia di Bidang Hukum Laut* / the Struggle of Indonesia on Law of the Sea / (Bina Cipta, 1979).

[8] For the background of this Workshop see Hasyim Djalal,'Indonesia and the South China Sea Initiative,' *Ocean Development & International Law* 32, no. 2 (2001): 97–103.

[9] An interview between the author and Dr. Hasjim Djalal can be accessed through Youtube: Foreign Policy Tapes—Wawancara Prof. Hasjim Djalal tentang Laut Tiongkok Selatan / Interview with Prof. Hasjim Djalal on South China Sea/, FPCI, 12/06/2019. https://www.youtube.com/watch?v=f9Lh0DF5JtM. Accessed 29/06/ 2023.

[10] Internal Note, 29/05/2003, On file with author.

assume that Indonesia's EEZ was free from any claim incompatible with UNCLOS 1982.[11]

In this regard, Indonesia overlooked an important point that China attempted to hide, i.e. whether the 9DL constituted a claim over the Natuna waters, which was neither specifically raised by Alatas nor revealed by Qichen. It appeared through later developments that the Chinese view was always silent if not ambiguous and was designed to be that way. A prominent Chinese scholar revealed that any attempt to clarify the dashed line would only lead to an escalation.[12]

Notwithstanding such an ambiguous answer, Indonesia kept its policy as a non-party to the dispute and continued its diplomatic lawfare under its non-claimant position. Thus, Indonesia sent an *Aide Memoire* protesting China's legislation of 1999 that drew straight baselines in the Paracel Islands, stating that this was contrary to UNCLOS 1982.[13] The intervention was merely an expression of concern over China's attempt to apply inappropriately straight baselines and was not intended to engage as a party to the SCS dispute. Further, in response to the issuance of Chinese passports in 2012 that depicted the 9DL, and bearing in mind that no legal explanation of the 9DL has ever been provided, Indonesia sent a protesting note but remained convinced that the 9DL did not affect Indonesia's long-standing belief that no dispute actually existed with China in the SCS.[14]

In 2010, Chinese fishing vessels operating in the Natuna waters within the 9DL were arrested by Indonesia, but the issue was eventually resolved discreetly by the two countries. It appears that no "battle of *note verbale*" had taken place in addressing the standoff. The diplomatic row had been managed carefully amid President Yudoyono's foreign policy that underlined a principle of "zero enemies thousand friends.[15] As requested by China, the incident was not publicly exposed and was addressed with a "don't ask don't tell" approach, ending with the release of the vessels. In order to avoid further misunderstandings, the two Governments established a bilateral mechanism under the Memorandum of Understanding on Maritime Cooperation on 23 March 2012. The bilateral dialogue was not intended to deal with the ambiguous claim, but instead to cooperate while setting aside the unclear claim. Similar incidents continued to happen in 2013 and were resolved discreetly by releasing the illegal fishing vessels.[16]

---

[11] Simon Sinaga, 'No problem with China over Natuna Isles, says Alatas,' *the Straits Times*, 27/06/1995: 15.

[12] Fu Ying, Wu Shicun, South China Sea: How We Got to This Stage, Understanding the Source of the Tension, *The National Interest,* 09/05/2016. http://nationalinterest.org/feature/south-china-sea-how-we-got-stage-16118?page=show. Accessed 26/06/2023.

[13] Ministry of Foreign Affairs of the Republic of Indonesia, 16/07/1996, *Aide Memoire.* On file with Author.

[14] The traditional position of non-claimant assertion by Indonesia in the SCS conflict has been widely criticized by some observers as "pretending to have no dispute," see for example Bill Hayton, op cit, note 7: xvii.

[15] Aaron L. Connelly, 'Indonesian foreign policy under President Jokowi' Lowy Institute, 214, p. 2.

[16] *Supra* note 4, 625–626.

Indonesia's complacency over the 9DL has changed dramatically since President Jokowi took office in 2014, putting maritime policy high on the domestic agenda, with a hardliner Minister of Fisheries, Susi Pudjiastuti, in charge of legal enforcement in fishing activities. Minister Susi, with her uncompromising policy against IUU fishing, took strong measures when a similar incident occurred on 19 March 2016. Under her instruction, Indonesia arrested the Chinese fishing vessels and towed them to the nearest port. On the way to the port, a Chinese Coast Guard rammed the vessels and aborted the legal enforcement process. Unlike the previous administration, Minister Susi exposed the incident using megaphone diplomacy, summoned the Chinese Ambassador and sparked a real diplomatic row between the countries.[17]

From this point, Indonesia suspected that the 9DL was not merely an ambiguous line on a map but had already been manifested clearly on the ground. It has added a new dimension to Indonesia's foreign policy, in which Indonesia became aware that China had a real claim, although it remained ambiguous, in Indonesia's EEZ.[18] The bilateral battle of *notes verbales* has been developing into a more direct and confrontational approach since then. The response was followed by a diplomatic protest in strong terms by the Indonesian government and triggered an intensive exchange of official statements between the two countries.[19]

The protesting note is no longer directed to the 9DL as a general concept but already refers to the application of the 9DL on the ground i.e. the Natuna waters and specifically questioning the so-called "traditional Chinese fishing grounds". It is interesting to note that China did not reply to the protesting note. Instead, China made some media statements through its spokesperson from the Ministry of Foreign Affairs with a classic formula that "Indonesia has no territorial claims over China's Nansha Islands, and China fully agrees that the Natuna Islands belong to Indonesia."[20] China's response through public media instead of diplomatic channels is apparently intended to tone down the escalation of the conflict between the two countries and focus more on the "battle" in public media, which at that time were massive attacking China over the standoff.

A similar situation was repeated with an incident on 19 December 2019, when an Indonesian Coast Guard vessel detected 63 Chinese fishing vessels, escorted by Chinese Coast Guard vessels, conducting illegal fishing in Natuna waters. The standoff has been the most intense diplomatic row and put relations at their lowest

---

[17] The Diplomat, 'Indonesia Summons Chinese Ambassador After South China Sea Stand-Off Near Natuna Islands' 21/03/2016. https://thediplomat.com/2016/03/indonesia-summons-chinese-ambassador-after-south-china-sea-stand-off-near-natuna-islands/.

[18] Munmun Majumdar, 'Beijing Raising the Ante in the Natunas: The Next Flash Point in the South China Sea' *India Quarterly: A Journal of International Affairs* 77, no. 3 (2021): 4.

[19] Katie Hunt, 22/03/2016, *South China Sea: Indonesia issues protest to China,* CNN. https://edition.cnn.com/2016/03/21/asia/indonesia-china-south-china-sea/index.html. accessed 25/06/2023; *Diplomatic Protest Note,* 01/03/2016, Ministry of Foreign Affairs of Indonesia, on file with Author.

[20] Regular Press Briefing, 21 & 22/03/2016, Ministry of Foreign Affairs of the People's Republic of China. https://www.Fmprc.gov.cn/. Accessed 28/06/2023.

level.[21] Indonesia again launched a *notes verbales*[22] attack on China over the incident. It has been publicly stated that the *note verbale* was countered by China through diplomatic channels, which thus might include a replying *note verbale* from China.[23]

It appears that the battle of *notes verbales,* which is normally confidential has been echoed on air in public media. The row has been characterized by an exchange of harsh words between the respective spokespersons in a "battle" of media statements and public gestures. To begin with, China started with a smart approach by offering a bilateral dialogue for managing disputes properly.[24] Indonesia rejected the proposal out of hand stating that Indonesia has no overlapping claim with China in Natuna waters and referred to the SCS Tribunal Award[25] as confirming this view, saying that any dialogue on this issue was therefore irrelevant. Further, Indonesia again requested China to clarify the meaning of the 9DL.

This statement angered China and pushed it to raise a strong and high-tone reaction, stating that:

> Whether the Indonesian side accepts it or not, nothing will change the objective fact that China has rights and interests over the relevant waters. The so-called award of the South China Sea arbitration is illegal, null and void and we have long made it clear that China neither accepts nor recognizes it. The Chinese side firmly opposes any country, organization or individual using the invalid arbitration award to hurt China's interests.[26]

In this regard, China not only avoided giving any clarification on its rights and interests over the relevant waters, but also revealed its sensitivity when Indonesia made reference to the SCS Tribunal Award. In its response, Indonesia reacted more aggressively through a public gesture with the visit of President Jokowi to Natuna Island on 8 January 2022 as a symbolic challenge to China. China suddenly took down its harsh tone and pursued a persuasive attitude, drawing attention to the coming 70th anniversary of diplomatic ties between the two countries and indicating that the two countries have been in communication with each other through diplomatic channels regarding recent maritime developments.[27] The incident began to fade away when China fishing vessels slowly left the Natuna waters.

---

[21] Damos Dumoli Agusman and Citra Yuda Nur Fatihah, 'Celebrating the 25th Anniversary of UNCLOS Legal Perspective: The Natuna Case' (2020) *Indonesian Journal of International Law 17*, No. 4.

[22] Ministry of Foreign Affairs of the Republic of Indonesia, 01/01/2020, *Press Release.* https://kemlu.go.id/portal/id/read/933/siaran_pers/ri-kembali-tegaskan-tolak-klaim-unilateral-rrt-atas-zee-indonesia. Accessed 25/06/2023,

[23] Regular Press Briefing, 08/01/2020, Ministry of Foreign Affairs of the People's Republic of China. https://www.Fmprc.gov.cn/. Accessed 28/06/2023.

[24] Regular Press Briefing, 30/12/2019, Ministry of Foreign Affairs of the People's Republic of China. https://www.Fmprc.gov.cn/. Accessed 28/06/2023.

[25] Award of Arbitral Tribunal Constituted under Annex VII to the 1982 United Nations Convention on the Law of the Sea between the Philippines and China, 12/07/2016.

[26] Regular Press Briefing, 02/01/2020, Ministry of Foreign Affairs of the People's Republic of China. https://www.Fmprc.gov.cn/. Accessed 27/06/2023.

[27] Regular Press Briefing, 07/01/2020, Ministry of Foreign Affairs of the People's Republic of China. https://www.Fmprc.gov.cn/. Accessed 27/06/2023.

However, following this latest incident, the battlefield on the ground has changed. China seems to avoid any unnecessary escalation with Indonesia, knowing that such escalation would only provoke criticism from the world with respect to the 9DL and would invite a never-ending public debate questioning the 9DL. China was also aware that a confrontation with Indonesia would only open the door for unexpected involvement by outside powers. Apparently, no further incident has been reported since then. While the Chinese Coast Guard was still patrolling the waters to sustain the 9DL claim, no Chinese fishing vessel has been detected in the waters. Indonesia is likely to regard the movement of the Coast Guard vessels as enjoying freedom of navigation in its EEZ, and will only take enforcement measures when it involves fishing activities escorted by the Coast Guard vessels.

The persistent protests continued over a number of subsequent actions by China. Indonesia has lodged a solemn presentation about the issuance of the Coast Guard Law in 2020 and the Marine Transportation Law in 2021. The two legislations define Chinese jurisdiction in an ambiguous manner covering an area that assumingly falls within the 9DL.

Amid public criticism of the effectiveness of the protesting notes, it is argued that such a note carries its own legal merits. Indonesia is of the view that the persistent protests constitute a persistent objection under international law, which is aimed at preventing the 9DL from becoming embryonic and consolidated and serve as a legal basis for Indonesia to claim under international law that the claim does not and will never bind Indonesia.[28]

2.2 *Diplomatic Lawfare Under the UN CLCS*

As briefly explained above, the lawfare in the form of a battle of *notes verbales* under the UN CLCS over the SCS has taken place consecutively and separately in 2009/ 2011 and 2019. The former was triggered by the Joint Submission by Malaysia and Vietnam to the UN CLCS on 6 May 2009 and the latter was triggered by Malaysia's partial submission of its extended continental shelf on 12 December 2019.

Indonesia has joined the orchestra of the international community in both battles of note verbale exchanges with some claimant States and other States having interests in the SCS. In response to the 2009's submission, China submitted its reply note attaching a map for which Indonesia then raised a protesting note. Indonesia stated in the note that the 9DL has no basis in international law and features in the SCS cannot generate EEZ and continental shelves, encroaching the legitimate interest of the international community.[29]

[28] *Supra* note 3, 636–637.

[29] United Nations Commission on the Limits of the Continental Shelf (UN CLCS), 08/07/2010, Communication of the Republic of Indonesia. https://www.un.org/depts/los/clcs_new/submissions_files/mysvnm33_09/idn_2010re_mys_vnm_e.pdf. Accessed 28/06/2023.

The Natuna incidents explained above apparently prompted a significant role of Indonesia in the following "battle notes" in 2019/2020. The battle was triggered by Malaysia's partial submission to the same Commission on 12 December 2019. In this battle, Indonesia made specific reference to the SCS Tribunal as confirming its persistent objection to the 9DL. The move has been considered by Chinese observers as "a little trick" that attempted to take advantage of the SCS Tribunal case.[30] Hong Thao[31] however argued that:

> Indonesia's robust participation in the battle of the diplomatic notes 2020 arguably encourages other States as well as the Association of Southeast Asian Nations (ASEAN) to create a consistent position based on the UNCLOS as the sole legal basis for defining maritime entitlements and resolving maritime disputes in the SCS.

Interestingly, unlike the 2009/2010 *notes verbales,* the current "battle" involves other countries not bordering the SCS, such as Germany, France, Australia, Canada, the United Kingdom and New Zealand. They have raised concerns about freedom of navigation under UNCLOS and also the issue concerning maritime entitlement. The dispute may affect their interests under UNCLOS or at least negate the sanctity of the Convention.

Even the US, which is not a party to UNCLOS, has mingled in the battle. The procedural barrier as a non-party to UNCLOS did not prevent the US from getting on board with the others. Instead of addressing to the UN CLCS, which only parties could do, the US sent its Note to the UN Secretary-General and requested the latter to post the Note on the UN Website.[32]Although through a different channel, the message of the US regarding the issue reached its audience.

3 Some Legal Questions Clarified

The 2019 "battle of *notes verbales*" addresses wide-ranging issues and highlights two distinct aspects of the SCS dispute, i.e. the dispute concerning sovereignty over the features under general international law (title to features) on the one hand, and the claims over maritime zones therefrom which falls under the purview of UNCLOS (maritime entitlement) on the other hand.

The intersection between the two is nevertheless plausible. The determination of a feature (located beyond 12 nm from any high tide features) as a low tide elevation or as an underwater feature renders it as a feature not capable of sovereignty claim. The SCS Tribunal award has demonstrated this delicate point. By declaring that Mischief

[30] Hanping Cheng, 04/08/2020, Indonesia should make comprehensive considerations on the South China Sea. *Global Times*. https://www.globaltimes.cn/content/1196714.shtml. Accessed 28/06/2023.

[31] Nguyễn Hồng Thao,'South China Sea: Battle of the Diplomatic Notes among China and Non-Claimant States ' (2023) *Asia–Pacific Journal of Ocean Law and Policy* 8, 133–134.

[32] United States' Letter to the UN Secretary-General dated 01/07/2020 (GA SC Doc. A/74/874-S/2020/483).

Reef and Second Thomas Shoal are low tide elevation outside 12 nm from any high tide feature, they are thus not capable of appropriation.[33] Hence, both features shall be removed from the list of claimed features.[34]

The core issue in the SCS dispute is about sovereignty over features. Unfortunately, this core dispute has seemingly been dragged out of the picture since the public discourse is inadvertently focused more on other issues, i.e. maritime entitlements including "historic rights within nine dashed lines." The unnecessary mix-up between the two has led to public confusion. While the notes focus much on the latter, the distinction between the two is apparently duly taken.

3.1 Title to Features

Claimants have asserted their claim over features in the SCS. At this stage, claimants have yet to elaborate the basis for their respective claims. Until now, claimants merely assert that each has indisputable sovereignty over feature(s) in SCS. China and Vietnam assert that the claim is supported by abundant historical evidence.[35] Meanwhile, non-claimants exercise restraint on this issue by not taking sides.

Some States highlight that underwater features are not subject to sovereignty claims or not capable of appropriation. They fall under the sovereignty/sovereign rights of the coastal states in whose territorial sea/sovereign rights those features are located. Vietnam and New Zealand refer to these features as low-tide elevations or submerged features.[36] Meanwhile, the US points out features that have already been determined by the SCS Tribunal, like Mischief Reef and Second Thomas Shoal (low-tide elevations), or Macclesfield Bank or James Shoal (submerged features) and thus not subject to appropriation.[37] Furthermore, Australia expresses its concern in relation to China's claims of "continuously and effectively" exercising sovereignty over low-tide elevations.[38] This view should not be construed as taking sides with particular claimants since it applies to all.

Some related issues were also raised. China particularly reiterates its legal position that there is no territorial dispute between China and Indonesia in the SCS.[39] The Philippines addresses the competing claim with Malaysia over North Borneo (Sabah),

---

[33] *Supra* note 25, Para 1203, B, (4).

[34] Damos Dumoli Agusman, *The South China Sea UNCLOS Tribunal Award 2016: What It Has Changed and What It Does Mean to Indonesia,* Indonesian J. Int'l L., Vol. 14, 2017, 143.

[35] China's *Note Verbale* No. CML/8/2011, CML/11/2020; *Vietnam's* Note Verbale No. 77/HC-2011, No. 22/HC-2020.

[36] *Supra* note 35, No. 22/HC-2020.

[37] *Supra* note 32.

[38] Australia's *Note Verbale* No. 20/026.

[39] China's *Note Verbale* No. CML/46/2020.

which was also raised in 2009's battle, arguing that it has never relinquished its sovereignty.[40]

3.2 Maritime Entitlements

On maritime entitlements, all States (except China) unanimously and explicitly agree on the illegality of the nine-dash line or any other claims made by China in contravention of UNCLOS.

Vietnam states that UNCLOS "provides the sole legal basis" to define the maritime entitlements in the SCS, and thus opposes any maritime claims that exceed the permitted range under the Convention[41] or in Malaysia's wording "exceeds the geographic and substantive limits of maritime entitlement under the Convention."[42]

Most states make reference to the SCS Tribunal award. The Philippines states that the tribunal has "conclusively settled the issue of historic rights and maritime entitlements."[43] The US,[44] Australia,[45] and New Zealand[46] amplify the award saying that the historic rights claim exceeds the permitted limit under international law as reflected in the Convention.Indonesia has objected to the claim of historic rights ever since the claim became known to it in the 1990s, and in this battle has borrowed the SCS Tribunal award's wording: "should there be any historic rights existing prior to the entry into force of UNCLOS, those rights were superseded by the provisions of UNCLOS."

Apart from the *historic rights* argument, China officially brought to the table its argument on offshore/continental archipelagos, which had been introduced before in some Chinese scholarly works.[47] In responding to the protests by Australia, the United Kingdom, Germany and France[48] on the application of straight baseline and archipelagic baseline in SCS, China argues that UNCLOS does not cover everything about the maritime order, and matters not so regulated continue to be governed by the rules and principles of general international law. China then concludes that the drawing of such baselines conforms to the UNCLOS and general international law.

[40] Philippine's *Note Verbale* No. 000819–2009, No. 000192–2020, No. 0929–2020; Malaysia's *Note Verbale* No. HA 41/09, No. 30/20.

[41] *Supra* note 35, No. 22/HC-2020. Under the Vietnam chairmanship of ASEAN, the role of UNCLOS 1982 has been endorsed in the Chairman Statement of ASEAN Foreign Ministers' Retreat, 01/2020 and thereafter in the 36th ASEAN Summit, 26/06/2020.

[42] Malaysia's *Note Verbale* No. HA 26/20.

[43] Philippine's *Note Verbale* No. 000191–2020.

[44] *Supra* note 32.

[45] *Supra* note 38.

[46] New Zealand's *Note Verbale* No. 08/21/02.

[47] Recent work see, Nong Hong, *Archipelagic Regime in the South China Sea: A Debate on the Rights of Continental States' Outlying Archipelagos,* Ocean Year Book 32, 2018.

[48] France, Germany, and UK's Joint *Note Verbale* No. 162/20 (UK), 2020–0,343,647 (France), 324/ 2020 (Germany).

On this particular issue, most States reject the drawing of archipelagic baselines in the SCS by emphasizing the specific and exhaustive conditions set forth in the Convention for the application of straight and archipelagic baselines which, according to the SCS Tribunal,[49] excludes the possibility of employing them in other circumstances.

Most states impose legal restrictions on features for their maritime entitlements, by emphasizing that no features in Spratly are capable of generating a continental shelf or an exclusive economic zone. Indonesia reiterates its position on the maritime status of the features that have already been stipulated in the *note verbale* of 2010 and adds reference to the SCS Tribunal award that confirms Indonesia's claim to this effect.[50] The emphasis on the maritime status of the features in the current battle is a new development, since none of the claimant States made an explicit statement on the matter during the 2009-2010's battle. Only Indonesia addressed the issue in the previous battle, arguing that features in the SCS could not have a continental shelf or exclusive economic zone on their own. Interestingly, after the SCS Tribunal award, while not making explicit reference to the award, Vietnam and Malaysia's statements mirror its substance. Referring to Article 121 (3) UNCLOS, Vietnam asserts that features in the SCS fall under the provision of that article.[51]

4 The Future of the South China Sea Dispute

The battle of *notes verbales* may continue in the foreseeable future. The SCS Tribunal award has stimulated the proliferation of legal clarification after being silent in the past. In this "battle", most claimants have indicated, if not disclosed, their newly clarified legal position pertaining to their claims in an official manner and in the public domain.

While the "battle" is not by itself ending the dispute, the significant role of the legal exchanges however should not be underestimated. The notes at least have successfully clarified the dispute, put the distinct elements in a proper setting, and gradually removed the conundrum. It is expected that transparency and clarification of the respective claims will enable those involved to understand the gap between their respective legal stances. In turn, this would make it easier for them to move forward for a peaceful settlement.

Some legal issues have been significantly clarified through these *notes verbales,* such as the maritime status of some features. Except for China, all claimants, supported by non-claimants involved in the battle, confirm the SCS Tribunal findings that none of the features met the criteria for "islands," and thus none of them is entitled to an exclusive economic zone or continental shelf. This clarified legal

[49] Para 575, Award of SCS Arbitral Tribunal 2016.

[50] Indonesia's *Notes Verbales* No. 126/POL-703/V/20 dated 26/05/2020 and No. 148/POL-703/VI/20.

[51] *Supra* note 35, No. 22/HC-2020.

position has resolved some puzzles concerning maritime entitlements that could be claimed by the claimants. They are no longer bothered with the question of whether there is any overlapping claim over an exclusive economic zone or continental shelf derived from the features, since none of them is entitled. They may now concentrate on the question of title to the high tide features, i.e. on the question of "which feature belongs to whom."

The position revealed by the claimants in the battle has also removed uncertainty for non-claimants in the SCS such as Indonesia. Before, it was unclear to Indonesia whether the Cuarteroon Reef, the nearest feature to Indonesia's Natuna island (about 377 Nm from the feature), was an island entitled to a 200 Nm maritime zone. The Tribunal finds that the Reef is a rock that is not entitled to a 200 Nm maritime zone and thus cannot overlap waters within the Natuna maritime zone. It would mean that no matter who will own the feature, it will not constitute an overlapping claim over maritime zones with Indonesia. It is not surprising to observe that Indonesia has flatly rejected China's proposal to open negotiations over what China defines as "overlapping maritime rights and interests in Natuna waters."[52] On the other hand, Vietnam, which claims the Cuarteroon Reef, has shown a gesture that it would respect the maritime status of the Reef as having no entitlement to 200 Nm. It turns out that Vietnam does not use the Reef as a basepoint to project its maritime entitlement viz. a viz. Indonesia.[53]

The clarified points resulting from the battle have also removed some doubts with regard to the position of third parties in the dispute. It has been China's long-standing view that the SCS dispute is between claimants only and the others should be neutral and restrained from taking sides in the dispute. Most third parties adhere to this neutrality when it comes to the dispute over ownership of the features. A neutral stance is no longer required with respect to some features that have been removed from the "disputed box," i.e. Mischief Reef and Second Thomas Shoal. Both features have been determined by the SCS Tribunal and confirmed by most claimants as low-tide elevations not capable of appropriation. They are therefore within the exclusive economic zone and continental shelf of (and automatically belong to) the Philippines.

This maritime status of both features is valid *erga omnes* in the sense that other states are bound to that legal determination and are not allowed to regard them otherwise. The US support to the Philippines in the standoff with China over Second Thomas Shoals throughout 2023 is based on a conviction that the US "interference"[54] should not (any longer) be considered as taking a side to the dispute, as the dispute over the Reef does not exist.[55] The same belief that such "interference" over Second

[52] Benar News, Indonesia Rejects Beijing's Offer for South China Sea Talks, 06/05/2020. https://www.benarnews.org/english/news/indonesian/no-negotiation-06052020155450.html.

[53] *Agreement* between Indonesia and Vietnam on Continental Shelf, 26/06/2003. https://treaties.un.org/doc/publication/unts/no%20volume/part/i-44165.pdf.

[54] US Department of State Press Statement, 10/11/2023, "U.S. Support for the Philippines in the South China Sea." https://www.state.gov/u-s-support-for-the-philippines-in-the-south-china-sea-6/.

[55] Pham Ngoc Minh Trang, 'Second Thomas Shoal, A Legal Perspective, Asia Maritime Transparency Initiative, 23/01/2024. https://amti.csis.org/second-thomas-shoal-a-legal-perspective/.

Thomas Shoals does not constitute "taking side" has been held by many States. Some other States such as the European Union, the UK, Germany, Australia, and Japan have issued statements accusing China of violating international law over the standoff. ASEAN Member States, while issuing a statement of concern over the tension, apparently have raised no reservations towards the US involvement in the region, as they normally had in the past. It demonstrates that the standoff is no longer a dispute over title to territory but has already constituted a violation of the maritime rights of the Philippines by China, to which the third parties are obliged to respond accordingly.

The clarified legal stances of claimants might help the negotiators in the ongoing negotiation of the code of conduct (COC) in the South China Sea to identify legal challenges that lie ahead. The negotiators shall be guided by the already-clarified map regarding the maritime status of the features and their entitlement. Consequently, the quest for defining the geographical scope of the application of the COC becomes a pivotal issue in the upcoming negotiations. The position of ASEAN and China would be mutually negated on this issue. China will inevitably not agree with the geographical scope as defined by the SCS Tribunal, in which the 9DL shall be ignored. Contrary to China's standpoint, ASEAN could not accept any geographical scope that implied the validity of the 9DL. The negotiators might avoid this delicate issue and will be compelled to accept the COC, which would be silent on the scope. This kind of approach might help ASEAN's and China's diplomats to escape from the dilemma but the unclear scope of application would only complicate the application of the COC on the ground.

5 Conclusion

While the battle will not end with any solution to the conflict, it will provide valuable insights into the legal position of the countries concerned and are a useful source in sorting out the positions of certain claimant States. Some legal clarifications might be derived from this exercise as follows:

First, the legal question of title to features becomes clear. While only claimants can solve it, the maritime status of the features can only be determined by the provisions of UNCLOS. It therefore paves the way for claimants to publicly (re)state which features they claim accordingly.

Second, on maritime entitlements, most claimants apparently reject the "historic rights" claim. They also generally agree that no feature in Spratly could generate a 200 nm maritime zone. Thus, the remaining issue among them is only concerning maritime delimitation projected from their mainland rather than from the disputed features. The delimitation between disputed features, if any, could only be carried out after their sovereignty status is determined.

The positions of most claimants deriving from the battle have significantly convinced Indonesia that it has no dispute with any claimant in the SCS. The current battle has confirmed the longstanding position of Indonesia against China's ambiguous claim over Natuna waters. The battle of *notes verbales* between Indonesia and China will continue with stronger support from the other claimants as well as the international community.

The position of the third parties not involved in the dispute is becoming clear. Some features have been clarified as low tide elevations forming part of an exclusive economic zone of a claimant. In this regard, the third parties will no longer be anxious about being accused of taking sides by China if they make a response that supports the States that are entitled to the zone. The rest of the features are clarified as having only a 12 Nm territorial sea. The maritime zones in the SCS are therefore becoming clear as nothing but high seas, economic exclusive zone and territorial seas, and thus provide legal certainty for the user States in enjoying freedom of navigation in relevant waters.

* * *

Chapter 12
State Jurisdiction Over Submarine Pipelines: Southeast Asian Practice from the Relevant Provisions of National Laws

Hai Dang Vu

1 Introduction

Pursuant to the United Nations Convention on the Law of the Sea (UNCLOS), 1982,[1] the jurisdiction of the coastal State over activities relating to submarine pipelines depends on which maritime zones these pipelines are located: territorial seas, archipelagic waters, exclusive economic zone or continental shelf. In territorial seas, in principle, the coastal State has 'sovereignty so all activities by other States to be undertaken in this area must have its agreement.[2] Other States can have the right to innocent passage[3] but they must respect the coastal State's laws and regulations adopted in conformity with UNCLOS relating to innocent passage in respect of, *inter alia*, the protection of pipelines.[4] The coastal State's sovereignty, in case where it is an archipelagic State,[5] also extends to archipelagic waters.[6] While an archipelagic State must respect existing submarine cables laid by other States and passing through its waters without making a landfall, a similar obligation does not exist for submarine

H. D. Vu (✉)
Diplomatic Academy of Viet Nam, Hanoi, Vietnam
e-mail: vuhaidang@dav.edu.vn

[1] United Nations Convention on the Law of the Sea, 10 December 1982, 1833 U.N.T.S. 3.

[2] United Nations Convention on the Law of the Sea, 10 December 1982, 1833 U.N.T.S. 3, Art. 2(1).

[3] United Nations Convention on the Law of the Sea, 10 December 1982, 1833 U.N.T.S. 3, Art. 17.

[4] United Nations Convention on the Law of the Sea, 10 December 1982, 1833 U.N.T.S. 3, Art. 21(1)(c).

[5] United Nations Convention on the Law of the Sea, 10 December 1982, 1833 U.N.T.S. 3, Art. 46(a).

[6] United Nations Convention on the Law of the Sea, 10 December 1982, 1833 U.N.T.S. 3, Art. 49(1).

L. A. T. Nguyen and H. D. Vu (eds.), *Viability of UNCLOS amid Emerging Global Maritime Challenges*, https://doi.org/10.1007/978-981-97-5838-8_4

pipelines.[7] In the exclusive economic zone and continental shelf, there is the freedom of laying submarine pipelines.[8] It was argued that this freedom covers not only the act of laying but also supporting, maintenance and repair activities.[9] However, in the continental shelf, the consent of the coastal State is required for the delineation of the course for the laying of submarine pipelines. When laying these pipelines, other States must have due regard to cables and pipelines already in position, not prejudicing possibilities of repairing them. At the same time, coastal States may not impede the laying or maintenance of submarine pipelines while undertaking activities to explore and exploit resources and to deal with pollution from pipelines.[10]

This chapter evaluates the practice of Southeast Asia in adopting domestic regulations relating to coastal State's jurisdiction over submarine pipelines. It does so by reviewing relevant provisions in legislations adopted by nine coastal ASEAN Member States and how they apply to submarine pipelines. The States to be reviewed are: Brunei, Cambodia, Indonesia, Malaysia, Myanmar, Philippines, Singapore, Thailand and Vietnam. It then provides an overall evaluation of the regional practice to see how the jurisdiction over submarine pipelines in the region is regulated by national laws.

2 Brunei

Legal provisions relating to jurisdiction over submarine pipelines in Brunei are provided in legislations relating to maritime jurisdiction and petroleum pipelines.

2.1 Maritime Jurisdiction Legislation

The coastal State jurisdiction of Brunei is stipulated in the Exclusive Economic Zone Proclamation, 1993.[11] In principle, Brunei claims a 12-nautical mile territorial sea, a 200-nauticale mile exclusive economic zone and a continental shelf of at least 200 nautical miles.[12] Pursuant to the Exclusive Economic Zone Proclamation,

---

[7] United Nations Convention on the Law of the Sea, 10 December 1982, 1833 U.N.T.S. 3, Art. 51(5).

[8] United Nations Convention on the Law of the Sea, 10 December 1982, 1833 U.N.T.S. 3, Arts 58(1) and 79(1).

[9] Hai Dang Vu, "Improving the Freedom of Repairing Telecommunication Submarine Cables in Southeast Asia: Next Steps for ASEAN" Asia–Pacific Journal of Ocean Law and Policy 6 (2021): pp.66–93 at 71.

[10] United Nations Convention on the Law of the Sea, 10 December 1982, 1833 U.N.T.S. 3, Art. 79 (2), (4) and (5).

[11] Exclusive Economic Zone Proclamation, 20 July 1993.

[12] For details about Brunei maritime claims, see Brunei's Continental Shelf Proclamation 30 June 1954, Brunei's Continental Shelf Proclamation 30 June 1954, The North Borneo (Definition of

Brunei exercises sovereign rights for the exploration, exploitation, conservation, and management of the resources and jurisdiction with regard to the establishment and use of artificial islands, installations and structures, authorization, and control of marine scientific research. It also states that the rights and jurisdiction that Brunei claims in this Proclamation do not go beyond what is permitted under the international law.[13]

2.2 Legislation Relating to Petroleum Pipeline

Regulations relating to petroleum pipeline in Brunei are provided in the Petroleum Pipeline Act, 1951.[14] In the Act, "pipeline" means pipeline used or intended to be used for conveying petroleum or the products of petroleum in bulk from a place of main storage to a point of distribution or a point of export from Brunei Darussalam. The same definition is adopted for "pipe".[15] Any person wants to use, lay or connect on any land in Brunei any pipes must apply for a permission from the Minister of Energy and Industry.[16]

2.3 Application to Jurisdiction Over Submarine Pipelines

The laying of oil submarine pipelines in the territorial seas, exclusive economic zone and continental shelf of Brunei needs permission from the Minister of Energy and Industry. The application for such a permission is accompanied by a plan of the lands showing, among other things, the course and direction of the pipeline and the position of any pumping station, tanks or other works in connection with it.[17]

3 Cambodia

Provisions relating to jurisdiction over submarine pipelines in Cambodia are found in legislation on maritime jurisdiction and petroleum.

Boundaries) Order in Council, No.1517, 11 September 1958, Sarawak (Definition of Boundaries) Order in Council No. 1518, 11 September 1958, Territorial Waters of Brunei Act, An Act to Declare the Limits of the Territorial Waters of Brunei Darussalam (10 February 1983) and Brunei's Exclusive Economic Zone Proclamation 20 July 1993.

[13] Exclusive Economic Zone Proclamation, 20 July 1993, Art.7.

[14] Brunei Petroleum Pipeline Act 2 of 1920, Chapter 45 of 1951.

[15] Brunei Petroleum Pipeline Act 2 of 1920, Chapter 45 of 1951, S2.

[16] Brunei Petroleum Pipeline Act 2 of 1920, Chapter 45 of 1951, S3.

[17] Brunei Petroleum Pipeline Act 2 of 1920, Chapter 45 of 1951, S3.

3.1 *Maritime Jurisdiction Legislation*

The nature of maritime entitlement claimed by Cambodia is determined mainly in the Statement issued by the Spokesman of the Ministry of Foreign Affairs on 15 January 1978[18] and the Decree of the Council of State of 1982, which determined different maritime zones of Cambodia and their status.[19] Pursuant to the Statement of the Spokesman of the Ministry of Foreign Affairs, 1978, Cambodia claims full and entire sovereignty over the territorial sea, exclusive sovereign rights for the purpose of exploring, exploiting, conserving and managing all natural resources in an exclusive economic zone. Cambodia also claims sovereign rights over the continental shelf for the purpose of exploring, exploiting, conserving and managing all natural resources of the seabed and subsoil.[20]

The Decree of the Council of State, 1982 further details the rights of Cambodia and third States in these maritime zones. For instance, pursuant to the Decree, in its exclusive economic zone, Cambodia has exclusive jurisdiction regarding the setting up and use of installations, devices and artificial island and marine research. In its continental shelf, Cambodia has the exclusive right to regulate the setting up and use of installations, devices and artificial islands or drilling on its continental shelf. All activities carried out by foreigners on the continental shelf, for whatever end, must be the object of authorization or an agreement by the Cambodian government.[21]

3.2 *Petroleum Legislation*

The management of activities relating to the exploitation of petroleum resources is provided in the Petroleum Law of Cambodia, 2019.[22] Pursuant to the Law, petroleum activity in Cambodia could be divided into upstream and downstream activities. The upstream activity is defined as the prospecting, exploration, development and production of petroleum. The downstream activity refers to the treatment, transportation, and storage of petroleum and petroleum products, except for the sale and exportation of petroleum in accordance with a petroleum agreement. For exploration, development, and production of petroleum, they must enter into a Petroleum Agreement with the Minister of Mines and Energy (MIME) with prior permission from the Prime Minister. For downstream activity, they must have a license or letter of permission

---

[18] Statement of the Spokesman of the Ministry of Foreign Affairs of the Democratic Kampuchea of 15 January 1978.

[19] Decree of the Council of State of the People's Republic of Kampuchea of 13 July 1982.

[20] Statement of the Spokesman of the Ministry of Foreign Affairs of the Democratic Kampuchea of 15 January 1978, ss1-3.

[21] Decree of the Council of State of the People's Republic of Kampuchea of 13 July 1982, Art.6.

[22] Law on Management of Petroleum and Petroleum Products (Petroleum Law) adopted by the National Assembly on 12 July 2019.

from MIME. They must also have a Certificate of Technical Safety before starting to construct the infrastructure.[23]

3.3 Application to Submarine Pipelines

Thus, the laying of oil submarine pipelines requires, depending on whether they are connected with upstream or downstream petroleum activities, the signature of an agreement with or permission from MIME. Both natural persons and legal entities, including foreign commercial companies operating their business activities in Cambodia, can participate in the petroleum activity.[24]

4 Indonesia

Provisions relating to jurisdiction over submarine pipelines in Indonesia are found in legislation on maritime jurisdiction and oil and gas pipelines.

4.1 Maritime Jurisdiction Legislation

The rights and duties of Indonesia and other States in the former's maritime zones are stipulated in the Law No. 6 of 1996 on Indonesia Waters,[25] Law No. 1 of 1973 on Continental Shelf[26] and Law No. 5 of 1983 on Exclusive Economic Zone.[27] Indonesia claims sovereignty over Indonesian waters (which includes inland waters, 12-nautical mile territorial waters and archipelagic waters),[28] a 200-nautical mile exclusive economic zone,[29] and a continental shelf extending to a depth of minimum 200 m.[30]

---

[23] BNG Legal, *Petroleum Law in Cambodia*, Newsletter (May 2020) online: BNG Legal <https://bnglegal.com/wp-content/uploads/2020/05/200522-Email-newsletter-Petroleum-Law-In-Cambodia.pdf> .

[24] BNG Legal, *Petroleum Law in Cambodia*, Newsletter (May 2020) online: BNG Legal <https://bnglegal.com/wp-content/uploads/2020/05/200522-Email-newsletter-Petroleum-Law-In-Cambodia.pdf> .

[25] Indonesia's Law no.6, 8 August 1996, on Indonesian Waters.

[26] Indonesia's Law No.1 of 1973 on Indonesia Continental Shelf.

[27] Indonesia's Law No.5 of 18 October 1983 on Indonesian Exclusive Economic Zone.

[28] See Indonesia's Law no.6, 8 August 1996, on Indonesian Waters, Art. 3. Art. 3 also defines inland waters as "all waters located on the land side of the low water line from the coasts of Indonesia" and archipelagic waters as "all the waters located on the innerside of the straight basic line of the archipelago without regard to the depth or the distance from the coast".

[29] Indonesia's Law No.5 of 18 October 1983 on Indonesian Exclusive Economic Zone.

[30] Indonesia's Law No.1 of 1973 on Indonesia Continental Shelf.

Pursuant to Law No. 6 of 1996 on Indonesia Waters, Indonesia has sovereignty over Indonesia waters, sea area and land underneath.[31] Law No. 1 of 1973 on Continental Shelf provides that the laws and regulations of Indonesia also apply to the construction, maintenance and use of installations and equipment on the continental shelf.[32] Law No. 5 of 1983 on Exclusive Economic Zone stipulates that Indonesia exercises jurisdiction over the construction and use of artificial islands, installations and other structures in its exclusive economic zone.[33] The freedom of laying submarine pipelines shall be respected in accordance with the principles of the international law of the sea.[34]

4.2 Oil and Gas Pipeline Legislation

Regulations relating to oil and gas pipelines in Indonesia are found in the Law on Petroleum and Natural Gas, 2001 and Government's Regulation on Oil and Gas, 2004, and the Minister of Energy and Mineral Resources' Regulation regarding Natural Business through Pipelines, 2009.[35] Pursuant to the Law on Petroleum and Natural Gas, which has its territorial scope limited to the territory of Indonesia,[36] pipelines are used both in the transport and commerce of oil and gas.[37] Government's Regulations on Petroleum and Natural Gas, 2001 stipulates that the corporate body that operates the business of transportation of oil, gas, oil fuel, gas fuel and/or processing output must have a transportation business license from the Minister of Energy and Mineral Resources.[38] Minister of Energy and Mineral Resources' Regulation regarding Natural Gas Business through Pipelines provides that natural gas

[31] Indonesia's Law no.6, 8 August 1996, on Indonesian Waters, Art.4.

[32] Indonesia's Law No.1 of 1973 on Indonesia Continental Shelf, Art.6.

[33] Indonesia's Law No.5 of 18 October 1983 on Indonesian Exclusive Economic Zone, arts 2 and 4.

[34] *Ibid.* note 38, art. 4(3).

[35] Law No.22/2001 Dated 23 November 2021 on Petroleum and Natural Gas; Government's Regulation No.36/2004 on Oil and Gas Downstream Business (14 October 2004); Minister of Energy and Mineral Resources Regulation No.19/2009 regarding Natural Gas Business through Pipelines.

[36] Law No.22/2001 Dated 23 November 2021 on Petroleum and Natural Gas, Art. 8(2) stipulates that the government shall guarantee the availability and smooth distribution of fuel oil being a vital commodity and controlling the life of public at large throughout the territory of Indonesia and Art. 46(2), the regulating agency shall function to regulate so that the supply and distribution of fuel oil and natural gas stipulated by the government can be guaranteed throughout the territory of Indonesia.

[37] Pursuant to Article 1(12) and (14) of the Law, transport are activities to move petroleum, natural gas and/or their processed products from the working area or storage and processing places, including the transport of natural gas through transmission and distribution pipeline and commerce, activities to purchase, sell, export and import petroleum, natural gas and/or their processed products, including commerce of natural gas through pipeline.

[38] Regulation No.36/2004 on Oil and Gas Downstream Business (14 October 2004), Art.26.

transportation business activities through pipes are carried out by a business entity after obtaining a business permit for the transportation of natural gas by pipe.[39]

4.3 Application to Submarine Pipelines

Indonesia requires a license or permit from the Minister of Energy and Mineral Resources for laying oil and gas submarine pipelines in its territorial sea and archipelagic waters but not in the exclusive economic zone and continental shelf. The land rights to construct oil and natural gas transportation pipelines will generally be obtained by negotiating with owners and occupiers.[40]

5 Malaysia

Provisions relating to jurisdiction over submarine pipelines in Malaysia are found in legislation on maritime jurisdiction and transportation of petroleum by pipelines.

5.1 Maritime Jurisdiction Legislation

Maritime jurisdiction legislation of Malaysia includes the Territorial Act, 2012, Continental Shelf Act, 1966 and Exclusive Economic Zone Act, 1984. Malaysia claims 12-nautical mile territorial sea, 200-nautical mile exclusive economic zone and a continental shelf of at least 200 nautical miles.[41] Pursuant to the Territorial Act, the sovereignty in respect of the territorial sea, its bed and subsoil, is vested in and excisable by the Yang di-Pertuan Agong (King) in right of Malaysia.[42] The Continental Shelf Act provides that activities to explore, prospect, bore for or carry on any operations for the getting of petroleum and minerals in the seabed or subsoil of the continental shelf will need a license from the Federal Government.[43] Pursuant to the Exclusive Economic Zone Act, no person shall lay submarine pipelines in the exclusive economic zone or on the continental shelf without the consent of the Malaysian

[39] Indonesia's Minister of Energy and Mineral Resources Regulation No.19/2009 regarding Natural Gas Business through Pipelines, Art.15.

[40] Fitriana Mahiddin, Syahdan Z. Aziz & Aninda Nurul Savitri, "Indonesia" in International Comparative Legal Guides, Oil and Gas Regulation 2021: A Practical Cross-Border Insight into Oil and Gas Regulation Work, 16th Ed., Ch.10.

[41] Territorial Sea Act, Act 750 of 2012; Continental Shelf Act, Act No. 57 of 28 July 1966, as Amended by Act No. 83 of 1972 and Act No. A351 of 2009, and Exclusive Economic Zone Act, Act No.311 of 31 December 1984 as amended by Act A1277 (1 May 2007) of 2006.

[42] Territorial Sea Act, Act 750 of 2012, s4.

[43] The Continental Shelf Act, 1966, ss3&4.

government as to the delineation of the course for laying such pipelines. Besides, the government may impose conditions for the maintenance of such pipelines in the exercise of its right to take reasonable measures for the exploration of the continental shelf, the exploitation of natural resources and the prevention, reduction and control of pollution from such pipelines.[44]

5.2 Legislation Relating to Transportation of Petroleum by Pipelines

The transportation of petroleum by pipelines in Malaysia is regulated by the Petroleum (Safety Measures) Act, 1984 and the Petroleum (Safety Measures) (Transportation of Petroleum by Pipelines) Regulations, 1985. The Petroleum (Safety Measures) Act, 1984 provides for the safety in the transportation, storage and utilization of petroleum. The Act defines "pipelines" as all parts of physical facilities through which petroleum moves in transportation including pipes, valves and other appurtenances attached to pipes, pumps, compressor units, meters, regulators and fabricated assemblies. "Pipeline works" refer to placing the pipeline or a length of pipeline, inspection, maintaining, adjusting, repairing, altering or renewing a pipeline or a length of pipeline; changing the position of a pipeline or a length of pipeline, or removing a pipeline or a length of pipeline onshore or offshore. Transportation means the action of taking petroleum from any place or vessel to any other place or vessel by any means or mode of transportation, including conveyance by pipelines offshore underwater.[45] Pursuant to the Act, any person who wants to undertake any pipeline works, including underwater in offshore areas must have an authorization granted by the Minister in charge of petroleum.[46] The Petroleum (Safety Measures) (Transportation of Petroleum by Pipelines) Regulations, 1985 further requires that any person who wants to operate any pipeline must obtain a written permission from the approving Authority.

5.3 Application to Submarine Pipelines

The laying of oil submarine pipelines in territorial sea, exclusive economic zone and continental shelf of Malaysia requires written authorization from the Minister in charge of petroleum. A permission from the approving Authority is further required for the operation of pipeline. To obtain the permission, this person must submit that the design, fabrication, installation, testing and the safety aspect of the operation and

[44] *Ibid.* note 58, Sect. 22.

[45] Malaysia Petroleum (Safety Measures) Act 1984, No. 302, S1.

[46] Malaysia Petroleum (Safety Measures) Act 1984, No. 302, S16.

maintenance of petroleum and gas pipeline shall meet the requirements of the American National Standard Institute Code for Liquid Petroleum Transportation Piping System ANSI/ASME B 31.4 or Pressure Piping Gas Transmission and Distribution Piping System ANSI/ASMEB 31.8.[47]

6 Myanmar

Provisions relating to jurisdiction over submarine pipelines in Myanmar are found in legislation on maritime jurisdiction and petroleum.

6.1 Maritime Jurisdiction Legislation

The Myanmar Territorial Sea and Maritime Zones Law provides the legal regime for Myanmar maritime zones. Pursuant to the Law, Myanmar claims 12 nautical mile territorial sea, 200 nautical mile exclusive economic zone and continental shelf up to the outer edge of the continental margin.[48] In its territorial seas, Myanmar has sovereignty, which also extends to the seabed, subsoil and airspace.[49] In its exclusive economic zone, Myanmar has the sovereign rights and authority for exploring, exploiting, conserving and managing the natural resources on the seabed and its subsoil, the waters superjacent to the seabed and the water level in the exclusive economic zone.[50] In its continental shelf, Myanmar has the sovereign right and jurisdiction over the conservation and protection of the marine environment, and reduction, prevention and control of marine pollution due to submarine cables, pipelines and its related facilities and underground tunnelling.[51] With regards to the rights and freedoms of other States in these areas, the Law states that in the exclusive economic zone, all States may enjoy the right of freedom of laying of submarine pipelines and its related facilities.[52] However, the Law also requires prior permission from the Myanmar government for excavating or drilling for any purpose in the exclusive economic zone as well as searching, excavating or drilling for any purpose and extending or maintaining submarine pipelines in the continental shelf.[53]

[47] Malaysia Petroleum (Safety Measures) (Transportation of Petroleum by Pipelines) Regulations 1985, SS5-6.

[48] Myanmar Territorial Sea and Maritime Zones Law, 4, 19, and 23.

[49] Myanmar Territorial Sea and Maritime Zones Law, 5.

[50] *Ibid.* note 49, Chapter V.

[51] *Ibid.* note 49, Chapter VI.

[52] *Ibid.* note 49, Chapter VI (21).

[53] *Ibid.* note 49, Chapter X 31(d) & 32(d).

6.2 Petroleum and Petroleum Product Law

Myanmar's Petroleum and Petroleum Production Law, 2017 provides regulations for the implementation of petroleum and petroleum product business activities. Pursuant to the Law, any person who wants to carry out petroleum and petroleum product business activities[54] must apply for a license. The license relating to the refining, transit and transport of petroleum and petroleum products by pipelines is to be issued by the Ministry of Commerce.[55]

6.3 Application to Submarine Pipelines

Myanmar requires license from the Ministry of Commerce for the refining, transit and transport of petroleum and petroleum products by pipelines. The Ministry shall determine the period, form, conditions and means of applying license, permitting authority and fees to be assessed for licenses.[56]

7 The Philippines

Provisions relating to jurisdiction over submarine pipelines in the Philippines are found in legislation relating to maritime jurisdiction and petroleum.

[54] Under the Petroleum and Petroleum Production Law, petroleum and petroleum product business activities mean the business activity of import, export, transport, transit, storage, possession, refining, sale and distribution, inspection and testing of petroleum and petroleum products, see The Petroleum and Petroleum Product Law, The Pyidaungsu Hluttaw Law No. 20, 2017, 1st August 2017, 2(f).

[55] The Petroleum and Petroleum Product Law, The Pyidaungsu Hluttaw Law No. 20, 2017, 1st August 2017, 8 & 30.

[56] The Petroleum and Petroleum Product Law, The Pyidaungsu Hluttaw Law No. 20, 2017, 1st August 2017, 8 & 30.

7.1 Maritime Jurisdiction Legislation

The Philippines claims inland waters, territorial seas based on a straight archipelagic baseline,[57] continental shelf[58] and a 200 nautical mile exclusive economic zone.[59] The Presidential Decree of No.1599 of 1978 establishing an Exclusive Economic Zone and for other purposes, it stipulates that in its exclusive economic zone, the Philippines has the sovereignty rights for the purpose of exploration and exploitation, conservation and management of the natural resources.[60] With regards to the rights and freedoms of other states in the exclusive economic zone, the Presidential Decree of 1978 recognizes that other states enjoy the freedom with respect to the laying of submarine pipelines.[61] However, no person shall carry out any search, research, excavation or drilling operations nor construct, maintain and operate any artificial island, offshore terminal, installation or other structure or device without agreement with or license granted by the Philippines.[62]

7.2 Petroleum Legislation

The development of petroleum resources in the Philippines is regulated by the Republic Act no. 387, the Petroleum Act of 1949.[63] Pursuant to the Act, a pipeline concession is needed to provide and operate pipeline systems for transporting petroleum in the territory of the Philippines.[64] The granting of a pipeline concession is obligatory upon the Government to the holder of an exploitation concession[65] when the manufacturing or transportation is directly related to the exploitation concession.

[57] Republic Act No. 9522, 10 March 2009, An Act to Amend Certain Provisions of Republic Act No. 3046, as Amended by Republic Act No. 5446, to Define the Archipelagic Baseline of the Philippines and for Other Purposes. All waters within this baseline are considered inland or internal waters.

[58] Presidential Proclamation No.370 of 20 March 1968 Declaring as Subject to the Jurisdiction and Control of the Republic of the Philippines all Mineral and other Natural Resources in the Continental Shelf.

[59] Presidential Decree No.1599 of 11 June 1978 establishing an Exclusive Economic Zone and for other purposes.

[60] Presidential Decree No.1599 of 11 June 1978 establishing an Exclusive Economic Zone and for other purposes, Section 2.

[61] *Ibid.* note 60, Section 4.

[62] *Ibid.* note 60, Section 3 (b) and (d).

[63] Republic Act no. 387 of 18 June 1949, An Act to Promote the Exploration, Development, Exploitation and Utilization of the Petroleum Resources of the Philippines, to encourage the conservation of such petroleum resources; to authorize the Secretary of Agriculture and Natural Resources to Create an Administration Unit and a Technical Board in the Bureau of Mines; To Appropriate Funds therefor and for Other Purposes (Petroleum Act of 1949).

[64] Petroleum Act of 1949, Art.10.

[65] The exploitation concession grants the concessionaire the exclusive right to develop petroleum production within a specified area, see Petroleum Act of 1949, Art. 10(c).

The granting of the pipeline concession to the holder of a refining concession[66] is also compulsory when the two concessions are directly related.[67] The law applies to all lands within the territorial limits of the Philippines including those submerged beneath the territorial waters or on the continental shelf.[68] The application for the pipeline concession must be filed with the Director of Mines and pay an application fee of 2000 pesos. The term of a pipeline concession does not exceed 25 years from the date of its issuance and could be renewable for another 25 years.[69]

In principle, only Filipinos or associations and corporations established under Philippine law can apply for petroleum concessions, including pipeline concessions.[70] However, since the adoption of the Republic Act no. 6479, 1998, the downstream oil industry is liberalized.[71] The Act defines the downstream oil industry as the business of importing, exporting, re-exporting, shipping, transporting, processing, refining, storing, distributing, marketing and/or selling crude oil, gasoline, diesel, liquefied petroleum gas, kerosene and other petroleum products.[72] Any person or entity may import or purchase any quantity of crude oil and petroleum products from a foreign or domestic source, lease or own and operate refineries and other downstream oil facilities provided that that person or entity gives prior notice to the Department of Energy.[73]

7.3 Application to Submarine Pipelines

The Philippines requires a concession from the Director of Mines for the installation and operation of oil submarine pipelines in its inland waters, territorial seas, archipelagic waters and continental shelf. A pipeline concessionaire acquires the non-exclusive right to transport petroleum, by means of and through a pipeline or systems of pipelines between the sources of production and/or refining and the places defined in the pipeline concession. The concession rights include the construction and operation of pipelines, pumping or compressing stations, storage tanks, gas tanks, power plants, shops, storehouses and other buildings, water supply and communication systems, roads and other equipment of facilities needed for the purpose of the concession.[74]

---

66 The refining concession grants the concessionaire the right to manufacture or refine petroleum, or to extract its derivatives, see Petroleum Act of 1949, Art. 10(d).

67 Petroleum Act of 1949, Art.11.

68 Petroleum Act of 1949, Art.14.

69 Petroleum Act of 1949, Arts 83–87.

70 Petroleum Act of 1949, Art.31.

71 Republic Act No. 8479, 10 February 1998, An Act Deregulating the Downstream Oil Industry, and for other Purposes.

72 Republic Act No. 8479, 1998, S4.

73 Republic Act No. 8479, 1998, S5.

74 Petroleum Act of 1949, Arts 83–87.

8 Singapore

Provisions relating to jurisdiction over submarine cables in Singapore are found in legislation on maritime jurisdiction, shipping, and gas.

8.1 Maritime Jurisdiction Legislation

Singapore has not officially declared any maritime zone beyond the territorial sea yet. However, the country made claims to exclusive economic zones through two official communications: a press release from the Ministry of Foreign Affairs in 1980 and a notification on the Government Gazette in 2008. In the press release of 1980, Singapore stated that since 1878, the country has adhered to the concept of a three-nautical mile territorial sea.[75] Notwithstanding, Singapore will exercise the right to extend its territorial sea limit up to 12 nautical miles as well as establishing an exclusive economic zone.[76] In the notification of 2008, while reaffirming its entitlement to a 12-nautical-mile territorial sea and exclusive economic zone, Singapore stated that the precise coordinates of these areas would be announced at an appropriate time.[77] Relating to the rights and freedoms in the exclusive economic zone, the press release of 1980 stated in a general manner that in this area States have jurisdiction and rights over resources.[78]

8.2 Shipping Legislation

Maritime regulations in Singapore are provided in two main Acts, namely the Singapore Merchant Shipping Act, 1995[79] and the Maritime and Port Authority of Singapore Act, 1996.[80] The Maritime and Port Authority of Singapore Act contains provisions relating to submarine cable activities. Section 81 of the latter requires any person to provide any marine service or facility to request a public license or an exemption granted by the Maritime and Port Authority of Singapore.[81]

---

[75] Based on the United Kingdom's Territorial Waters Jurisdiction Act of 1878, see Territorial Waters Jurisdiction Act, 16 August 1878.

[76] Ministry of Foreign Affairs, "Exclusive Economic Zone", Singapore Government Press Release No.09–0/80/09/15 (15 September 1980).

[77] "Singapore Maritime Zones", Government Gazette No. 1485 (28 May 2008).

[78] "Exclusive Economic Zone", *supra* note 76.

[79] Singapore Merchant Shipping Act (Chapter 179) Act 19 of 1995, revised edition 30 April 1996.

[80] Maritime and Port Authority of Singapore Act 1996, 2 February 1996 (as revised in 2020).

[81] Maritime and Port Authority of Singapore Act 1996, 2 February 1996 (as revised in 2020), S81.

8.3 Gas Legislation

There are no specific regulations on the construction and operation of oil pipelines in Singapore, except those from general environmental, health and safety requirements.[82] Meanwhile, gas pipelines in Singapore are regulated by the Gas Act, 2002 and a number of Codes were issued by the Energy Market Authority of Singapore to implement the Act.

The Gas Act provides provisions for the safety, technical and economic regulation of the transportation and retail of gas.[83] The Gas Act defines gas pipelines as "a gas transmission pipeline, a gas main or a gas service pipe" and gas pipeline network as "a gas transmission network, a gas mains network and gas service pipes".[84] Pursuant to the Act, to transport gas through a gas pipeline or gas pipeline network to any premises a person needs to apply for a gas transporter license.[85] The gas transporter may undertake to install in, on, over, under, upon, along or across any land, premises, street or waters and inspect, maintain, adjust, repair, alter, restore, replace or remove any gas pipeline which is or is to be part of its gas pipeline network.[86] No person shall carry out any earthwork within the vicinity of any gas pipe in a gas pipeline network owned by a gas transporter without giving a written notice not less than seven days before the commencement of the work and obtaining from the gas transporter necessary information on the location of the gas pipe. The person who carries out such work has the duty to comply with all reasonable requirements of the gas transporter for the prevention of damage to the gas pipe.[87]

The Gas Supply Code was issued by the Energy Market Authority of Singapore in February 2008 to set out the obligations of gas licensees to comply with standards and procedures for the safe operation of the gas supply system.[88] The Code requires the gas transporter to keep an up-to-date record of gas pipeline networks installed and under public places and highways, in such form as is accessible by other utility service providers or such other persons who reasonably require such information.[89]

---

[82] Kelvin Wong, Tan Wee Meng and Yeo Boon Kiat, *Oil and Gas Regulation in Singapore: Overview* (1 October 2020) online: Thomson Reuters <https://uk.practicallaw.thomsonreuters.com/6-637-5122?transitionType=Default&contextData=(sc.Default)&firstPage=true> .

[83] Singapore's Gas Act (Chapter 116A) Act 11 of 2001, 31st July 2002.

[84] Singapore's Gas Act (Chapter 116A) Act 11 of 2001, 31st July 2002, 10.

[85] Singapore's Gas Act (Chapter 116A) Act 11 of 2001, 31st July 2002, 6(1)(a).

[86] Singapore's Gas Act (Chapter 116A) Act 11 of 2001, 31st July 2002, 27.

[87] Singapore's Gas Act (Chapter 116A) Act 11 of 2001, 31st July 2002, 32.

[88] Gas Supply Code (February 2008), online: Energy Market Authority of Singapore <https://www.ema.gov.sg/cmsmedia/About-Us/Gas_Supply_Code.pdf>.

[89] Gas Supply Code (February 2008), online: Energy Market Authority of Singapore <https://www.ema.gov.sg/cmsmedia/About-Us/Gas_Supply_Code.pdf>, 13.1.

8.4 Application to Submarine Pipelines

Singapore requires the possession of a gas transporter's license issued by the Market Energy Authority of Singapore and the Maritime and Port Authority of Singapore to carry out works relating to gas submarine pipelines. From the wording of the Gas Act, 2002, these requirements do not apply beyond Singapore's territorial waters. Any person who willfully, recklessly or negligently causes damage to any submarine gas pipeline in the territorial waters of Singapore shall be guilty of an offence punishable of a fine of up to two million SGD or imprisonment of up to 5 years.[90]

9 Thailand

Provisions relating to jurisdiction over submarine cables in Thailand are found in legislation on maritime jurisdiction and oil and gas.

9.1 Maritime Jurisdiction Legislation

The maritime jurisdiction of Thailand is provided in the Proclamation Establishing the Breadth of the Territorial Waters, 1966[91]; the Royal Proclamation establishing the Continental Shelf of the Kingdom of Thailand in the Gulf of Thailand, 1973[92]; and the Royal Proclamation establishing the Exclusive Economic Zone of the Kingdom of Thailand, 1981.[93] According to the Proclamation of 1966, the territorial waters of Thailand extend 12 nautical miles from the baseline used for measuring the breadth of the territorial sea. Thailand has sovereignty over the waters, airspace, bed and subsoil of this area.[94] The Royal Proclamation of 1981 provides that the exclusive economic zone of Thailand extends 200 nautical miles from the baseline used for measuring the breadth of the territorial sea.[95] In the exclusive economic zone, Thailand has sovereign rights for the purpose of exploring and exploiting, conserving and managing the natural resources, whether living or non-living, of the seabed and subsoil and the superjacent waters and with regard to other activities for the economic exploration and exploitation of the zone. With regards to the rights and freedoms of

---

[90] Singapore's Gas Act (Chapter 116A) Act 11 of 2001, 31st July 2002, 36.

[91] Proclamation establishing the Breadth of the Territorial Waters, 6 October 1966.

[92] Royal Proclamation establishing the Continental Shelf of the Kingdom of Thailand in the Gulf of Thailand, 18 May 1973.

[93] Royal Proclamation establishing the Exclusive Economic Zone of the Kingdom of Thailand, 23 February 1981.

[94] Proclamation establishing the Breadth of the Territorial Waters, 6 October 1966.

[95] Royal Proclamation establishing the Exclusive Economic Zone of the Kingdom of Thailand, 23 February 1981, s1.

other States in Thailand's exclusive economic zone, it states that the freedom of the laying of submarine pipelines should be governed by international law.[96]

9.2 Oil and Gas Legislation

Regulations relating to oil and gas activities in Thailand are found in the Petroleum Act, 1971[97] and the Energy Industry Act, 2007.[98] The Petroleum Act defines petroleum business as the exploration, production, storage, transportations, sale or distribution of petroleum.[99] Pursuant to the Act, any person who explores or produces petroleum in any area in Thailand must obtain a concession from the Minister in charge of energy.[100] The concessionaire has the right to store and transport petroleum in accordance with the provisions of the concession.[101] The concessionaire also has the right to sell and distribute the petroleum produced by it.[102] In conducting petroleum operations in offshore areas, the concessionaire shall not hinder the laying of submarine cables or pipelines or cause damage to existing submarine cables or pipelines.[103]

The Energy Industry Act defines natural gas business as natural gas transportation through pipelines via a natural gas transmission system, natural gas storage and transformation from liquid to gas, natural gas procurement and wholesale, or natural gas retail via a natural gas distribution system. A natural gas transmission system is defined as a pipeline system used for receiving natural gas from a natural gas purchasing point and for transmitting it to a natural gas distribution point or a natural gas distribution system or a power plant. A natural gas distribution system is defined as a pipeline system connecting with a natural gas transmission system, including the equipment or anything else necessary for distributing natural gas.[104] Pursuant to the Act, the operation of an energy business in Thailand needs a license from the Energy Regulatory Commission.[105] The Commission also grants the approval for construction of gas pipelines.[106] The licensee shall maintain, repair and fix the energy network system, equipment and tools used for energy business operation

---

[96] *Ibid.* note 131, s3.

[97] Petroleum Act, B.E. 2514 (1971) as amended until Petroleum Act (no. 6), B.E. 2550 (2007).

[98] Energy Industry Act B.E. 2550 (2007).

[99] Petroleum Act, B.E.2514 (1971), S4.

[100] Petroleum Act, B.E. 2514 (1971), S23.

[101] Petroleum Act, B.E. 2514 (1971), S54.

[102] Petroleum Act, B.E. 2514 (1971), S56.

[103] Petroleum Act, B.E. 2514 (1971), S74.

[104] Energy Industry Act B.E. 2550 (2007), S5.

[105] Energy Industry Act B.E. 2550 (2007), S47.

[106] David Tennant & Adam Brown (eds), Gas Regulation 2021, online: Chandlermhm <https://www.chandlermhm.com/content/files/pdf/publications/GAS%20Regulation%20-%20Thailand%20-%20GETTING%20THE%20DEAL%20THROUGH%202021.pdf> 10.

to ensure their efficient operations and compliance with standards. In the case of damage or breakdown, action shall be taken to restore them to a working condition promptly.[107]

9.3 Application to Submarine Pipelines

In territorial seas, Thailand requires concession from the Ministry of Energy for the laying of oil pipelines. For laying gas pipelines, Thailand requires a license from the Energy Regulatory Commission. Beyond territorial seas, Thailand follows international law with respect to the freedom of laying submarine pipelines.

10 Vietnam

Provisions relating to jurisdiction over submarine pipelines in Vietnam are found in legislation on maritime jurisdiction and oil and gas.

10.1 Maritime Jurisdiction Legislation

Pursuant to Vietnam's Law on maritime zones, 2012, Vietnam has a 12 nautical mile territorial sea, 200 nautical mile exclusive economic zone and a continental shelf of minimum 200 nautical miles. The Law stipulates that Vietnam exercises full and absolute sovereignty over the waters, air space over and seabed and subsoil of the territorial sea.[108] Vietnam respects the right to lay submarine pipelines by other states in its continental shelf and exclusive economic zone. However, Vietnam requires consent in writing from Vietnamese competent authorities for the laying of submarine pipelines in its continental shelf and exclusive economic zone.[109]

---

[107] Energy Industry Act B.E. 2550 (2007), S74.

[108] Law on Maritime Zones, Art. 12.

[109] *Ibid.* note 146, articles 16 (2) and 18 (4).

10.2 Oil and Gas Legislation

In Vietnam, oil and gas activities are regulated by the Oil and Gas Law, 2022,[110] the Regulations of exploitation of oil and gas, 2010,[111] and National Technical Regulations on Classification and Technical Supervision of Subsea Pipeline System, 2014.[112] The Oil and Gas Law provides for the oil and gas activities in land, island and waters of Vietnam. Oil and gas activities are defined as exploration, development, exploitation of oil and gas and removal of oil and gas constructions, including pipelines. Pursuant to the Regulations for the exploitation of oil and gas, before engaging in the exploitation of oil and gas, the operator must submit to the Prime Minister a Plan for Mine Development, in which information relating to structures and equipment to be used must be provided. These structures and equipment must be certified to be safe and environmentally friendly.[113] With regards to submarine pipelines, the operator must comply with the National Technical Regulations on Classification and Technical Supervision of Subsea Pipeline System. The Vietnam Register Administration of the Ministry of Transport is in charge of controlling, inspecting and monitoring the safety and environmental friendliness of the design, construction, repair, import and use of the submarine pipelines.[114]

10.3 Application to Submarine Pipelines

The laying of submarine pipelines for oil and gas activities in Vietnam's territorial seas, exclusive economic zones and continental shelf requires the submission of a Plan for Mine Development to the Prime Minister for agreement. Submarine pipelines also need to follow National Technical Regulations on the Classification and Technical Supervision of Subsea Pipeline System.

---

[110] Oil and Gas Law No.12/2022/QH15 dated 14 November 2022 of the National Assembly.

[111] Decision no.84/2010/QD-TTg dated 15 December 2010 of the Prime Minister issuing the Regulations for the exploitation of oil and gas.

[112] National Technical Regulation for Classification and Technical Supervision of Subsea Pipeline System, QCVN 69: 2014/BGTVT, issued by the Circluar no.06/2014/TT-BGTVT dated 7 April 2014 of the Ministry of Transport.

[113] Regulations for the exploitation of oil and gas, Arts 5 and 44.

[114] National Technical Regulations on Classification and Technical Supervision of Subsea Pipeline System, S4.

11 General Evaluations

Based on the analysis of domestic provisions relating to the national jurisdiction over submarine pipelines of nine coastal ASEAN Member States above, the following observations could be made.

First and foremost, there is no harmonization in complying with UNCLOS' freedom of laying submarine pipelines between the Southeast Asian States. Indonesia, Malaysia, Singapore and Thailand do not require authorization for the laying of submarine pipelines in the exclusive economic zone and continental shelf. Meanwhile, Cambodia, Myanmar, the Philippines and Vietnam require prior agreement from relevant authorities to do so. The prior agreement could take the form of either permission, license, concession, authorization or control. In the case of Vietnam, there is a requirement for both authorization and control.

Second, in some cases, there is a difference between the stated principle and the concrete rule. In principle, it is declared that the freedom of laying submarine pipelines by other countries in the coastal waters is respected. However, in the concrete rule, there is a requirement for prior agreement by national authority. This is the case with Myanmar and Vietnam.

Third, there is also no uniformity in terms of the type of submarine pipelines regulated in the domestic law of Southeast Asian States. Indonesia, Thailand and Vietnam's law apply to both oil and gas pipelines. Among those, in Indonesia and Vietnam, the same law would apply to oil and gas pipelines whereas in Thailand, there are two different laws for oil and gas pipelines. Cambodia, Malaysia, Myanmar and Philippines' law apply only to oil pipelines. Singapore's law only applies to gas pipelines.

Fourth, there is a difference in the level of granting authorization for laying submarine pipelines between the Southeast Asian States. In the Philippines, Thailand, and Singapore, the authorization is granted by an authority under the ministerial level. In Brunei, Indonesia, Malaysia, and Myanmar, the authorization is granted at the ministerial level. In Cambodia and Vietnam, the involvement of the Prime Minister is necessary for the approval of the work.

Finally, in many Southeast Asian States, the authorization process for laying submarine pipelines requires more than one procedure. In Cambodia, the laying of oil submarine pipelines in connection with the development and production of petroleum requires a Petroleum Agreement with MIME with prior permission from the Prime Minister. In Malaysia, laying an oil pipeline requires authorization from the Minister in charge of petroleum and written permission from an approving Authority. In Singapore, the laying of gas submarine pipelines needs a public license (or an exemption) granted by the Maritime and Port Authority of Singapore and gas transporter license granted by the Energy Market Authority of Singapore. In Vietnam, the laying of submarine pipelines requires agreement by the Prime Minister for the Plan for Mine Development and control from the Vietnam Register—Ministry of Transport for the safety and environmental friendliness of the design, construction, repair, import and use of pipes.

12 Conclusion

This Chapter evaluates stipulations relating to jurisdiction over submarine pipelines in national legislation of nine coastal ASEAN Member States to evaluate how Southeast Asia has been implementing relevant UNCLOS provisions relating to submarine pipelines. The evaluation reveals that the freedom of laying submarine cables is not uniformly respected throughout the region and that there are a number of differences in concrete regulations relating to laying submarine pipelines between each Southeast Asian State. These could present an opportunity for ASEAN to take action to improve the freedom of laying submarine pipelines and the harmonization of their regulations in the region.

Correction to: Viability of UNCLOS amid Emerging Global Maritime Challenges

Lan Anh T. Nguyen and Hai Dang Vu

Correction to: L. A. T. Nguyen and H. D. Vu (eds.), *Viability of UNCLOS amid Emerging Global Maritime Challenges*, https://doi.org/10.1007/978-981-97-5838-8

The original version of the content in front matter was inadvertently published without the funding statement

"This material has been funded by UK International Development from the UK government; however, the views expressed do not necessarily reflect the UK government's official policies" and inclusion of UK International Development logo in cover page, which have now been updated. The front matter and cover page have been updated with the changes.

The updated version of the book can be found at
https://doi.org/10.1007/978-981-97-5838-8

L. A. T. Nguyen and H. D. Vu (eds.), *Viability of UNCLOS amid Emerging Global Maritime Challenges*, https://doi.org/10.1007/978-981-97-5838-8_13

Conclusion

The book "UNCLOS: Viability Amid Emerging Global Maritime Challenges" provided a critical review of the role of UNCLOS as the most important legal framework governing our ocean in modern time through the lenses of a number of world's leading scholars in the law of the sea. Their analysis offers three important insights into the place of UNCLOS in the international legal order today. First, they confirm that the Convention is still very much the comprehensive legal instrument that regulates all activities of States at sea. Second, the "UNCLOS ecosystem" which includes UNCLOS itself, its implementing agreements and its institutional structure, are working hard to overcome all the gaps, unclarities and limits of the provisions of the Convention as well as to adapt them to new challenges that face the ocean today. Third, in the specific case of the South China Sea, where there are most complicated sovereignty and maritime disputes in the world, UNCLOS has played a very important role of serving as the "golden standard" through which the marine region's coastal States use to base their maritime claims. Along with these discussions, a number of interesting observations have been made.

Despite the fact that it is virtually impossible to amend its provisions, UNCLOS could still be considered "living treaty" which can adapt to changing circumstances and address new challenges unforeseen at the time it was negotiated. UNCLOS could do so thanks to five mechanisms: implementing agreements, rule-making by bodies under UNCLOS, incorporating generally accepted international rules and standards, subsequent state practices, and using the development of the law by international courts and tribunals. The successful adoption of the Agreement under the United Nations Convention on the Law of the Sea on the Conservation and Sustainable Use of Marine Biological Diversity of Areas Beyond National Jurisdiction recently has been clear evidence of the use of UNCLOS implementing agreements to deal with a very new challenge in the ocean.

One of the most important achievements under UNCLOS was the establishment of a mandatory system for the settlement of maritime disputes. This system has been able to balance between the preservation of state sovereignty and the insurance of peace and legality in the ocean. In particular, the mechanism of Advisory Opinion of ITLOS has contributed to the advancement of the law of the sea. This could be

L. A. T. Nguyen and H. D. Vu (eds.), *Viability of UNCLOS amid Emerging Global Maritime Challenges*, https://doi.org/10.1007/978-981-97-5838-8

witnessed with the Advisory Opinions given by the tribunal on the responsibilities of States sponsoring persons and entities for activities in the Area. This mechanism could potentially be used to deal with disputes with regards to *erga omnes* obligations to overcome the challenge to determine who has the standing to initiate the dispute settlement procedures and who would be bound by the resulting decision.

The solution of "freezing baselines" in response to sea-level rise, in spite of its broad support by the international community, should only be considered a temporary solution to preserve maritime entitlements. The reason is that such a solution could lead to abuses by setting precedents to validate the primacy of particular interest which could undermine the integrity of UNCLOS. For the long-term interest of preserving the legal order of the ocean, the solution to deal with sea-level rise should be worked out in a multilateral context with the incorporation of compatible norms and principles. The good news is that our best legal minds in the International Law Committee and International Law Association have been studying the issue of impacts of sea-level rise on maritime entitlements.

Cooperation in marine scientific research seems to receive a lot of support. Indeed, it is generally considered as a non-sensitive area for cooperation in areas in disputes. Furthermore, science plays a critical role in addressing the challenges that our ocean is currently facing, in particular the protection of the marine environment. As a matter of fact, SDG 14 "Life below water" calls for increasing scientific knowledge, research and technology for improving the ocean health Cooperation in marine science research should be done through existing international and regional institutions such as International Hydrographic Organisation, Intergovernmental Ocean Commission, International Seabed Authority to take advantage of their cooperation infrastructures.

Another issue relating to marine scientific research is that there is a need to update and adapt existing rules relating to marine scientific research. First, there are many types of marine data collection which do not fit in the regime of marine scientific research of UNCLOS, namely; operational oceanography, data collection using remote sensing satellite, hydrographic surveys, exploring underwater cultural heritage exploration, environmental monitoring and assessment, military and intelligence activities, biologging, and citizen science. Each of these either is under a specific legal regime or lacks any controlling legal authority that would render them subject to foreign regulation.

Finally, with regards to the South China Sea, UNCLOS has helped to clarify national claims and reduce the disputed areas. Two UNCLOS mechanisms contributed to this endeavour: the Commission on the Limits of the Continental Shelf and the Arbitral Tribunal of Annex VII. For the first case, the submission of Malaysia to the Commission on the Limits of the Continental Shelf triggered the issuance of notes verbales by both South China Sea and outside States expressing their views on the limit of coastal states' maritime entitlements in the marine region. For the second case, the South China Sea arbitral award in 2016 helped turn a very large sea area considered disputed water because of Chinese claims of nine-dash line and Spratlys' "relevant waters" to non-disputed waster. It thus opens the possibility for the South China Sea to have a portion of high sea and the opportunity for regional States to engage in cooperation in areas beyond national jurisdiction.

Based on these observations, it could be predicted that in a foreseeable future, UNCLOS will continue to be the most comprehensive legal framework to govern all activities at sea and the most important legal basis for resolving maritime disputes between States.

The manufacturer's authorised representative in the EU is Springer Nature Customer Service Centre GmbH, Europaplatz 3, 69115 Heidelberg, Germany. If you have any concerns regarding our products, please contact ProductSafety@springernature.com

Printed and bound by CPI Group (UK) Ltd, Croydon, CR0 4YY
01/10/2026
02225858-0004